WITTGENSTEIN ON MEANING

Aristotelian Society Series

Colin McGinn

Wittgenstein on Meaning

An Interpretation and Evaluation

Aristotelian Society Series
Volume 1

Basil Blackwell

© Colin McGinn 1984

First published 1984
First published in paperback 1987
Reprinted 1989

Basil Blackwell Ltd.
108 Cowley Road, Oxford OX4 1JF, England

Basil Blackwell, Inc.
3 Cambridge Center
Cambridge, Massachusetts 02142, USA

in cooperation with The Aristotelian Society
King's College, London WC2

British Library Cataloguing in Publication Data

McGinn, Colin
Wittgenstein on meaning.
1. Wittgenstein, Ludwig   I. Title

192   B3376.W564
ISBN 0-631-13764-5
ISBN 0-631-15681-X Pbk

Photoset by Photobooks (Bristol) Ltd
Printed in Great Britain by
Billing & Sons Limited, Worcester

Contents

Preface

I had always found Wittgenstein's *Philosophical Investigations*
a baffling work, and commentaries upon it did little to improve
my understanding. Consequently, I never made a careful study
of Wittgenstein's writings.

When I first read Saul Kripke's *Wittgenstein on Rules and
Private Language* it seemed to me to make clear sense, at last, of
Wittgenstein's text: I felt that Kripke had clarified the
Investigations to the point at which it was now actually possible
to consider whether Wittgenstein's doctrines were correct;
moreover, Kripke's clarification seemed to reveal a set of
powerful and challenging arguments, disturbing but difficult to
dispose of. I decided (in 1982) to give a seminar on the topic,
with Malcolm Budd. In the course of re-reading Wittgenstein
with Kripke's interpretation in mind I came, to my surprise, to
have considerable doubts about the correctness of that
interpretation; in particular, I could not see that Wittgenstein
introduced the community into his account of meaning and
rule-following, in the way Kripke suggests. At the same time, I
began to think that the arguments Kripke develops were less
impregnable than had first appeared to me. As a result of
nurturing these doubts, I arrived at a quite different understanding of Wittgenstein's aims and doctrines. I resolved to
write a paper, or possibly two, setting out my disagreements
with Kripke, never intending to spend a great deal of time on
the project. However, it gradually became clear to me that, if I
was to do the job properly, it would require something a bit

more substantial; in the end it turned out to be a book.

My main aim in this book is to give a clear and accurate account of what Wittgenstein actually thought, with a view to critically evaluating his ideas. In pursuance of this aim, I have perforce included a good deal of quoted material and commented closely on Wittgenstein's actual words; I invite the reader to check for himself whether Wittgenstein is really saying what I say he is. I hope the book will be useful to students, as well as to their teachers; indeed, I have tried to write in a way that does not presuppose any prior knowledge of Wittgenstein's later philosophy.

My greatest debt in the composition of this work is to Malcolm Budd. We discussed Wittgenstein protractedly, and I was constantly reassured by the happy convergence of our views. His extensive knowledge of Wittgenstein's corpus and his sure grasp of its contents were a great help to me. He directed me to certain important passages in Wittgenstein, and saved me from more than one error of interpretation. He also read and commented upon the first draft and made several very helpful comments. It is seldom that one has the benefit of such disinterested and agreeable cooperation from a fellow philosopher.

Other people also helped me to work out my ideas. Audiences of seminars I gave at University College London, the University of Southern California, Bielefeld University and Stanford University made helpful comments which led to various improvements. Conversations with Rogers Albritton, Anita Avramides, Jim Hopkins, Ian McFetridge, Marie McGinn, David Pears, Richard Warner and Crispin Wright (who commented in writing on my first draft) were also much appreciated. Peter Hacker generously made detailed critical comments on my penultimate draft; I am very grateful to him for undertaking this labour and for the correspondence which ensued. I am also grateful to Martin Davies for his encouragement and his efficient editorial work. Lastly, I am again grateful to Katherine Backhouse for typing the work and for her good humour in doing it.

Colin McGinn
10 June 1984

Note on References

References to Wittgenstein's *Philosophical Investigations* (Blackwell: Oxford, 1974) are given simply by citing section numbers, or page numbers where appropriate. Other works of Wittgenstein are cited by using initial letters of their titles followed by section or page numbers, according to the following system:

TLP   : *Tractatus Logico-Philosophicus* (Routledge and Kegan Paul: London, 1961)

Z   : *Zettel* (1981)

BB   : *The Blue and Brown Books* (1969)

RFM   : *Remarks on the Foundations of Mathematics* (1978)

OC   : *On Certainty* (1979)

PG   : *Philosophical Grammar* (1974)

RPP   : *Remarks on the Philosophy of Psychology* (1980)

WLFM   : *Wittgenstein's Lectures on the Foundations of Mathematics*, ed. C. Diamond (Harvester Press: Sussex, 1976)

All of these books (except for the first and last) are published by Basil Blackwell, Oxford.

Introduction

However much interpreters of Wittgenstein's philosophy may disagree, there is one point in which no dispute is to be expected: that Wittgenstein held that the proper way of understanding and resolving philosophical problems lies in arriving at a correct conception of language. Both the *Tractatus* and the *Investigations* are concerned first and foremost with the topic of meaning. So the philosophy of language is not, for Wittgenstein, merely one department of the subject, its results bearing in no essential way upon enquiry in other areas of philosophy; it is, rather, to be conceived as anterior and foundational.[1] We need to be clear about the nature of meaning before we can hope to be clear about anything else. It follows that if we are to be in a position to understand and assess Wittgenstein's philosophy we need to acquire a firm grasp of his view of language. With respect

---

[1] Compare the following remarks from the *Tractatus* and the *Investigations*, respectively: 'Most of the propositions and questions of philosophers arise from our failure to understand the logic of our language' (*TLP* 4.003), 'All philosophy is a "critique of language" (though not in Mauthner's sense)' (*TLP* 4.0031); 'Philosophy is a battle against the bewitchment of our intelligence by means of language' (109), 'The problems arising through a misinterpretation of our forms of language have the character of *depth*. They are deep disquietudes; their roots are as deep in us as the forms of our language and their significance is as great as the importance of our language' (111). Note that in *both* works philosophy is conceived as an effort to correct the misunderstandings our forms of language generate in us.

to Wittgenstein's later philosophy, this involves understanding the celebrated but nebulous slogan 'meaning is use'.[2]

It is not that this question has been neglected; far from it. But it is my belief that Wittgenstein's later views on meaning and related notions have not yet received a fully satisfactory exegesis; and in consequence it is still unclear whether those views should be accepted. To speak plainly: I have found that commentaries on Wittgenstein's later conception of meaning typically tend towards the obscure and impressionistic.[3] Recently, however, the study of Wittgenstein's later philosophy has received something of a fillip from the publication of Saul Kripke's *Wittgenstein on Rules and Private Language*.[4] What this book so notably does is to present an articulated and coherent structure of argument leaving one in no doubt about what is being asserted and denied. Kripke emphasises the importance of the sections of the *Investigations* concerned with the notion of grasping and following a rule (roughly 138–242), and he takes Wittgenstein to be putting forward a definite conception of how this notion is to be understood. I want to agree with Kripke (and others[5]) about the centrality of those sections, but I do not believe that the interpretation he offers is correct. The clarity of Kripke's interpretation does, however, make it an excellent foil against which to put forward an alternative interpretation: studying Wittgenstein's text with Kripke's interpretation in mind provides a focus enabling one to discern better what it is that Wittgenstein is really saying. In the present work, I shall suggest an interpretation of Wittgenstein which seems to me to accord with the text, using Kripke's interpretation as a foil, with a view to critically assessing Wittgenstein's views.[6]

---

[2] 'Every sign *by itself* seems dead. *What* gives it life? – In use it is *alive*' (432); 'if we had to name anything which is the life of the sign, we should have to say that it was its *use*' (*BB* p. 4).

[3] I do not, of course, mean to suggest that there is nothing of value in the secondary literature; indeed, I think there are a number of illuminating studies of Wittgenstein's later work on meaning. However, none seems to me both clear and wholly accurate; and many are obscurantist.

[4] Blackwell: Oxford, 1982. An earlier version appeared in I. Block, ed., *Perspectives on the Philosophy of Wittgenstein* (Blackwell: Oxford, 1981).

[5] Notably Crispin Wright in *Wittgenstein on the Foundations of Mathematics* (Duckworth: London, 1980).

[6] I shall be focusing in what follows upon the text of the *Investigations*, using Wittgenstein's other works as corroborative rather than as independently authoritat-

What follows is divided into four parts. In Chapter 1 I shall give a more or less elementary exposition of Wittgenstein's views on meaning, rules, understanding and related notions, keeping as close to the text as possible. This exposition will be disciplined by the following constraint: views will be attributed to Wittgenstein just on the condition that textual evidence can be found which directly supports the attribution in question. Too often, I think, expositors of Wittgenstein allow their fancies to carry them away from what Wittgenstein actually says; I wish my interpretation to be maximally sensitive to what is to be found in the text. I will not, therefore, be particularly concerned to discover in Wittgenstein intimations of theses directly relevant to contemporary debates; nor will I assume that Wittgenstein's opponents are as numerous as ever. In fact I believe that contemporary philosophical opinion has absorbed a very great deal of Wittgenstein's views, and that much of his criticism of various philosophical doctrines is accordingly of only historical importance. (This is not to say that I think Wittgenstein's views have *no* relevance to contemporary philosophy; I am merely warning against a temptation anachronistically to read into Wittgenstein's text issues and concerns which are not his.) Keeping an historical perspective will act as an antidote to the response to some proposed interpretation which runs: 'How could Wittgenstein be saying that? *Nobody* (today) would hold the view allegedly being criticised'. It is, in other words, no objection to a proposed interpretation of Wittgenstein that the interpretation makes Wittgenstein *obviously* right (by our contemporary lights). I shall also at this stage of my discussion shun exegetical polemics, though anyone familiar with rival interpretations of Wittgenstein will appreciate that I am writing with these interpretations in mind; the advantage of this is that we shall be able to approach Wittgenstein's text without the distractions of exegetical disputation. It perhaps goes without saying that the interpretation of Wittgenstein is (in principle) a virtually endless process, so that my own efforts are not to be taken as

---

ive. It should always be remembered that Wittgenstein himself saw fit to publish only this work from his later corpus; and also that there are some significant changes of view in the later period, which makes an eclectic approach somewhat hazardous.

exhaustive or definitive; my main aim is to highlight Wittgenstein's principal contentions and to spell out their interrelations. Once I have presented the interpretation I prefer I shall turn (in Chapter 2) to Kripke's interpretation and explain where and why I think it is mistaken: if the interpretation offered in Chapter 1 has carried conviction, this should not prove a long or difficult task – indeed, it should be necessary only to indicate and emphasise the points of contrast between the two interpretations. The differences are, I think, radical, though they may be disguised by certain ambiguities and unclarities of formulation. In Chapter 3 I move on to questions of evaluation: my intention here is to offer some assessment of Wittgenstein's views as I have interpreted them. Naturally this will involve us in further issues of interpretation, but the aim is to separate as far as possible questions of interpretation from questions of evaluation. I cannot hope in this chapter to provide decisive rebuttals of those views of Wittgenstein that I find myself disinclined to accept, nor indeed to provide conclusive arguments for those of Wittgenstein's claims that strike me as plausible; what I hope to do is to isolate clearly the points at issue and indicate the sorts of considerations that are relevant to resolving the questions raised. (One difficulty here is that Wittgenstein does not always tell us his *reasons* for maintaining what he does, so we can be at a loss to undertake an evaluation of the cogency of his case for the claim in question.) In Chapter 4 I return to Kripke, this time with the aim of critically assessing the arguments he puts forward in their own right: irrespective of their correctness as interpretation, are they in themselves convincing arguments? I shall contend that they are not. Possibly some readers will not be persuaded of their incorrectness as exegesis until this stage of my discussion has been reached, since they will, I surmise, be reluctant to construe Wittgenstein as holding views to which there are objections of the kind I shall be urging. While this stance is in general methodologically suspect, I would not discourage adopting it in the present case; for I believe that the objections I shall raise against Kripke's arguments do serve to underline the remoteness of Kripke's interpretation from Wittgenstein's real position. In this respect at least issues of interpretation are not completely over with until the end.

1

Wittgenstein's Views:
Meaning, Understanding, Rules

In essaying an interpretation of Wittgenstein's views there are
two cautionary points to keep in mind; these points are familiar
enough, but it is easy to under-stress them and so misrepresent
what Wittgenstein is about. The first is that Wittgenstein's
aims are primarily negative: he sees himself as dislodging
certain natural and tempting misconceptions of the matter at
hand, as protecting us from certain sorts of error. In the case of
meaning these temptations to error are particularly inviting,
and the correct conception correspondingly difficult for us to
rest with. We should not, then, expect from Wittgenstein the
sort of positive theory of meaning characteristically proposed
by philosophers whose intentions are less therapeutic: Wittgenstein is not out to give a 'theory of meaning' in the usual sense
of that phrase. Such a project is indeed the target of remarks
such as 'The mistake is to say that there is anything that
meaning something consists in' (Z 16). Insofar as Wittgenstein
has a positive account of meaning, it is an account whose chief
purpose is to act as an antidote to mistaken or misleading
conceptions of meaning. So if the positive account we find in
Wittgenstein looks to us unsatisfyingly thin, this is not
necessarily to be taken as showing that the interpretation is
superficial or that Wittgenstein's views are trivial; it is, rather, a
reflection of the philosophical perspective from which the
positive account issues. It is of the essence of Wittgenstein's

approach to these questions that the truth should not be
surprising.[1]

The second point is that it is not an accident that
Wittgenstein's text does not take the form of a conventionally
structured argument. We must avoid the temptation to regard
the text as a sort of cipher through which we must penetrate to
reveal the linearly ordered argument beneath. It is not that
Wittgenstein really has an argument of orthodox form which
for some inscrutable reason he chose to present in a disguised
fashion. We must take seriously his prefatory remark that his
investigations go 'criss-cross in every direction', and that this is
'connected with the very nature of the investigation'.[2] This
feature of Wittgenstein's method of presentation poses obvious
problems for the expositor, and I cannot in my own case be
entirely sure that I have proceeded in a way which sufficiently
respects this point. However, I think the dangers of misrep-
resentation will be minimised if we see Wittgenstein's discussion
as organised around certain *themes*, which recur in different
connexions and with varying sorts of significance. These
themes together conspire to produce a conception of the
subject which it is Wittgenstein's aim to promote – not by
taking us from premises to conclusion in the usual way, but by
being exhibited at appropriate junctures.[3] Thus it is in the spirit
of Wittgenstein's methodological intentions to expound him as
putting forward a number of themes and elaborating upon
their implications and significance; and it will I think do no
harm to express these in the form of definite *theses* about
meaning and related notions. Let us then, with these cautions
in mind, proceed immediately to state in summary form the

[1] 'Philosophy simply puts everything before us, and neither explains nor deduces
anything. – Since everything lies open to view there is nothing to explain. For what is
hidden, for example, is of no interest to us' (126); 'If one tried to advance *theses* in
philosophy, it would never be possible to debate them, because everyone would agree
to them' (128).
[2] Preface, p. viii.
[3] It is this feature of Wittgenstein's method that explains the *repetitiveness* of his
work; he comes repeatedly at the same fundamental points from different directions.
This repetitiveness is unavoidably echoed in Wittgenstein exegesis; and in the present
case it is compounded by my separation of questions of interpretation and of
evaluation. I hope that my readers will not find this too tedious; I have tried, when
expounding essentially the same point in different places, to state the point in a way
that deepens or extends it, rather than merely repeating my earlier words – but a certain
amount of repetition is inevitable.

main themes of Wittgenstein's treatment of meaning; we shall then elaborate upon each in turn, trying to bring out their interrelations.

We can separate out three negative theses and one positive thesis, as follows:

(i)   To mean something by a sign is not to be the subject of an inner state or process.

(ii) To understand a sign is not to interpret it in a particular way.

(iii) Using a sign in accordance with a rule is not founded upon reasons.

(iv) To understand a sign is to have mastery of a technique or custom of using it.

Thesis (i) is perhaps the most accessible and well-understood of Wittgenstein's negative contentions; it does, however, need to be articulated with some care. It is useful to divide it into two sub-theses, corresponding to two different notions of the 'inner': on the one hand, there is the rejection of the idea that meaning something consists in certain *conscious* or *experiential* states and processes; on the other, there is the rejection of the idea that meaning or understanding is a state or process of one's 'mental apparatus', i.e. of the nervous system or some other kind of subconscious mechanism. The first of these rejections is much the more important in Wittgenstein's writings; he returns to this theme again and again, subjecting it to sustained criticism; whereas the second rejection occurs in relatively few laconic passages. The reason for this dispro-portionate treatment is that he thinks that the 'mentalistic' version of the rejected conception is much more attractive to us than the 'mechanistic' version: it is something his readers will be more tempted to hold, and so its dislodgement calls for correspondingly more work. It is also, of course, historically more prominent. Wittgenstein's most characteristic formulation of the conception he is against is in terms of something which 'comes before the mind': what he is denying is that meaning something consists in some item coming before one's mind. And the central version of this idea is the view that meaning something is having an *image* of it before one's mind – for example, to mean *cube* by 'cube' is to have before one's mind the image of a cube. Thus meaning is construed as a species of

picturing, where the picture occurs in the medium of consciousness. Wittgenstein's hostility to this idea is expressed in the
following (representative) passages:

> What is essential is to see that the same thing can come before
> our minds when we hear the word and the application still be
> different. Has it the *same* meaning both times? I think we shall
> say not. (140)

> Try not to think of understanding as a 'mental process' at
> all.—For *that* is the expression which confuses you. But ask
> yourself: in what sort of case, in what kind of circumstances, do
> we say, "Now I know how to go on," when, that is, the formula
> *has* occurred to me?—
> In the sense in which there are processes (including mental
> processes) which are characteristic of understanding, under-
> standing is not a mental process.
> (A pain's growing more or less; the hearing of a tune or a
> sentence: these are mental processes.) (154)

> Meaning is as little an experience as intending.
> But what distinguishes them from experience?—They have
> no experience-content. For the contents (images for instance)
> which accompany and illustrate them are not the meaning or
> intending. (p. 217)

> Meaning is not a process which accompanies a word. For no
> *process* could have the consequences of meaning.
> (Similarly, I think, it could be said: a calculation is not an
> experiment, for no experiment could have the peculiar con-
> sequences of a multiplication.) (p. 218)[4]

Wittgenstein is not here denying that there are characteristic
experiential *accompaniments* to meaning and understanding –
for images and the like do sometimes come before our minds
when we utter or understand words – but he is denying that
such experiential phenomena could *constitute* understanding.
Experiences are at most a symptom or sign of understanding;
they are not understanding itself. The mistake of the traditional
empiricist conception of meaning was thus to take as
constitutive what is in reality only symptomatic. Neither is
Wittgenstein denying that such experiential episodes may be
psychologically irresistible for human beings, that there is a

[4] *Cf.* also: *Z* 26, 45, 72, 82, 84, 163, 236, 446, 669; *BB* pp. 3–4, 5, 40, 65, 78, 86, 113, 117, 144.

psychologically natural association for us between particular meanings and particular images; his point is a logical or conceptual one – that the notion of meaning is not the notion *of* such experiential episodes.[5] Put differently, meaning something is not an exercise of the imagination, though the imagination *may* be brought into play *when* something is meant. It follows from this negative contention that meaning the same thing by a given sign on different occasions does not consist in the recurrence of a particular conscious content, and that teaching someone the meaning of a sign does not consist in establishing an association between the sign and such a content. Wittgenstein is thus resisting the assimilation of the concepts of meaning and understanding to the concepts of experience, sensation and imagination; we need to recognise that these are concepts of quite different kinds.

Wittgenstein advances three sorts of reasons for rejecting the idea that meaning is a kind of experience. First, he observes that there are 'grammatical' differences between, e.g., depression, pain and excitement on the one hand, and understanding on the other: that is to say, the two categories of concepts relate to other concepts in logically different ways. Thus *temporal* concepts interact with concepts of experience and the concept of understanding differently: we speak of being in continuous pain, or of a pain being interrupted for five minutes, or of suddenly ceasing to feel pain; but we do not regard understanding (like knowledge) as clockable in these ways.[6] Similarly, concepts of *intensity* apply to experiential phenomena – as when a pain is described as intense or an emotion as strong – but it is 'ungrammatical' to speak of understanding in this way. What Wittgenstein is here pointing to is the kind of distinction that is gestured at by the customary distinction between 'occurrent' and 'dispositional' concepts; and his claim, in these (not totally satisfactory) terms, is that understanding is a dispositional and not an occurrent condition of the person. This kind of point has been overlooked, he thinks, because of

[5] He sometimes puts the point by distinguishing two sorts of 'terminus', which he calls 'logical' and 'psychological' (see 140, Z 231): we may indeed be psychologically compelled to use a mental picture in a certain way, but this is not to be confused with logical compulsion. Wittgenstein is not concerned merely with the (empirical) psychology of meaning something by a word, but rather with the *concept* of meaning.
[6] See p. 59 (*a*), (*b*); Z 71–86, 472, 488.

the tendency to identify understanding with its characteristic experiential accompaniments – this along with a general temptation to assimilate together different psychological concepts.

Wittgenstein's second argument is that it is not in fact a *necessary* condition of understanding that some particular item come before one's mind. For a great variety of images, feelings, etc. may accompany understanding a particular word, either for the same person on different occasions or for different people; no *one* of these experiences seems to be *essential* for understanding the word in a particular way.[7] And even if there were a *de facto* uniformity, possibly as a result of some psychological law, we could still *conceive* of cases of the same understanding in which a different conscious content is present. The failure to appreciate this point stems from concentrating upon the most common or typical kinds of accompaniment and erecting this correlation into a necessity – an error that arises from assuming that understanding *must* consist in a distinctive type of experience. And Wittgenstein's point is that introspection just does not bear out this theoretical assumption. Furthermore, introspection cannot even be relied upon to produce *any* kind of experience when a sign is understood: we sometimes understand a sign without any item coming before our mind – our inner consciousness is, so to speak, a blank. Again, this is something that would only be overlooked by someone who was antecedently convinced that understanding must be a kind of experiencing. If you conduct an unprejudiced introspective investigation ('look and see'[8]) you will find that the empiricist theory is a mere dogma. It is no more necessary to understanding that one entertain an inner mental picture than it is that one possesses an external physical picture.[9]

Wittgenstein's third and most important point is that it is not *sufficient* for meaning a sign in a particular way that some item come before one's mind, e.g. a picture of a cube when one uses

---

[7] See 35, 172–8; *BB* pp. 149–50.

[8] The phrase is from 66, in which Wittgenstein is urging that there is not something that is common to all games.

[9] See *BB* pp. 4–5: here Wittgenstein advises us always to replace the supposed mental picture with a physical one, so that we shall better appreciate the impotence of the mental picture – the replacement prevents us investing the image with an 'occult' power to determine meaning.

the word 'cube'. This is not sufficient because the picture does not in itself *determine* the correct use of the associated word; we cannot read off the associated picture how the word is to be applied. This is readily seen if we consider physical pictures: we need to be told which aspects of the picture are relevant and how they are to be interpreted. Presented with a picture we can always contrive a variety of meanings it could be taken to determine; *in itself* it is semantically inert.[10] The reason for this is that a picture associated with a sign is really just another sign which itself stands in need of its meaning being fixed. Wittgenstein's claim is that inner mental pictures are logically no different: a mental image does not *dictate* the use of a word, since it is itself susceptible of a variety of interpretations. There is no logical route from the intrinsic properties of an image to the meaning of an associated word, because of the possibility of deviant applications of the image: even an image of red could be employed as a sign for some other colour if we consider some sort of mapping from red to that other colour (compare Wittgenstein's discussion of deviant 'methods of projection'[11]). A vivid way to see this point is to imagine someone who has been conditioned to entertain a specific mental image whenever he hears a certain word – say an image of a cube whenever he hears the word 'cube': such a person has not thereby been put in a position to use the word 'cube' with the meaning *cube*, since there is nothing *in* the image that tells him to apply 'cube' to cubes and not to other shapes which bear certain (definable) relations to cubes. It is of course true that images naturally *suggest* applications to us, but this is a psychological not a logical fact: there is no incoherence in the idea that two people could understand a word differently though the same images came before their minds.

Once this point about sufficiency has been clearly made it can (I take it) hardly be denied, but Wittgenstein connects it with another claim which is less familiar and less straightforward; and this other claim takes us to an important and difficult aspect of Wittgenstein's thinking about meaning. So far we have considered the incapacity of what might be called *quotidian* conscious contents to determine meaning – the commonplace items that make up the introspectible contents

[10] See 73–4, 139–141; *Z* 236; *BB* pp. 36–7.
[11] E.g., *BB* p. 33.

of consciousness; but Wittgenstein also addresses himself to the assumption of *queer* or magical mental acts, which are supposed to effect what the merely quotidian fail to bring off.[12] The felt inadequacy of ordinary conscious contents to determine meaning leads us to postulate a special sort of conscious content, one which magically *contains* that which the ordinary contents fail to determine, *viz.* use. Thus there arises a temptation to credit the mind with states in which the whole of use comes before its inner gaze, in order to avoid the objection that there is a logical gap between use and what (in the quotidian way) comes before the mind. Such queer mental states are then naturally conceived as somehow *hidden*. Wittgenstein here sees the case of understanding as a special case of a more general temptation: the temptation to regard the mind as *presently* containing or surveying what lies in the future. When the ascription of a psychological predicate (e.g. 'expects') has implications for future behaviour we tend to suppose a state of mind in which that future behaviour is presently somehow an object of consciousness; the future behaviour is thus seen as the unfolding of what is presently there. In this way the use of a sign, which is spread over time, is supposed magically contained in my present understanding by dint of a special mental act in which the whole course of temporally extended use comes before my mind – a mental act in which my future use is somehow *anticipated*.[13] Some light is shed on the kind of mistake Wittgenstein thinks we are inclined to make here by his discussion of machines and their possibilities of movement. His claim is that we think of possible (including future) movements of a machine as mysteriously present in the machine as shadows of actual movements:

> When does one have the thought: the possible movements of a machine are already there in it in some mysterious way?— Well, when one is doing philosophy. And what leads us into thinking that? The kind of way in which we talk about

[12] See 187–97.

[13] This is connected with the problem Wittgenstein raises in 138–9, *viz.* how I can understand a word when I hear or say it, given that the use of the word is extended over time. He rejects the idea that this is accomplished by way of a queer mental act or process consisting in a magically condensed series of *thoughts* corresponding to each possible occasion of use. Wittgenstein's own answer to this question, to be filled out later, invokes the idea of an *ability* to use a word on future occasions, an ability which gets exercised when I now hear or say the word with understanding.

machines. We say, for example, that a machine *has* (possesses) such-and-such possibilities of movement; we speak of the ideally rigid machine which *can* only move in such-and-such a way.—What is this *possibility* of movement? It is not the *movement*, but it does not seem to be the mere physical conditions for moving either—as, that there is play between socket and pin, the pin not fitting too tight in the socket. For while this is the empirical condition for movement, one could also imagine it to be otherwise. The possibility of a movement is, rather, supposed to be like a shadow of the movement itself. But do you know of such a shadow? And by a shadow I do not mean some picture of the movement—for such a picture would not have to be a picture of just *this* movement. But the possibility of this movement must be the possibility of just this movement. (See how high the seas of language run here!) (194)

Wittgenstein is here diagnosing a misleading conception we are disposed to have of what is actually absent but possible or future: we tend to think of the absent as really present but in a shadowy way, so that when the possible is actualised there is something like a revelation of what was already in existence.[14] Thus we think of future or possible use as present 'in a queer way', by being *already contained* in what the mind does when something is meant – in particular, by being present to consciousness after the manner of an image. Wittgenstein thinks that this mythology of queer acts of mind comes from, *inter alia*, adherence to the idea that understanding is like, or is a kind of, imagining; it is a desperate (though natural) attempt to preserve this model in the face of the demonstrable incapacity of quotidian conscious contents to determine meaning. And this tendency is, he thinks, part of a more general tendency to fall back on the magical and queer when we have got ourselves onto the wrong track:

> In our failure to understand the use of a word we take it as the expression of a queer *process*. (As we think of time as a queer medium, of the mind as a queer kind of being.) (196)

---

[14] One might reasonably speculate that Wittgenstein here has in mind his own earlier conception of possibility in the *Tractatus*: 'In logic nothing is accidental: if a thing *can* occur in a state of affairs, the possibility of the state of affairs must be written into the thing itself' (*TLP* 2.012), 'Objects contain the possibility of all situations' (*TLP* 2.014). Indeed the whole earlier conception of logical space lends itself to the suspect idea of possibilities as shadowy forms of actuality.

Wittgenstein's rejection of an experiential conception of understanding is, in fact, only part of a broader campaign to discourage parallel conceptions of other psychological concepts; it is not just where *meaning* is involved that there is a powerful tendency to construe psychological concepts as expressing states of consciousness. Thus we find him in different places rejecting such a conception of knowing, believing, attending, recognising, comparing, reading, wishing, intending, willing.[15] None of these concepts stands for conscious experiential contents, either quotidian or queer, as the empiricist (Humean) tradition had supposed: what we call the 'psychological' is not a homogeneous domain.

So much for Wittgenstein's opposition to the first version of thesis (i); let us turn now to the version which construes understanding as some kind of *non-conscious* inner state or process. Wittgenstein typically represents this idea as a sort of fallback position for someone who wants to insist that meaning is something inner but has been persuaded that it is not inner in the state-of-consciousness sense; thus an internal 'mental apparatus' is introduced to harbour what consciousness was seen not to be able to. This mental apparatus can either be conceived as a physical mechanism located in the nervous system or as some kind of unconscious but non-physical mental mechanism. The claim Wittgenstein here wishes to reject is that the difference between one who understands and one who does not understand consists in their being in different unconscious or physical states. In the *Investigations* there is little which bears directly upon Wittgenstein's attitude towards this claim; the following remarks all but exhaust his treatment of the topic:

> Now we should of course like to say: What goes on in that practised reader and in the beginner when they utter the word *can't* be the same. And if there is no difference in what they happen to be conscious of there must be one in the unconscious workings of their minds, or, again, in the brain.—So we should

[15] Discussions of these concepts can be found in the following places: knowing, 148; believing, *Z* 75, *BB* pp. 144–5; attending, 33–4, *Z* 90–1; recognising, *BB* p. 165; comparing, *BB* pp. 85–7; reading, 156–178; wishing, *BB* pp. 41–2; intending, 591, p. 217; willing, *BB* pp. 150–2. It would thus be a mistake, in view of the generality of Wittgenstein's point, to treat the case of meaning as for him unique; there is a large family of psychological concepts which invite the same kind of misconstrual as the concept of meaning does.

like to say: There are at all events two different mechanisms at work here. And what goes on in them must distinguish reading from not reading.—But these mechanisms are only hypotheses, models designed to explain, to sum up, what you observe.   (156)

But in the case of the living reading-machine "reading" meant reacting to written signs in such-and-such ways. This concept was therefore quite independent of that of a mental or other mechanism.—Nor can the teacher here say of the pupil: "Perhaps he was already reading when he said that word". For there is no doubt about what he did.—The change when the pupil began to read was a change in his *behaviour*; and it makes no sense here to speak of 'a first word in his new state'.   (157)

But isn't that only because of our too slight acquaintance with what goes on in the brain and the nervous system? If we had a more accurate knowledge of these things we should see what connexions were established by the training, and then we should be able to say when we looked into his brain: "Now he has *read* this word, now the reading connexion has been set up".——And it presumably *must* be like that—for otherwise how could we be so sure that there was such a connexion? That it is so is presumably a priori—or is it only probable? And how probable is it? Now, ask yourself: what do you *know* about these things?——But if it is a priori, that means that it is a form of account which is very convincing to us.   (158)

Elsewhere, however, we find a fuller statement of Wittgenstein's view of the relation between the psychological and the physical:

No supposition seems to me more natural than that there is no process in the brain correlated with associating or with thinking; so that it would be impossible to read off thought-processes from brain-processes. I mean this: if I talk or write there is, I assume, a system of impulses going out from my brain and correlated with my spoken or written thoughts. But why should the *system* continue further in the direction of the centre? Why should this order not proceed, so to speak, out of chaos? The case would be like the following—certain kinds of plants multiply by seed, so that a seed always produces a plant of the same kind as that from which it was produced—but *nothing* in the seed corresponds to the plant which comes from it; so that it is impossible to infer the properties or structure of the plant from those of the seed that it comes out of—this can only be done from the *history* of the seed. So an organism might come into being even out of something quite amorphous, as it were causelessly; and there is no reason why this should not really hold for our thoughts, and hence for our talking and writing.   (Z 608)

It is thus perfectly possible that certain psychological phenomena *cannot* be investigated physiologically, because physiologically nothing corresponds to them.   (Z 609)

I saw this man years ago: now I have seen him again, I recognize him, I remember his name. And why does there have to be a cause of this remembering in my nervous system? Why must something or other, whatever it may be, be stored up there *in any form*? Why *must* a trace have been left behind? Why should there not be a psychological regularity to which *no* physiological regularity corresponds? If this upsets our concepts of causality then it is high time they were upset.   (Z 610)

Putting these sections in *Zettel* together with what is said in the *Investigations*, we can conclude that Wittgenstein would deny that understanding requires any basis in a person's physical states: there need not exist any such basis, and even if there is a physical basis it is quite irrelevant to the concept of understanding.

So far we have interpreted Wittgenstein as objecting to the idea of understanding as an inner or internal state; but there is at least one passage in which he goes further than this:

(a) "Understanding a word": a state. But a *mental* state?— Depression, excitement, pain, are called mental states. Carry out a grammatical investigation as follows: we say
"He was depressed the whole day".
"He was in great excitement the whole day".
"He has been in continuous pain since yesterday".—
We also say "Since yesterday I have understood this word". "Continuously", though?—To be sure, one can speak of an interruption of understanding. But in what cases? Compare: "When did your pains get less?" and "When did you stop understanding that word?"   (p. 59)

Here Wittgenstein is apparently opposing talk of understanding as a state of mind; and his reason appears to be that only concepts of conscious states deserve to be so described and understanding is not a concept of this category. To call understanding 'mental' would be to risk assimilating it to pain, depression and excitement, thus inviting the erroneous 'inner state' conception. In order to discourage this assimilation Wittgenstein advises us not to think of understanding as something 'mental' at all.[16]

One upshot of accepting thesis (i) is that we shall no longer think of meaning and understanding as 'parallel processes' occurring simultaneously with the hearing or uttering of a sentence: to understand what is said is not for something to *go on* in you as you hear the utterance – neither conscious, unconscious, nor physical. Thus acceptance of thesis (i) is intimately connected with those sections in which Wittgenstein warns against conceiving understanding and related notions as a sort of inward counterpart to hearing or speaking; for example:

> For neither the expression "to intend the definition in such-and-such a way" nor the expression "to interpret the definition in such-and-such a way" stands for a process which accompanies the giving and hearing of the definition   (34)[17]

Thesis (ii), that understanding a sign is not interpreting it, is given less space than thesis (i) in Wittgenstein's text, though it occurs in some especially significant sections of the *Investigations*, notably in connexion with the notion of grasping a rule. The passages in question are these:

> "But how can a rule shew me what I have to do at *this* point? Whatever I do is, on some interpretation, in accord with the rule."—That is not what we ought to say, but rather: any interpretation still hangs in the air along with what it interprets, and cannot give it any support. Interpretations by themselves do not determine meaning.   (198)

> This was our paradox: no course of action could be determined by a rule, because every course of action can be made out to accord with the rule. The answer was: if everything can be made out to accord with the rule, then it can also be made out to conflict with it. And so there would be neither accord nor conflict here.

> It can be seen that there is a misunderstanding here from the mere fact that in the course of our argument we give one interpretation after another; as if each one contented us at least for a moment, until we thought of yet another standing behind

[16] *Cf.* 693; *Z* 26; *BB* pp. 3, 78.
[17] *Cf. BB* p. 148.

it. What this shews is that there is a way of grasping a rule which is *not* an *interpretation*, but which is exhibited in what we call "obeying the rule" and "going against it" in actual cases.

Hence there is an inclination to say: every action according to the rule is an interpretation. But we ought to restrict the term "interpretation" to the substitution of one expression of the rule for another.   (201)

Wittgenstein supplies us with precious little guidance as to his use of 'interpretation' in these passages; his sole elucidatory comment is the advice to 'restrict the term "interpretation" to the substitution of one expression of the rule for another'.[18] From this comment, however, it is sufficiently evident that Wittgenstein means by an interpretation of a sign simply *another sign*, and by interpreting he in effect means *translating* one sign into another. Some further light is shed on Wittgenstein's intentions here by going back to 85–6:

A rule stands there like a sign-post—Does the sign-post leave no doubt open about the way I have to go? Does it shew which direction I am to take when I have passed it; whether along the road or the footpath or cross-country? But where is it said which way I am to follow it; whether in the direction of its finger or (e.g.) in the opposite one?—And if there were, not a single sign-post, but a chain of adjacent ones or of chalk marks on the ground—is there only *one* way of interpreting them?—So I can say, the sign-post does after all leave no room for doubt. Or rather: it sometimes leaves room for doubt and sometimes not. And now this is no longer a philosophical proposition, but an empirical one   (85)

Imagine a language-game like (2) played with the help of a table. The signs given to B by A are now written ones. B has a table; in the first column are the signs used in the game, in the second pictures of building stones. A shews B such a written sign; B looks it up in the table, looks at the picture opposite, and so on. So the table is a rule which he follows in executing orders.—One learns to look the picture up in the table by receiving a training, and part of this training consists perhaps in the pupil's learning to pass with his finger horizontally from left

[18] *Cf.* also: *Z* 229, 230, 231, 234, 235; *BB* pp. 4–5, 33–4. These passages make it quite clear that an 'interpretation' is always, for Wittgenstein, another symbol; thus he says: 'Whenever we interpret a symbol in one way or another, the interpretation is a new symbol added to the old one' (*BB* p. 33).

to right; and so, as it were, to draw a series of horizontal lines on the table.

Suppose different ways of reading a table were now introduced; one time, as above, according to the scheme:

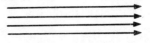

another time like this:

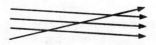

or in some other way.—Such a schema is supplied with the table as the rule for its use.

Can we not now imagine further rules to explain *this* one? And, on the other hand, was that first table incomplete without the schema of arrows? and are other tables incomplete without their schemata?   (86)

An interpretation is thus what Wittgenstein calls in 84 'a rule determining the application of a rule', where examples of rules are things like signposts and tables.[19] So we can say that part of Wittgenstein's point in these passages is to deny that understanding a sign consists in translating it into some other sign, no matter of what kind. His point is not, of course, that understanding *never* involves such translation; his point is that it cannot *always* do so. This point is of a piece with his frequent observation that 'explanations come to an end somewhere' (1): when we explain the meaning of a word to someone we presuppose that he understands the words of our explanation, and no explanations of meaning would be possible unless some words were understood without (verbal) explanation. Under-

[19] Wittgenstein says: 'Tables, ostensive definitions, and similar instruments I shall call rules, in accordance with ordinary usage. The use of a rule can be explained by a further rule' (*BB* p. 90). Whether this is really in accordance with the ordinary usage of the word 'rule' is not perhaps clear; what is clear is that Wittgenstein intends no significant distinction to be drawn between 'rule' and 'expression of a rule', so that a 'rule for determining the application of a rule' is to be understood as one *sign* determining the application of another, i.e. an 'interpretation' in the sense defined.

standing must ultimately rest upon more than (or less than) the association of one symbol with another.

This is not, however, all that Wittgenstein means by denying that understanding is interpreting, for the notion of interpretation has I think other connotations for him. Thus consider his use of 'interpret' in the sections dealing with seeing-as:

> Do I really see something different each time, or do I only interpret what I see in a different way? I am inclined to say the former. But why?—To interpret is to think, to do something; seeing is a state.
>
> Now it is easy to recognize cases in which we are *interpreting*. When we interpret we form hypotheses, which may prove false. (p. 212)

To judge from these remarks Wittgenstein invests the notion of interpreting with the ideas of thinking, forming hypotheses, doing something – as opposed to literal seeing, receiving what is given to one, being cognitively passive. And of course this is an entirely natural and correct way to employ the notion: to interpret is to bring something to bear upon the 'data', to *take* what is given in a certain way – in such a way as to add to or enrich what is presented. Seeing-as, according to Wittgenstein, is not in this sense interpreting what one sees; it enters right into what one sees. Now it is interesting to compare Wittgenstein's non-interpretative view of seeing-as with his like view of linguistic understanding. It is clear that Wittgenstein does not have in mind the translational notion of interpretation in his discussion of seeing-as, but I think it is reasonable to find in his use of that notion in his discussion of understanding some echo of the force it has for him in connexion with seeing-as: for it is an important element in Wittgenstein's conception of rule-following that it be represented as unreflective and automatic (see below p. 19f), not as the forming of a hypothesis upon the basis of evidence – rule-following does not involve *taking thought*. One accordingly does not *choose* to understand a sign in a certain way, as one does not choose to see something as a such-and-such. Use of the notion of interpretation imports an overly 'intellectualist' conception of the phenomena of seeing and understanding; it underestimates the primitiveness of what is going on. If we combine this aspect of the notion of interpretation with the explicit directions Wittgenstein gives in 201 about this notion, then we can say the following: Wittgenstein is rejecting the idea that understanding (grasping a rule) consists in forming a *hypothesis* about the correct *translation* of the sign to be understood. Such a conception misrepresents the character of the phenomenon and also involves insuperable logical difficulties (the threat of an infinite regress). (It is not that understanding is, according to Wittgenstein, a *sort* of seeing-as – and hence is opposed to interpreting just in virtue of this subsumption; the point is rather that understanding is *analogous* to seeing-as with respect to the contrast it presents with genuine interpreting.)

Wittgenstein's stated reason for denying that understanding is a kind of translating is that 'any interpretation still hangs in the air along with what it interprets, and cannot give it any support' (198). This point is elaborated in 201 with the observation that a mere association of signs cannot determine what is a correct and what an incorrect use of those signs: meaning fixes correct use, but interpretations cannot determine linguistic correctness, so meanings cannot be interpretations. In other words, a sign is in itself just a piece of lifeless syntax, and syntax can never add up to meaning; so it is hopeless to conceive of grasp of meaning as the association of signs. For no sign is *intrinsically* meaningful.

It may fairly be asked why Wittgenstein would think it worth stressing this point: why does he attach such weight to what appears to be a rather obvious point? I think that there are two sorts of reasons why Wittgenstein makes so much of this point; and when these are appreciated it will seem less surprising that he insisted upon what may appear quite undeniable – something no philosopher in his right mind would dispute. The first reason has to do with the enterprise of analysis, as exemplified by Russell's logical atomism and by Wittgenstein's earlier conception of an underlying ideal language in the *Tractatus*.[20] For analysis precisely consists in the association of signs with signs; definition is nothing other than the substitution of one sign for another. The picture was that there is a basic or deep level of language whose semantics is perspicuous

[20] See Russell's 'The Philosophy of Logical Atomism', in *Logic and Knowledge*, ed. R.C. Marsh (George Allen and Unwin: London, 1956); and *TLP*, e.g. 3.201, 4.221, 5.5562.

and requires no explanation – a level of self-interpreting signs, one might almost say. Correlatively, understanding the familiar signs of unanalysed ordinary language consists in a mental operation of translation into the ideal language, this being somehow antecedently understood. Now I think Wittgenstein wants to say that the motivating and sustaining presupposition of this whole picture is that there are signs which, so to speak, take care of their own meaning – that have their meaning somehow written into them; but this idea is seen to be manifestly incoherent once it is made explicit, since signs considered in themselves can never determine (correct) use – and whatever meaning is, it must determine use.[21] And once this point is properly absorbed the project of analysis loses the significance it appeared to have: analysis as such cannot determine meaning but must always presuppose some independent determination of meaning; so it cannot play the foundational role assigned to it by Russell and the earlier Wittgenstein. A philosophically illuminating account of meaning will therefore have to take a quite different form. Thus it seems to me that Wittgenstein's apparently elementary logical point has quite considerable significance when seen in its historical and philosophical context.

The second reason why I think Wittgenstein attaches such importance to his rejection of the interpretational conception of understanding is that he sees a connexion between this conception and the idea that meaning consists in something coming before the mind. The connexion goes both ways: an interpretation, e.g. an algebraic formula, is something that comes before one's mind; and an item that comes before one's mind has the logical status of an interpretation. The first of these points shows that the conception of understanding as translation is committed to viewing meaning as an (intentional) *object* of consciousness (or of the unconscious if the translation operation is supposed to be somehow unconscious), and so inherits all of the objections to be raised against that view. The second point is less obvious and of greater significance for Wittgenstein: it amounts to the suggestion that anything that

---

[21] When I say that meaning must, for Wittgenstein, determine use, I am not, of course, using 'determine' in a causal sense; I am using it rather in the sense of 'fix', i.e. in a quasi-logical sense, as when one says (e.g.) that the logical form of an argument determines whether it is valid.

comes before one's mind is logically in the same case as a mere symbol. Thus Wittgenstein's nonsufficiency argument against meaning as an object of consciousness (e.g. an image) is paralleled by his argument against the interpretational conception: both sorts of item are susceptible of indefinitely many ascriptions of meaning, so they fail to determine what counts as a correct use of the sign in question. Signs and pictures can be *applied* in all sorts of ways, so they cannot dictate what is the *right* way to apply them. In view of this parallel we can take Wittgenstein's opposition to the interpretational conception to be intended to subsume any account of meaning as something coming before the mind; for what comes before the mind is just, in effect, another sign. This subsumption is made most explicit in a passage from the *Blue Book*:

> As a part of the system of language, one may say, the sentence has life. But one is tempted to imagine that which gives the sentence life as something in an occult sphere, accompanying the sentence. But whatever accompanied it would for us just be another sign. (*BB* p. 5)

A conscious content is an accompaniment to the hearing of a sign, and an accompanying process is in the same logical position as a sign – it stands in need of having its application fixed. This thesis is by no means trivial, since it cuts against a dominant conception of meaning: Wittgenstein's claim is that (e.g.) the empiricist view of meaning really reduces to an interpretational conception, and so is open to the *reductio* he directs against that conception. By generalising the notion of a sign in this way Wittgenstein's rejection of the idea that understanding is translating acquires a greater significance than it might otherwise appear to have. In the light of this point, and the previous point about the role of analysis, I think we can see that it is no objection to our interpretation of Wittgenstein that the target of thesis (ii) is a position that (once made explicit) is obviously false: on the contrary, Wittgenstein takes it that the conception he exposes as unworkable lies behind certain dominant and tempting views of langauge and understanding.

Wittgenstein's third negative thesis concerns what might be called the epistemology of rule-following. He wishes to give a

characterisation of what it is actually like to follow a rule, to
remind us of the 'phenomenology' of (e.g.) using a word; and
so to get away from certain natural philosophical misconceptions of what sort of activity rule-following is.[22] His main
thesis is that obeying a rule is not ultimately based upon
reasons; when we apply words to things we do not do so
because we have some *reason* for thinking that this is the right
application, something we could produce to show that our
application is justified if someone were to throw down a
sceptical challenge. Thus he says:

> How can he *know* how he is to continue a pattern by
> himself—whatever instruction you give him?—Well, how do I
> know?——If that means "Have I reasons?" the answer is: my
> reasons will soon give out. And then I shall act, without
> reasons. (211)

> "How am I able to obey a rule?"—If this is not a question
> about causes, then it is about the justification for my following
> the rule in the way I do.
> If I have exhausted the justifications I have reached bedrock,
> and my spade is turned. Then I am inclined to say: "This is
> simply what I do."   (217)

> He must go on like this *without a reason*. Not, however,
> because he cannot yet grasp the reason but because—in *this*
> system—there is no reason. ("The chain of reasons comes to an
> end.")   (Z 301)[23]

If I were pressed to demonstrate that how I am inclined to go
on is the correct way, I would be at a loss; my application of

---

[22] Wittgenstein does not himself use the word 'phenomenology' in this connexion. I
do not mean to suggest, in using this word, that Wittgenstein is concerned with the
condition of consciousness when a rule is being followed, as a phenomenologist might
be; I mean merely that he is concerned to give a theoretically unprejudiced description
of the actual phenomena of following a rule – to remind us of what really goes on when
a rule is being followed.

[23] *Cf.* also: *BB* pp. 14–15, 87–89, 143, 148-9. It might seem that in these passages
Wittgenstein gives inequivalent formulations of his thesis about the lack of reasons; for
he says now that my reasons come to an *end* and now that I act *without* reasons; and the
first of these claims does not entail the second. Light is shed on this by the following
remark: 'If on the other hand you realize that the chain of *actual* reasons has a
beginning, you will no longer be revolted by the idea of a case in which there is *no*
reason for the way you obey the order' (*BB* p. 15). I think this remark makes it
sufficiently clear that Wittgenstein's basic thesis is that acting in accordance with a rule
is (typically) acting *without* a reason; his point is that even in the cases in which a reason
can be produced, this reason cannot itself be based upon some further reason – at the
foundation there must be rationally ungrounded ways of acting.

signs does not rest upon a foundation of justifying reasons in the sort of way envisaged by classical foundationalist conceptions of knowledge.[24] Wittgenstein puts essentially the same point in terms of the notion of *guidance*:

> Whence comes the idea that the beginning of a series is a visible section of rails invisibly laid to infinity? Well, we might imagine rails instead of a rule. And infinitely long rails correspond to the unlimited application of a rule.   (218)
>
> "We see a series in just *one* way!"—All right, but what is that way? Clearly we see it algebraically, and as a segment of an expansion. Or is there more in it than that?—"But the way we see it surely gives us everything!"—But that is not an observation about the segment of the series; or about anything that we notice in it; it gives expression to the fact that we look to the rule for instruction and *do something*, without appealing to anything else for guidance.   (228)

It is not that in following a rule I consult something ('rails') which *tells me* that a certain application or continuation of the rule is correct, as I might consult a recipe in making a cake; I am, so to speak, on my own.[25] The interpretational conception of understanding *would* provide just the sort of guidance Wittgenstein says there is not, since a further sign would be something I might consult to determine how a given sign is to be applied – wondering how to go on applying S I observe that it is translated by S' and that S' is to be applied in *this* way. But of course this just transfers the epistemological problem onto S' – I must know how to apply *it* without guidance from some other sign. An especially tempting picture of such guidance,

---

[24] *Cf.* 'The limits of empiricism are not assumptions unguaranteed, or intuitively known to be correct: they are ways in which we make comparisons and in which we act' (*RFM* p. 387). In effect, Wittgenstein is saying that empiricists, in so far as they are foundationalists, make the mistake of locating epistemic bedrock either in (mysteriously) self-evident judgements or in nothing at all (hence scepticism); they fail to see that the (adequate) bedrock consists in how we unreflectively act – this being what grounds our possession of concepts ('The limit of the empirical – is *concept-formation*' (*RFM* p. 237)). That, at any rate, is Wittgenstein's view.

[25] Of course it is not false to say that I am guided in my actions by the rule itself, e.g. by an order or a mathematical formula; the error is to suppose that I need to turn to anything *else* for guidance. The feeling that I do need to turn to something else arises from the fact that the rule I am following could in principle be *interpreted* in indefinitely many ways, it being just a sign. Wittgenstein's claim is that when I am presented with such a sign (i.e. with the 'expression of a rule') I act unhesitatingly and am not paralysed by the lack of guidance from elsewhere – and not because my actions are somehow *irrational*.

one which might seem to overcome the inherent impotence of the interpretational conception, invokes the notion of inner intuition; but Wittgenstein is quick to point out the inadequacy of this idea:

> So it must have been intuition that removed this doubt?—If intuition is an inner voice—how do I know *how* I am to obey it? And how do I know that it doesn't mislead me? For if it can guide me right, it can also guide me wrong.
> ((Intuition an unnecessary shuffle.))   (213)

The voice of intuition must either be admitted to raise the same epistemological question or it is a manifestation of the tendency to resort to the magical and mythological when the ordinary and quotidian will not do.

It is important to Wittgenstein that my ultimate lack of reasons is not an occasion for genuine doubt: that my rule-following inclinations do not rest on a bedrock of reasons does not imply that I can or should entertain doubts about those inclinations:

> When someone who I am afraid of orders me to continue the series, I act quickly, with perfect certainty, and the lack of reasons does not trouble me.   (212)

> "But this initial segment of a series obviously admitted of various interpretations (e.g. by means of alegbraic expressions) and so you must first have chosen *one* such interpretation."— Not at all. A doubt was possible in certain circumstances. But that is not to say that I did doubt, or even could doubt. (There is something to be said, which is connected with this, about the psychological "atmosphere" of a process.)   (213)

Wittgenstein is here insisting, in opposition to traditional epistemology, that the notions of reason and doubt are not correlative: we are not to suppose that one has no doubts just in case one has good reasons. Doubt can be out of place (not indicated) even when it has not been removed by reasons; for in some cases the bringing to bear of reasons is deemed inappropriate – it is just not part of the language-game. In fact I think Wittgenstein would want to say something stronger: that where the bringing to bear of reasons *is* appropriate the possibility of doubt is correspondingly real. For when reasons are appropriately brought to bear we are dealing with beliefs and actions which are *reflective*, with respect to which reasons may be weighed and evaluated; and where the question of the goodness of a reason is appropriately raised it will be appropriate to entertain doubts about the quality of the reasons one has. But when an activity is as undeliberative as using language is it lies outside the sphere of the reason-based and doubt-ridden.

The absence of doubt is in turn connected with the absence of the phenomenon of *choice* from the activity of rule-following: I do not have to *select* from a range of possibilities which pattern of use is required by the meaning of a sign, as it were plumping for one alternative over a range of others between which it is necessary for me to choose. Thus Wittgenstein says:

> "All the steps are really already taken" means: I no longer have any choice. The rule, once stamped with a particular meaning, traces the lines along which it is to be followed through the whole of space.——But if something of this sort really were the case, how would it help?
>
> No; my description only made sense if it was to be understood symbolically.—I should have said: *This is how it strikes me.*
>
> When I obey a rule, I do not choose.
> I obey the rule *blindly*. (219)
>
> "But surely you can see. . . .?" That is just the characteristic expression of someone who is under the compulsion of a rule. (231)

To obey a rule 'blindly' is to obey it without guidance, and guidance is what one needs in order to have one's doubts removed when faced with the necessity to choose; but since there is no choice of this kind to be made one simply *acts* in the way that is natural and spontaneous. ("This is simply what I do"). It is thus essential for Wittgenstein that what is natural in following a rule should present itself as inevitable, immediate, unreflective, automatic:

> One does not feel that one has always got to wait upon the nod (the whisper) of the rule. On the contrary, we are not on tenterhooks about what it will tell us next, but it always tells us the same, and we do what it tells us. (223)
>
> The rule can only seem to me to produce all its consequences in advance if I draw them as a *matter of course*. As much as it is a

matter of course for me to call this colour "blue". (Criteria for
the fact that something is 'a matter of course' for me.)   (239)[26]

The general picture Wittgenstein is here advocating is a sort of
anti-intellectualism about the activity of using signs in a rule-
governed way: he wishes to emphasise the *habitual* character of
rule-following and to discourage an overly rationalistic
conception of the nature of this form of behaviour. To put his
view crudely: we do better to compare our use of language with
the trained behaviour of a dog when it puts out its paw than
with the reflections of a scientist weighing evidence and doing
experiments (of course this is really *too* crude, but perhaps it
serves to get the point across).[27]

It is instructive to compare Wittgenstein's view of the
epistemology of rule-following with his attitude towards
induction. In fact, Wittgenstein makes this comparison himself
(324–6): he rejects the traditional demand for a justification of
our expectations and fears, comparing this rejection with his
analogous rejection of the idea that we need reasons to
continue a series as we naturally do. He says of our inductive
certainty that a book will fall to the ground when released that
'we don't need any grounds for *this* certainty either. What
could justify the certainty *better* than success?' (324). And he
writes, in a way very reminiscent of 211 on my lack of reasons
for continuing a series as I do, 'We expect *this*, and are
surprised at *that*. But the chain of reasons has an end.' (326)
Wittgenstein's intention here is to contest the very *appropriate-
ness* of the sort of question that leads to the classical problem of
induction – as he wishes to discourage raising the sorts of
epistemological questions which threaten to lead to scepticism
about the correctness of our use of language. In a later series of
remarks (472–486) Wittgenstein expands upon his attitude
towards inductive knowledge, his fundamental contention
being that philosophers have supposed an epistemological
problem here because of an inappropriate and tendentious
notion of a reason: we should simply *describe* our actual

[26] *Cf.* 'One follows the rule *mechanically*. Hence one compares it with a mechanism.
"Mechanical" – that means: without thinking. But *entirely* without thinking? Without
reflecting' (*RFM* p. 422).
[27] Wittgenstein does in fact make this comparison himself; he says: 'The child learns
this language from the grown-ups by being trained to its use. I am using the word
"trained" in a way strictly analogous to that in which we talk of an animal being
trained to do certain things' (*BB* p. 77; *cf.* also *BB* pp. 89–90).

practice in arriving at attitudes towards the future and not insist that these attitudes be grounded in something other than what we ordinarily *take* to be their grounds.[28] The parallelism between Wittgenstein's account of rule-following and his account of induction thus reflects an insistence that we learn to accept the fact that our justifications come to an end, and not worry as philosophers that this threatens to undermine our habitual confidence in what we do. (Wittgenstein's strategy in the two cases is well seen in his asking us to consider not just cognitive attitudes towards the future but also affective attitudes: thus in 212 and 473 he invites us to think of how *fear* makes the sceptical problems of rule-following and induction, respectively, look unreal; and this is part of his attack on the intellectualist conception of these matters.)

From these passages it is abundantly clear that thesis (iii) is not intended sceptically; quite the contrary. Wittgenstein means to be *rejecting* the traditional sceptical move from the lack of reasons (or their soon petering out) to the unavailability of knowledge and warranted certainty; he rejects the demand for a *demonstration* of our knowledge-claims in terms of (roughly speaking) Cartesian foundations. In fact what we have in the *Investigations*, in these passages on rule-following and elsewhere, is the germinal form of the sort of epistemology most fully set out in *On Certainty*; and this latter work is manifestly anti-sceptical. The following passages give the flavour of Wittgenstein's general epistemological position:

> What *counts* as its test?—"But is this an adequate test? And, if so, must it not be recognizable as such in logic?"—As if giving grounds did not come to an end sometime. But the end is not an ungrounded presupposition: it is an ungrounded way of acting. (*OC* 110)

> Giving grounds, however, justifying the evidence, comes to an end;—but the end is not certain propositions' striking us immediately as true, i.e. it is not a kind of *seeing* on our part; it is our *acting*, which lies at the bottom of the language-game. (*OC* 204)

In the case of rule-following our natural ways of acting with signs provide an adequate basis for the epistemic claims we

---

[28] See esp. 480–4; note also: 'Justification by experience comes to an end. If it did not it would not be justification' (485).

make about the correctness of what we do; they give us the *right*
to have the confidence we actually do have.

Wittgenstein's attitude towards self-ascriptions of correct
rule-following may also be compared with his view of self-
ascriptions of sensations – and in two respects. First, we can
note that Wittgenstein takes a parallel view of the kind of
warrant we have for the two kinds of self-ascription: I do not
mean by this that he regards our knowledge that we are
following a rule correctly as knowledge of a kind of sensation
we have – that would be quite wrong; I mean that in both cases
he insists that a lack of reasons is not a lack of epistemic right.
About my use of 'I am in pain' he says:

> "When I say 'I am in pain' I am at any rate justified *before
> myself*."—What does that mean? Does it mean: "If someone
> else could know what I am calling 'pain', he would admit that I
> was using the word correctly"?'
>
> To use a word without justification does not mean to use it
> without right.   (289)

And this last sentence is a motto he might well have adopted to
summarise his view of our knowledge of how to follow a rule:
the purport of the motto is that to lack a justification for a
claim is not necessarily to suffer an epistemological defect.
The second point of comparison is that Wittgenstein suggests
in both cases that the model of *description* is not the most
appropriate to capture the significance of these self-ascriptions.
Thus he says of the sentence 'Now I know how to go on':

> *This is how these words are used*. It would be quite misleading,
> in this last case, for instance, to call the words a "description of
> a mental state".—One might rather call them a "signal"; and
> we judge whether it was rightly employed by what he goes on to
> do.   (180)

> "Now I know how to go on!" is an exclamation; it
> corresponds to an instinctive sound, a glad start. Of course it
> does not follow from my feeling that I shall not find I am stuck
> when I do try to go on.—Here there are cases in which I should
> say: "When I said I knew how to go on, I *did* know." One
> will say that if, for example, an unforeseen interruption
> occurs. But what is unforeseen must not simply be that I
> get stuck.   (323)

That is, the significance of self-ascriptions of understanding (grasping a rule) is not that of describing a mental state one is in but is rather that of an *expression*. Compare this passage:

> How do words *refer* to sensations?—There doesn't seem to be any problem here; don't we talk about sensations every day, and give them names? But how is the connexion between the name and the thing named set up? This question is the same as: how does a human being learn the meaning of the names of sensations?—of the word "pain" for example. Here is one possibility: words are connected with the primitive, the natural, expressions of the sensation and used in their place. A child has hurt himself and he cries; and then adults talk to him and teach him exclamations and, later, sentences. They teach the child new pain-behaviour.
>
> "So you are saying that the word 'pain' really means crying?"—On the contrary: the verbal expression of pain replaces crying and does not describe it.   (244)

Here Wittgenstein is suggesting an expressive view of self-ascriptions of pain; such self-ascriptions come to occupy the place of more primitive reactions to pain – they do not serve to *describe* those reactions, or that pain. Although Wittgenstein does not explicitly say as much, one might conjecture that a parallel account of 'Now I can go on' would come naturally to him: this utterance comes to *replace* the more primitive behaviour of actually following rules as the result of suitable training; the non-verbal expressions of understanding get augmented with saying that one understands, and so this saying bears the imprint of its origins – it acts as a 'signal' of understanding.

Thesis (iii) is not unconnected with theses (i) and (ii); for both the inner state model and the interpretational conception encourage the idea of a foundation of reasons for applying signs as one does. Suppose you are challenged to justify your application of a word: according to the views Wittgenstein rejects, you could meet the challenge by observing that an appropriate item was then before your mind, guiding you in the correct use of the word in question. For example, you applied 'red' to a red object because that object matched in colour the image that came before your mind when you uttered 'red'. That is, your use of words is justified by the fact that there are certain mental accompaniments of use which provide you with reasons for using words as you do – much as you have reasons for using words of a foreign language as you do, namely that those words mean the same as words of your native language and *their* correct use is such-and-such. When in doubt about how a word is to be used you can consult the state of consciousness that word prompts in you and see what it recommends: paradigmatically, you introspect which mental *picture* the word evokes and apply the word to what fits that picture. We know what Wittgenstein's view of this whole idea is: such pictures, even if present, do not supply the desired justification since they are themselves susceptible of various interpretations – so they do not serve to remove the doubt. This point is clearly made in 239:

> How is he to know what colour he is to pick out when he hears "red"?—Quite simple: he is to take the colour whose image occurs to him when he hears the word.—But how is he to know which colour it is 'whose image occurs to him'? Is a further criterion needed for that? (There is indeed such a procedure as choosing the colour which occurs to one when one hears the word ". . . .")
>
> " 'Red' means the colour that occurs to me when I hear the word 'red' "—would be a *definition*. Not an explanation of *what it is* to use a word as a name.   (239)

So theses (i) and (ii) have to be established before thesis (iii) will be acknowledged; and of course Wittgenstein does place his advocacy of thesis (iii) after his demolition of the inner state model and the interpretational conception. Conversely, it is important for Wittgenstein that his anti-foundationalist epistemology be accepted if his readers are to be happy with theses (i) and (ii): for the cogency of his case for those theses leaves us in danger of scepticism unless the sceptic's presuppositions have been successfully undermined – we have to cease to hanker after what theses (i) and (ii) say we can't have. (This interdependence of the three theses bears out a point I emphasised earlier – namely, that Wittgenstein's discussion connects and overlaps as it progresses through what may at first seem like separate stages.)[29]

Wittgenstein's presentation of his own positive view of

[29] One might wonder which of Wittgenstein's negative theses is the basic one – which mistakes underlies the others? Wittgenstein does not, I think, suggest any particular ordering of basicness: the three mistakes are interrelated and mutually supporting, so that each has to be undermined separately if the whole package is to be convincingly refuted.

meaning and rule-following is interwoven with his criticism of views he rejects; one might almost say that his rejection of these views and his advocacy of the view he prefers are but aspects of a single movement of thought.[30] And this is connected with the fact, noted at the outset, that the point of Wittgenstein's positive suggestions is primarily negative: accepting the correct view of the matter consists mainly in seeing that other tempting views are wrong. There is thus a sense in which Wittgenstein's positive view is *unexplanatory*: he does not purport to give a *theory* of meaning, or necessary and sufficient conditions for rule following, but rather aims to get the reader to see the phenomena in the right way. We should remember such passages as this:

> A main source of our failure to understand is that we do not *command a clear view* of the use of our words.—Our grammar is lacking in this sort of perspicuity. A perspicuous representation produces just that understanding which consists in 'seeing connexions'. Hence the importance of finding and inventing *intermediate cases*.
>
> The concept of a perspicuous representation is of fundamental significance for us. It earmarks the form of account we give, the way we look at things. (Is this a 'Weltanschauung'?)
> (122)

Wittgenstein's aim is to say just so much about meaning as is necessary to protect us from seeing it wrongly; he wishes to describe the 'grammar' of the notions that give us trouble in such a way that we shall form a clear view of them – and this will involve the *connecting of concepts*. What we thereby come to see may strike us as truistic or even as trivial, as just an emphatic restatement of what we already knew; but Wittgenstein's point is that this is as it should be, since we need to resist the temptation to dig deeper than the phenomena allow.[31] This

---

[30] The reason I say this is that it is the failure of inner interpretational states to fix a unique use that is the fundamental flaw in the conception Wittgenstein rejects, and his positive view is precisely that meaning is fixed by use: only use itself can determine use, as it were.

[31] Thus he says: 'I want to say here that it can never be our job to reduce anything to anything, or to explain anything. Philosophy really *is* "purely descriptive"' (*BB* p. 18); 'Our method is *purely descriptive*; the descriptions we give are not hints of explanations' (*BB* p. 125). This conception of philosophy is of a piece with the contrast Wittgenstein draws between science and philosophy, as the context of the first of these quotations makes explicit.

is not to say that we shall find everything Wittgenstein says uncontroversially true; it is rather to register an important feature of Wittgenstein's intended method which must guide whatever interpretation we give of him. What Wittgenstein takes to be a mere description of our use of words may be something it requires philosophical effort to see our way clear to accepting; or it may be that Wittgenstein is simply wrong to characterise the grammar of the concepts with which he is concerned in the way he does. In any case it is not a good objection to a proposed interpretation of Wittgenstein that the interpretation represents his positive view as platitudinous (judged from a standpoint which is other than his).

It seems to me useful to divide Wittgenstein's positive account into two parts, corresponding to the notion of *technique* and the notion of *custom*, though Wittgenstein himself does not treat these two notions separately when advancing his positive account. Let us consider his introduction of the notion of technique first.

Wittgenstein frequently associates the notion of understanding with the notion of a *capacity* to do something and with knowing-how: to understand a sign is to have an ability, to be master of a technique, to possess a practical skill. Following a rule is *exercising* this kind of know-how. Thus he says:

> The grammar of the word "knows" is evidently closely related to that of "can", "is able to". But also closely related to that of "understands". ('Mastery' of a technique.)   (150)

> To understand a sentence means to understand a language. To understand a language means to be master of a technique.
> (199)

> "But it is just the queer thing about intention, about the mental process, that the existence of a custom, of a technique, is not necessary to it. That, for example, it is imaginable that two people should play chess in a world in which otherwise no games existed; and even that they should begin a game of chess—and then be interrupted."
> But isn't chess defined by its rules? And how are these rules present in the mind of the person who is intending to play chess?   (205)[32]

---

[32] *Cf. BB* pp. 112–15; *PG* p. 50; *Z* 421.

In addition to these explicit invocations of the notion of mastery of a technique Wittgenstein is often to be found characterising grasp of a rule by such phrases as 'he can go on' (see, e.g., 151 and 154). The intended effect of characterising understanding in this way is to forge a direct connexion between understanding and use: understanding is essentially connected with use because it precisely is the capacity *to do* certain things with signs. By contrast, the conception of understanding as a state of consciousness does not build use right into that which allegedly constitutes understanding; use must be supposed to come in at a later stage, in virtue of something that *associates* a conscious content with a particular pattern of use. The idea that understanding is a capacity to use a sign in a certain way does not therefore introduce the sort of gap between understanding and use which Wittgenstein argues to be fatal to the inner process conception. As a corollary of this, the notion of capacity directs us to consider the outer criteria for ascriptions of understanding: instead of trying to find understanding in a person's inner states we look to see what he does with signs, since this is the test of what abilities he possesses. The emphasis on behaviour comes out in this passage on 'reading':

> But in the case of the living reading-machine "reading" meant reacting to written signs in such-and-such ways. This concept was therefore quite independent of that of a mental or other mechanism—Nor can the teacher here say of the pupil: "Perhaps he was already reading when he said that word". For there is no doubt about what he did.—The change when the pupil began to read was a change in his *behaviour*; and it makes no sense here to speak of 'a first word in his new state'.   (157)

Similarly, to think of understanding through the notion of ability is to see its essential connexions with behaviour and to distance oneself from the idea of understanding as an inner state whose connexion with behaviour is only (so to say) fortuitous. We get the grammar of 'understands' right if we classify it along with being able to play chess, sing a tune, appreciate a piece of music, employ a tool – instead of assimilating it to having a visual experience, imagining a face, having a feeling of confidence, thinking up a hypothesis. Episodes of consciousness are neither necessary nor sufficient for possessing an ability, and understanding is best seen as an ability.[33]

The suggestion that knowledge of a language is mastery of a set of techniques of use – that it is a practical skill – no longer has the power to surprise: no doubt this is partly because Wittgenstein's ideas have become absorbed into contemporary philosophical consciousness and no longer strike us as novel or revolutionary; but it is also, I think, partly because this suggestion *is* intrinsically unsurprising – once enunciated it is scarcely disputable. Here, then, is an instance of what I anticipated above: the insistence upon the philosophical significance of the truistic. Controversy can be expected only when we enquire what such a capacity consists in, or into how the notion of capacity is to be understood generally. And in fact Wittgenstein does not confine himself to connecting the concept of understanding with ability concepts; he also makes some non-trivial claims about the notion of ability itself. We need to command a clear view of the grammar of ability concepts themselves if they are to shed the correct light upon the connected notion of understanding. Not surprisingly Wittgenstein wishes to discourage the idea that possessing an ability consists in being in some sort of internal state. The most extensive discussion of ability concepts occurs in *The Brown Book*, a sample of which is the following:

> Isn't it clear that the statement "B can continue . . ." is not the same as the statement that the formula $a_n = n^2 + n - 1$ comes into B's mind? This occurrence might have been all that actually took place. (It is clear, by the way, that it can make no difference to us here whether B has the experience of this formula appearing before his mind's eye, or the experience of writing or speaking the formula, or of picking it out with his eyes from amongst several formulae written down before-hand.) If a parrot had uttered the formula, we should not have said that he could continue the series.—Therefore, we are inclined to say "to be able to . . ." must mean more than just uttering the formula—and in fact more than any one of the

[33] Suppose someone understands 'red', and suppose that the correct use of 'red' consists (in part) in applying 'red' to red things. Then the ability suggestion makes a direct connexion between understanding and use in just this way: to understand 'red' is (akin to) having the ability to apply 'red' to red things – the correct use is thus built into the specification of the ability. (This does not mean, of course, that there is any 'logical connexion' between having the ability and actually exercising it – *that* connexion is causal at best.)

occurrences we have described. And this, we go on, shows that saying the formula was only a symptom of B's being able to go on, and that it was not the ability of going on itself. Now what is misleading in this is that we seem to intimate that there is one peculiar activity, process, or state called "being able to go on" which somehow is hidden from our eyes but manifests itself in those occurrents which we call symptoms (as an inflammation of the mucous membranes of the nose produces the symptom of sneezing). This is the way talking of symptoms, in this case, misleads us. When we say "Surely there must be something else behind the mere uttering of the formula, as this alone we should not call 'being able to . . .'", the word "behind" here is certainly used metaphorically, and 'behind' the utterance of the formula may be the circumstances under which it is uttered. It is true, "B can continue . . ." is not the same as to say "B says the formula . . .", but it doesn't follow from this that the expression "B can continue . . ." refers to an activity other than that of saying the formula, in the way in which "B says the formula" refers to the well-known activity.   (*BB* p. 113)

We are justified in saying that the sentence "He can continue . . ." has a different meaning from this: "He knows the formula". But we mustn't imagine that we can find a particular state of affairs 'which the first sentence refers to', as it were on a plane above that on which the special occurrences (like knowing the formula, imagining certain further terms, etc.) take place. (*BB* p. 115)

Wittgenstein is recommending that we think of abilities in terms of the *tests* we employ to judge whether someone has an ability; we should not think of abilities as states that somehow lie behind what they are abilities to do. In particular, we should not think of abilities as hidden interior performances of what we observe when someone overtly exercises an ability: to be able to sing a tune, for example, is not to have sung it through in one's mind already, so that all one needs to do is make overt what has already been done covertly.[34] The same kind of point is being made in 187 of the *Investigations*:

"But I already knew, at the time when I gave the order, that he ought to write 1002 after 1000."—Certainly; and you can also say you *meant* it then; only you should not let yourself be

[34] See 184; *Z* 2. In the same way, to mean a word in a certain way is not already to have covertly applied it, in the inner realm, as one will go on to apply it overtly in the future; no more so than being able to swim involves imagining acts of swimming in various future circumstances.

misled by the grammar of the words "know" and "mean". For you don't want to say that you thought of the step from 1000 to 1002 at that time—and even if you did think of this step, still you did not think of other ones. When you said "I already knew at the time . . ." that meant something like: "If I had then been asked what number should be written after 1000, I should have replied '1002'." And that I don't doubt. This assumption is rather of the same kind as: "If he had fallen into the water then, I should have jumped in after him".—Now, what was wrong with your idea?   (187)

Here the suggestion is that meaning something is best conceived in terms of the sorts of counterfactuals which provide the criteria for judging whether a sign is meant in a certain way; and this is also Wittgenstein's approach to abilities in general. If we put together the association of understanding with ability concepts and the employment of counterfactuals to specify when a sign is meant in a certain way, then we can say that Wittgenstein wishes to characterise the abilities in which understanding consists in counterfactual terms – where the relevant counterfactuals speak of the use to which signs are put. He does not want us to think of abilities in terms of underlying states; rather, he emphasises the *behavioural* implications of the ascription of abilities. He does not suppose that the counterfactuals about behaviour need to be *grounded* in any categorical facts about the person; indeed, as *Zettel* 608 indicates, he seems prepared to suppose that the truth of counterfactuals can be *independent* of the intrinsic states of an object – things could have the *same* intrinsic states and yet differ in the counterfactuals true of them. In particular, he seems prepared to allow that two people could agree in their internal states, both conscious and physical, and yet differ in their dispositions to use signs. *This* aspect of his view of understanding is by no means truistic: for it reflects a tendency of thought that can I think only be described as behaviouristic.[35]

The second element of Wittgenstein's positive view is

---

[35] I do not mean to suggest that Wittgeinstein is some kind of classical reductionist behaviourist; I mean only that he is prepared to tie the ascription of psychological concepts to behaviour, independently of any inner or internal states. This is quite compatible with acknowledging, or insisting, that the intended notion of 'behaviour' essentially involves psychological notions, i.e. must be psychologically characterised, e.g. as the intentional action of a person.

encapsulated in the word 'custom': and it is this element that contains what is really distinctive in Wittgenstein's view. The passages in which the idea of custom occurs are among the most forthright in Wittgenstein's treatment of meaning and rules:

> Let me ask this: what has the expression of a rule—say a sign-post—got to do with my actions? What sort of connexion is there here?—Well, perhaps this one: I have been trained to react to this sign in a particular way, and now I do so react to it.
>
> But that is only to give a causal connexion; to tell how it has come about that we now go by the sign-post; not what this going-by-the-sign really consists in. On the contrary; I have further indicated that a person goes by a sign-post only in so far as there exists a regular use of sign-posts, a custom. (198)

> Is what we call "obeying a rule" something that it would be possible for only *one* man to do, and to do only *once* in his life?—This is of course a note on the grammar of the expression "to obey a rule".
>
> It is not possible that there should have been only one occasion on which someone obeyed a rule. It is not possible that there should have been only one occasion on which a report was made, an order given or understood; and so on.—To obey a rule, to make a report, to give an order, to play a game of chess, are *customs* (uses, institutions). (199)

> The application of the concept 'following a rule' presupposes a custom. Hence it would be nonsense to say: just once in the history of the world someone followed a rule (or a signpost; played a game, uttered a sentence, or understood one; and so on). (*RFM* pp. 322–3)

> The words "language", "proposition", "order", "rule", "calculation", "experiment", "following a rule" relate to a technique, a custom. (*RFM* p. 346)

It is to be noted that Wittgenstein also uses the notion of a 'practice' to state his positive view, and indeed his use of 'custom' is virtually interchangeable with his use of 'practice'; thus consider:

> And hence also 'obeying a rule' is a practice. And to *think* one is obeying a rule is not to obey a rule. Hence it is not possible to obey a rule 'privately': otherwise thinking one was obeying a rule would be the same thing as obeying it. (202)

Language, I should like to say, relates to a *way* of living.

In order to describe the phenomenon of language, one must describe a practice, not something that happens once, *no matter of what kind*. (*RFM* p. 335)

Only in the practice of a language can a word have meaning. (*RFM* p. 344)

Our question now is what Wittgenstein intends by describing rule-following as a custom or practice: what picture of grasping and following a rule does he mean to suggest? I think there are three inter-linked ideas that he means to hit off by 'custom' and 'practice', and they are as follows.

The first thing Wittgenstein wants to get across is that rule-following takes place in the sphere of actual behaviour and not in the inner recesses of a person's consciousness or mental mechanism. The overt use of signs is not a contingent external manifestation of understanding, as the symptoms of a disease might be supposed to manifest its presence; rather, the operations of understanding consist in what one overtly does with signs. When a person follows a signpost (say) his behaviour *is* his rule-following; it is not that *real* rule-following takes place internally and then gets subsequently translated into action. So rule-following is not a hidden process: it is something you observe when you observe sign-using behaviour – not something of which behaviour is merely a symptom. We should resist the dualistic picture of an inner operation which is the locus of authentic rule-following and a parallel outer operation which is merely the publication of the genuine article; we should instead take literally the commonsense idea that overtly using signs just is what following rules consists in and not try to reinterpret this in terms of the dualistic picture. To say that rule-following is a practice is thus, in part, to insist that it is nothing other than what it appears to be, though it is difficult to resist trying to get behind the appearances: 'For here there is an overwhelming temptation to say something more, when everything has already been described' (*RFM* p. 323). We might put Wittgenstein's position this way: we should not think of rule-following as what *explains* practice, since rule-following is nothing over and above (or behind) practice, i.e. use. A non-misleading account of rule-following will accordingly limit itself to describing practice; it will not search for the hidden essence which underlies practice.

The second point is perhaps the main thesis of the passages we have quoted: this is the contention that rules can be grasped only if they are actually obeyed repeatedly. We find this point made most clearly in a number of passages in *Remarks on the Foundations of Mathematics*; for example:

> It is possible for me to invent a card-game today, which however never gets played. But it means nothing to say: in the history of mankind just once was a game invented, and that game was never played by anyone. That means nothing. Not because it contradicts psychological laws. Only in a quite definite surrounding do the words "invent a game" "play a game" make sense.
>
> In the same way it cannot be said either that just once in the history of mankind did someone follow a sign-post. Whereas it can be said that just once in the history of mankind did someone walk parallel with a board. And that first impossibility is again not a psychological one. (*RFM* p. 356)

It is clear from these passages that Wittgenstein intends his claim to be weaker than that for *each* rule there has to be more than one occasion on which *it* is obeyed; what he says is just that if any rules are to be grasped *some* must be obeyed more than once. This is to allow for the possibility that I might, e.g., invent a game with rules and never actually play it; but what Wittgenstein is not willing to allow is that *all* the rules I grasp should be thus inert. For rules to exist at all some must be followed – though some may lay idle. This claim – let us call it the 'multiple application thesis' – connects with another contention of Wittgenstein's, namely that our conception of grasping a rule *at* a time essentially involves the idea of applications of the rule *over* time. The repeated use that is required for there to be meaning is something spread out over time; meaning is, so to say, an essentially *diachronic* concept.[36] This is why Wittgenstein says of his fantasy of the two-minute

---

[36] *Cf.* 'I will now use an awful expression. I wanted to talk of a stationary meaning, such as a picture that one has in one's mind, and a dynamic meaning. I was going to say, "No dynamic meaning follows from a stationary meaning". But that is very badly put and had better be forgotten immediately' (*WLFM* p. 184). As the context makes plain, a 'dynamic meaning' consists in a pattern of use spread out over time. The same kind of point is also made in respect of the notion of pointing to a shape and not to a colour in 35: this depends upon 'what happened before and after the pointing', not upon what occurred simultaneously with the pointing.

England (*RFM* p. 336) that it is doubtful that we have enough going to attribute any meaning in such temporally truncated circumstances: the notion of determinate meaning gets a grip only when we consider a period of time sufficient for linguistic practice to provide it with a foothold. So Wittgenstein wishes the notion of 'custom' to capture the multiple application thesis, and hence to register the diachronic character of meaning: understanding a sign cannot be a one-off temporally isolated affair – it comes to be (so to speak) only in the fullness of time and use. And indeed the words 'custom' and 'practice' carry precisely the implication with which Wittgenstein wishes to invest them: we say that it is someone's custom to take a stroll on Sunday mornings, meaning that this is something he does regularly and repeatedly; and we likewise say such things as 'I will do it this once, but I do not intend to make a practice of it', with the same sort of implication. Customs and practices are things that get established by, or consist in, regularities in behaviour, and so they involve an appropriate spread of time: there would not for Wittgenstein really be customs and practices in two-minute England. It is I think this feature of the notions of custom and practice that Wittgenstein primarily wishes to stress when he introduces the terms; in fact, it is no exaggeration to say that these terms are introduced precisely as a *gloss* on the multiple application thesis and its consequential claim about meaning and time. For Wittgenstein first enunciates that thesis and then infers, by way of putting the thesis into a word, that obeying a rule is a *custom*. And this is the most explicit observation he makes about his use of 'custom' and 'practice': if there is one thing that is sure about Wittgenstein's positive view it is his advocacy of the multiple application thesis. We therefore do well to take it with full seriousness if we wish to discover what it is that Wittgenstein wants to maintain when he characterises rule-following as a custom.

It is to be noted that Wittgenstein's thesis does not concern merely the nature of third-person criteria for ascriptions of understanding; it is not a point about how I tell what you mean. Wittgenstein makes this clear:

> "But how often must a rule have actually been applied, in order for one to have the right to speak of a rule?" How often must a human being have added, multiplied, divided, before we

can say that he has mastered the technique of these kinds of calculation? And by that I don't mean: how often must he have calculated right in order to convince *others* that he can calculate? No, I mean: in order to prove it to himself. (*RFM* pp. 334–5)

Nor would it be right to think that Wittgenstein's claim concerns merely the *epistemology* of ascriptions of rules, if this is taken to contrast with what *constitutes* grasping a rule: he is not saying (just) that both first- and third-person ascriptions require repeated use over time if we are to *know* what someone means; his point is rather, as the passages I have quoted make plain, that the very *existence* of meaning requires repeated use. *What it is* to grasp a given rule cannot be divorced from actually obeying it or some other rule.

The third element in Wittgenstein's notion of custom that I want to bring out is the idea, already encountered, that using and reacting to signs is properly seen as habitual and unreflective, not as the upshot of ratiocination. A custom, like a habit, is something that gets established, not through the deliverances of reason, but on the basis of what we might call a *tradition*: when a kind of behaviour is described as traditional or customary it is implied that its inception and continuance depend upon factors other than reason. Traditions and customs become established and entrenched by dint of regularities in behaviour in which people come to acquiesce. This contrast with reason-based behaviour is implicit in such remarks as 'I do not do this for any *reason*; it is just a tradition/custom'. Customs are things people *find* themselves conforming to; it comes naturally to behave in accordance with custom, though no considerations of reason can be adduced to justify this behaviour. So Wittgenstein is, in part, amplifying his thesis that rule-following is not founded upon reasons when he says that it is a custom.[37]

The opposition between reason and custom is also, of course, a theme of Hume's.[38] Hume held that philosophers

[37] This is connected with the role of training in establishing understanding in the pupil: one is trained to conform to a custom or practice, and this training does not consist in the provision of *reasons* to behave in a certain way, but rather in encouragement, example, imitation, etc.

[38] See Hume's *A Treatise of Human Nature*, ed. L.A. Selby-Bigge (Clarendon Press: Oxford, 1978), pp. 104, 134, 183. See also Barry Stroud, *Hume* (Routledge and Kegan Paul: London, 1977), chap. X.

tend to regard our beliefs as founded upon reason, but that
when such a foundation is seriously sought nothing adequate
can be found to justify our commonsense beliefs – our beliefs
about causation and the future being perhaps the most
notorious in this regard. Hume's positive view of such beliefs
is that they have their foundation in our given *nature* as it
interacts with our 'training': that is to say, we believe what we
do by dint of custom. And by this Hume meant to suggest
the effects of repeated experience upon the mind with its
natural propensities. Thus Hume assigns to habit, custom and
nature what other philosophers take to belong to the province
of reason; he is opposed to an unduly rationalistic or
intellectualistic conception of the mind. To this extent I think
Wittgenstein agrees with Hume: he too thinks that philosophers
have underestimated the natural and customary and over-
estimated the ratiocinative and intellectual. The two philosophers differ however over the place of scepticism: Hume takes
the absence of reasons to lead to radical scepticism, whereas
Wittgenstein thinks that knowledge and certainty do not
require the sort of rational foundations the sceptic argues not
to exist. Nevertheless, there is I think a significant analogy
between Hume and Wittgenstein: both may be said to favour
what may be called epistemological naturalism. Wittgenstein's
naturalism is evident in such passages as these:

> It is sometimes said that animals do not talk because they lack
> the mental capacity. And this means: "they do not think, and
> that is why they do not talk." But—they simply do not talk. Or
> to put it better: they do not use language—if we except the most
> primitive forms of language.—Commanding, questioning,
> recounting, chatting, are as much a part of our natural history
> as walking, eating, drinking, playing. (25)

> What we are supplying are really remarks on the natural
> history of human beings; we are not contributing curiosities
> however, but observations which no one has doubted, but
> which have escaped remark only because they are always before
> our eyes. (415)[39]

[39] See also Part II xii, in which concept formation is said to depend upon 'facts of
nature'. Unfortunately, Wittgenstein says almost nothing about the kinds of fact he
has in mind here. It is reasonable to suggest, however, that these invocations of 'natural
history' and 'facts of nature' are connected with what he says in 185, in which he speaks
of what 'comes natural' to a person in continuing a series and compares this with the

The customs and practices of mankind are part of its natural history; and part of Wittgenstein's point in describing rule-following as conformity to a custom is to locate this activity in the context of this natural history.

This theme of naturalism relates to the tendency Wittgenstein diagnoses to 'sublime' language, a tendency most prominent in the *Tractatus*:

> 'A proposition is a queer thing!' Here we have in germ the subliming of our whole account of logic. The tendency to assume a pure intermediary between the propositional *signs* and the facts. Or even to try to purify, to sublime, the signs themselves.—For our forms of expression prevent us in all sorts of ways from seeing that nothing out of the ordinary is involved, by sending us in pursuit of chimeras. (94)[40]

The cure for this temptation to seek the sublime and occult in language is to see language as a natural phenomenon, continuous with other forms of behaviour seemingly more mundane. Characterising language as a set of customs or practices is thus intended to deflate these subliming tendencies, to discourage the hunt for the queer and mythological.[41] This again suggests an analogy with Hume: for Hume also saw himself as rooting out the occult and magical, recalling us to the mundane and natural. His view of the origin of our causal beliefs dispenses with the (allegedly) mysterious idea of 'powers' and favours a naturalistic explanation of how we acquire such beliefs – along with a diagnosis of why we fall into the error of embracing the occult. Wittgenstein for his part is against seeing language as 'transcendental' (see *Tractatus*, 6.13) and as harbouring a hidden essence ('logical grammar'); he wants to bring language down to earth by seeing it as a

---

case of a person who 'naturally reacted to the gesture of pointing with the hand by looking in the direction of the line from finger-tip to wrist, not from wrist to finger-tip.' Wittgenstein explicitly links his notion of custom with that of our natural history when he says of our acceptance of a proof: 'this is simply what we *do*. This is use and custom among us, or a fact of our natural history' (*RFM* p. 61).

[40] See also 38, 97, 192, 389.

[41] This is also a main purpose of Wittgenstein's consideration of simple language games: see 5. Exhibiting the interaction between speech and extra-linguistic behaviour can help in bringing language down to earth; hence the emphasis upon the place of language in our lives (in marked contrast to the *Tractatus* conception).

natural phenomenon whose real character is open to view. So we can say that both Hume and Wittgenstein suggest naturalism as an antidote to the mythologising which results from an unduly rationalistic picture of the phenomena. Language is not, for Wittgenstein, a Platonic entity of whose underlying essence we have but a dim grasp; it is rather a form of natural behaviour.[42] This theme is well expressed in 454:

> "Everything is already there in. . . ." How does it come about that this arrow ⋙⟶ *points*? Doesn't it seem to carry in it something besides itself?—"No, not the dead line on paper; only the psychical thing, the meaning, can do that."— That is both true and false. The arrow points only in the application that a living being makes of it.
>
> This pointing is *not* a hocus-pocus which can be performed only by the soul. (454)

That is, if we consider the arrow as employed by an agent equipped with certain natural propensities, we shall be better able to refrain from regarding its meaning as magical.

We can now sum up the negative and positive strands in Wittgenstein's discussion of understanding: understanding is not an *inner process* of supplying an *interpretation* of a sign which *justifies* one in reacting with the sign in a certain way; it is, rather, an *ability* to engage in a *practice* or *custom* of *using* a sign *over time* in accordance with one's *natural propensities*. Let us now apply this interpretation of Wittgenstein to two important and disputed sections of the *Investigations*, *viz*. 201 and 202.

In 201 Wittgenstein contrasts the interpretational conception of understanding with what he takes to be the correct view. He begins by setting out a paradox, *viz*. the paradox that rules can have no normative force since anything can be made out to conflict with a rule or to conform to it. He follows this up by saying that the paradox results from a 'misunderstanding', and that this misunderstanding stems from giving interpretations of rules and hoping they will determine the right use of the rule. He then remarks: 'What this shows is that there is a way of

---

[42] This is not, of course, incompatible with recognising that language is in some sense 'conventional'. It is true (in some sense) that words mean what they do in virtue of conventional relations between them and the world; but this does not imply that our nature makes no contribution to what we mean – indeed, one might well hold that the conventions are *underlain* by our nature.

grasping a rule which is *not* an *interpretation*, but which is exhibited in what we call "obeying the rule" and "going against it" in actual cases'. So: grasping a rule is not interpreting it, in the sense of translating it into another sign; it is rather that which we exhibit when we apply the rule. And what is it that is thus exhibited? It is, as we have seen, mastery of the technique of applying the sign, having the hang of a custom or practice. Wittgenstein's position, clearly, is that the paradox that destroys the interpretational conception will not threaten the alternative conception of a technique exhibited in use; and the reason for this difference (he thinks) is that the paradox results directly from trying to get signs themselves to determine use. Hence the observation that we should not call an *action* in accordance with a rule an 'interpretation'. Grasping a rule *determines* use precisely because it is nothing other than what gets *displayed* in use; it is not something for which we need a further step to reach use, as on the interpretational conception. Understanding, we might say, is an unmediated propensity to act.[43]

Section 202 is notoriously cryptic and laconic, and it is a bold man who claims to be perfectly sure what it means. It is reasonable to suppose that 202 does not introduce any radically new themes, not anticipated by the passages leading up to it; we should expect it to be generally in line with what Wittgenstein has already been saying. And the plausibility of an interpretation of this section must be tested against the background of an overall interpretation of Wittgenstein's position. Here, then, is my interpretation of 202, taking it sentence by sentence. The first sentence, 'And hence also "obeying a rule" is a practice', recapitulates what was said in 198–201, namely that obeying a rule is a practical activity, something overtly done over time; correlatively, to grasp a rule is to be master of such a practice, i.e. to have a certain capacity. The second sentence, 'And to *think* one is obeying a rule is not to obey a rule', says that it does not follow from the fact that one thinks one is obeying a rule that one really is: one could believe oneself to be master of a practice and to be exercising

---

[43] On the idea of unmediated action, see *BB* pp. 3, 87. It is the postulation of an interpretational intermediary which creates the paradox, since there is no logical connexion between it and a use; if we drop this intermediary, then we have, in effect, already crossed the logical gap that led to the paradox.

such mastery and one in fact not be, i.e. self-ascriptions of rule-following are fallible. This fallibility is only to be expected on Wittgenstein's positive view, since skills are just not the sorts of things about which one has infallible self-knowledge: you can think you have (e.g.) the ability to swim but in fact you don't; an impression of a capacity is not the same thing as (entails) having the capacity. Thus the evident fallibility of self-ascriptions of understanding (grasp of a rule) is *explained* by the thesis that understanding is an ability, given that abilities generally are not infallibly known.[44] The third sentence, 'Hence it is not possible to obey a rule "privately": otherwise thinking one was obeying a rule would be the same thing as obeying it', expands upon this theme of fallibility, by observing that if rule-following were a 'private' occurrence, i.e. a state of consciousness, it would not have the fallibility it evidently does have – it *would* follow from the fact that one believes one is following a rule that one is. This is simply because self-ascriptions of conscious states, e.g. of mental images, are *not* fallible – or at least not fallible in the way self-ascriptions of understanding are fallible. If understanding were just the coming before one's mind of some sign or quasi-sign, then understanding would be certifiable simply by introspection – you just scan the contents of consciousness to find the appropriate experience. Since the contents of consciousness are infallibly given it cannot be that one judges oneself to understand when one does not, as one cannot judge one is in pain and not be. To put it yet another way, the conception of rule-following as a private act of consciousness, logically independent of what one goes on to do, gets the epistemology of self-ascriptions of rule-following wrong: it cannot register, or make room for, the fact that we can be mistaken when we take ourselves to be exercising mastery of a rule. 202 is thus saying this: self-ascriptions of rule-following are fallible, as the capacity view acknowledges; but the inner process conception fails to have this consequence – it would make understanding as introspectively accessible as pain or having an image of red. This interpretation fits the letter of the section and it is in the

---

[44] This is particularly true of the ability to do the *same* thing on different occasions: that I have the ability to apply a sign in the same way over time is not something that is introspectively accessible. This point is especially significant for the question of the possibility of a private language, as we shall shortly see.

spirit of what we have seen to be Wittgenstein's general position. I think its plausibility is confirmed by substituting for 'obeying a rule' such allied notions as 'meaning something', 'exercising a concept', 'grasping the sense of a sign': these substitutions will be seen to preserve the significance and truth-value of the section and to make the interpretation I have suggested seem natural and predictable. The section is in effect insisting again upon the differences between these sorts of psychological concepts and the concepts of conscious experiential contents.

In fact there are intimations of what I take to be the main point of 202 earlier; thus consider:

> Must I *know* whether I understand a word? Don't I also sometimes imagine myself to understand a word (as I may imagine I understand a kind of calculation) and then realize that I did not understand it? ("I thought I knew what 'relative' and 'absolute' motion meant, but I see that I don't know.")
> (p. 53)

> "But how can it be? When *I* say I understand the rule of a series, I am surely not saying so because I have *found out* that up to now I have applied the algebraic formula in such-and-such a way! In my own case at all events I surely know that I mean such-and-such a series; it doesn't matter how far I have actually developed it."—
> Your idea, then, is that you know the application of the rule of the series quite apart from remembering actual applications to particular numbers. And you will perhaps say: "Of course! For the series is infinite and the bit of it that I can have developed finite." (147)

> But what does this knowledge consist in? Let me ask: *When* do you know that application? Always? day and night? or only when you are actually thinking of the rule? do you know it, that is, in the same way as you know the alphabet and the multiplication table? Or is what you call "knowledge" a state of consciousness or a process—say a thought of something, or the like? (148)

And there are other places in which Wittgenstein makes it clear that the sincere exclamation 'Now I can go on?' does not (logically) imply that the person really can (*cf.* 181). His underlying point is that the criteria for having grasped a rule, e.g. the principle of an arithmetical series, consist in the applications a person goes on to make in the fullness of time; what happens contemporaneously in the rule-follower's consciousness cannot render these criteria superfluous by providing a sort of immediate access to the condition of understanding, as the inner process model in effect supposes. Wittgenstein can and will agree that the 'characteristic accompaniments' of understanding – the feelings and experiences that are symptoms of understanding – are known infallibly, but he will point out that these are not the understanding itself, and that *its* (first-person) epistemology differs fundamentally from that of its characteristic conscious symptoms.

I think my interpretation of 202 can be further strengthened by considering Wittgenstein's interpolated discussion of 'reading'. Reading, in Wittgenstein's sense, is a kind of rule-following; it is going from marks to sounds according to rules (understanding the words is not required for reading in this sense). Now Wittgenstein's main point in 156–178 is that reading is not a 'special conscious activity of mind' (156). There are, to be sure, characteristic sensations that accompany reading – introspectible *marks* of reading – but these do not *constitute* reading. Rather, Wittgenstein describes reading as 'reacting to written signs in such-and-such ways', so that 'the change when the pupil began to read was a change in his *behaviour*' (157). Wittgenstein's basic point is that obeying rules for reading is exercising a (behavioural) *skill*, and having a skill is not a matter of enjoying certain sorts of experience – it is not a condition of consciousness. Accordingly, we need to recognise that a person can in principle be wrong about whether he is reading: thus Wittgenstein allows that someone could think he is reading when he is not and think he is not when he is (160).[45] To be reading is not the same thing as to have the impression of reading: the conscious activity conception cannot allow this, because of the immediate introspective accessibility of states of consciousness, whereas the skill conception provides a natural account of this aspect of the

[45] Thus Wittgenstein is denying both that reading is infallibly known and that it is self-intimating. Interestingly enough, he confines himself to the former denial when discussing understanding; I know of no place where he asserts that a person could understand a sign and yet believe he did not. However, I think it would be reasonable, and consonant with his claims about reading, for him also to deny the self-intimating character of understanding.

epistemology of reading. We could thus say that on Wittgenstein's view reading is not a 'private' occurrence, not something you do privately, i.e. within the sphere of consciousness in logical independence of behaviour; rather, reading is a practice in that it consists in overtly doing something. So reading is a special case of the obeying of rules with which 202 is concerned, and Wittgenstein's specific claims about reading are consonant with the general purport of 202 as I have interpreted it: reading is a practice; hence thinking one is reading does not entail reading; so reading is not something 'private', or else you *would* be infallible about whether you are reading. The key point here is that Wittgenstein uses 'private' to mean 'inner' and so in contrast with 'outer' or 'public'; we shall see in the next chapter that this construal of 'private' marks a great divide between the interpretation I favour and certain other interpretations.[46]

It is natural to suppose that there must be some connexion between 202 and the later sections concerned with the possibility of 'private language' (243f). For, first, there is the use of the notion of privacy in the earlier and the later passages; and, second, there is a concern for the distinction between seeming to follow a rule and really doing so in both parts of the *Investigations*. Thus, in the course of considering the idea that I name a sensation by concentrating my attention upon it, Wittgenstein says:

> A definition surely serves to establish the meaning of a sign.—Well, that is done precisely by the concentrating of my attention; for in this way I impress on myself the connexion between the sign and the sensation.—But "I impress it on myself" can only mean: this process brings it about that I remember the connexion *right* in the future. But in the present case I have no criterion of correctness. One would like to say: whatever is going to seem right to me is right. And that only means that here we can't talk about 'right'. (258)

> Are the rules of the private language *impressions* of rules?—The balance on which impressions are weighed is not the *impression* of a balance. (259)

[46] It is in this sense of 'private' that Wittgenstein considers the question whether thinking is 'an event in private consciousness' (*BB* p. 16). A consequence of this private conception of thinking or reading or understanding is that the claim of others to know or observe whether one is thinking, reading or understanding comes to seem problematic: driving these inward to the sphere of inner consciousness makes them dubiously accessible to others – they then became epistemologically private.

The point being made in these well-known sections is that in a putative private language, i.e. one that only I can understand, the distinction between real and apparent rule-following breaks down; and the conclusion drawn is that the idea of such a language is incoherent since this distinction is *essential* to anything we can call a language. Now it is not my aim in this work to offer any very thorough exposition of Wittgenstein's argument against private language, still less to criticise it; I will therefore confine myself to a brief sketch of the argument for purposes of comparison with the general views on meaning I have attributed to Wittgenstein on the basis of earlier sections. Wittgenstein's fundamental point in the sections following 243 is that in a putative private language neither the speaker nor the hearer has a criterion for telling whether the rules of the language are being obeyed correctly; there is thus no *check* on whether the words which only I (the speaker) understand are being employed with a constant meaning from occasion to occasion. And this is because the speaker himself has only an *impression* of constancy to go on, which does not itself entail that any rule is *really* being consistently followed, while the hearer cannot tell whether a given word is being applied to the same sensation from occasion to occasion since (*ex hypothesi*) he cannot know what sensations the speaker has. In the case of public physical objects, by contrast, the hearer *can* observe that it is the same (kind of) object that a word is being applied to over time; but where the referent of a word is unknowable there is no such way of telling from the third-person viewpoint whether it is being applied to the same or to different (kinds of) things. In a private language there would therefore be no criterion of semantic regularity in use, and so nothing that might be used to corroborate the speaker's impression, based upon his apparent memories, that he is using words in a consistent and regular way. Wittgenstein infers that in a private language there would *be* no distinction between real and apparent rule-following: for without a criterion for applying this distinction the supposition that it nevertheless exists is inadmissible.[47] It follows that any genuine (rule-governed)

---

[47] So, on this interpretation, the argument has a verificationist assumption: namely, that without a way of *telling* whether a rule is being consistently followed it is inadmissible to suppose there to be a fact of the matter about this. Without the assumption the argument would not go through, as I have presented it.

language must refer only to things and properties whose presence can be publicly verified: in particular, there must be public criteria for the presence of sensations if meaningful sensation words are to be possible. And in point of fact such criteria *do* figure in our actual acquisition of sensation language, since we use (e.g.) 'pain' precisely as a *replacement* for the kind of behaviour which provides others with a warrant for ascribing pain to us (see 244).

Now it should be clear even from this brief sketch of 'the private language argument' that it is not the same as the conclusion reached in 202. The basic point of 202 is that grasping a rule (understanding a sign) is not a condition that is infallibly given, as a state or process of consciousness is; the basic point of 258–9 is that words for private (unknowable-to-others) sensations cannot be associated with determinate semantic rules since there would be no criterion for whether such rules were being conformed to. Both passages say that an impression of a rule is not the same thing as a rule, but the reasons for saying this are different in the two cases and the consequences drawn relate to separate questions. In particular, I do not think that 202 is intended already to rule out the possibility of a private language in the sense later discussed, nor indeed could it under the interpretation I have placed upon it. For, all that 202 positively asserts is that following a rule is a practice, mastery of a technique; and this does not in and by itself exclude the possibility that one might have a practice of applying words *to private objects* – an ability to identify one's sensations from occasion to occasion and to apply sensation words in a regular manner. That is, 202 says only that following a rule is an ability to use a sign, not the occurrence or recurrence of a distinctive state of consciousness – and this is not yet to claim that all such abilities must be *checkable by others*. The two conceptions rejected by Wittgenstein are indeed logically independent both ways: it does not immediately follow from the inner state model of understanding that my understanding is unknowable to others – it could be just as knowable as the conscious experiences I have; and it does not follow from the unknowability to others of what my words mean that my understanding is not mastery of a practice – for it has not yet been excluded that my understanding of sensation words might consist in the possession of a *private* practice (i.e. a practice unknowable to others).[48] In other words, extra arguments are needed if the possibility of a private language is to be excluded; and Wittgenstein does, I think, produce novel considerations when he comes to consider sensation language – he does not simply indicate how his earlier general considerations, culminating in 202, already suffice to rule out the possibility of a private language.

If 202 is making a different point from 258–9 and does not imply it, then what is the relation between the two passages – are they simply irrelevant one to the other? I think that there is a significant relationship between them but that it is indirect. By 202 Wittgenstein has developed an account of meaning and rules which makes a sharp distinction between feelings or impressions of rule-following (prompted by the characteristic experiential marks of having grasped a rule) and the real thing, which consists in conditions independent of what happens in one's consciousness; this distinction must hold in *any* system of rule-governed signs, and hence in any language endowed with meaning. Now when we consider only signs for publicly accessible objects this distinction has verifiable content, since observers can tell whether a word is being used in application to the same thing over time; but matters are less straightforward for sensations – here criteria for the distinction must involve the behavioural *expression* of sensations. If there were no such behavioural criteria, then the distinction would not have verifiable content, and so, for Wittgenstein, would be a spurious distinction. What the sections culminating in 202 do is to *set the stage* for this argument by introducing and insisting upon the distinction between real and merely seeming rule-following; the private language argument then sets out to show what is needed for this distinction in the case of words for sensations. Put it this way: without the antecedent expectation of the distinction the private linguist might take refuge in the claim that in a private language there *is* no distinction between real and apparent rule-following; so it is tactically useful to

---

[48] Thus consider the beetle in the box (293): I might have a practice of applying a word to this unknowable-to-others object – it is not merely that I have a certain inner state, e.g. an image of the beetle, whenever I use the word – but this practice cannot become an object of evaluation for others. It is one thing to show that all linguistic understanding involves mastery of a practice; it is a further step to show that the mastery of a practice must always be publicly displayable.

have argued for the distinction ahead of confrontation with this issue. Only if we already have shown the importance of the distinction can we deploy it to challenge the possibility of a private language: it functions, we might say, as a condition of adequacy upon a conception of a genuine language, a condition which the idea of a private language is hard put to it to meet. 202 does not then already *state* the private language argument: what it does is to establish the necessity for a distinction which the later sections then argue to be impossible for the case of a private language. We might be tempted to think that the desired distinction could be made out for a private language simply by invoking the general point that thinking one is exercising a capacity does not entail really doing so; but the point of the later sections is that this will not do, since there would be no public criterion for whether the speaker really does have the capacity he takes himself to have – others would not be in a position to provide a check on his claim to be exercising such an ability on different occasions. Thus 202 *prepares us* for the private language argument while not by itself amounting to an anticipatory *statement* of that argument.

It may be that there is a further connexion between the rejection of the inner state model of understanding and coming to a proper view of sensation language, though I cannot claim that I have any hard textual support for the attribution to Wittgenstein of appreciation of this connexion. The connexion I have in mind is this: that it is *more* tempting to believe that understanding sensation words consists in something experiential than it is to believe that understanding words for physical objects consists in such a thing. Suppose one thinks that meaning something is paradigmatically being *confronted* by it, e.g. by seeing it as one utters its name: meaning an object is at its least problematic when the meant object is actually within one's sights.[49] Then it will seem to one that anything short of such direct ostensive presentation poses a problem: how can an *absent* object be meant? How can the mind get the meant object in its sights if it is just not present to be sighted? And a tempting reply to this worry might be that the trick is turned by somehow *approximating* to the condition of direct confrontation: thus

[49] This conception is discussed in *BB* pp. 38–9; it is also what lies behind the remark: 'Here meaning gets imagined as a kind of mental pointing, indicating' (*Z* 12).

what comes before one's mind when an absent object is meant
is not the object itself but an image or picture of the object,
which serves as a proxy or simulacrum for the absent object.
Hence one arrives at the idea, which is of course one of
Wittgenstein's chief targets, that meaning something is having
something like an image of it come before the mind: if we can't
have the object itself in our sights we can at least sight (by the
mind's eye) an object that *resembles* that object. Wittgenstein's
critique of this whole way of thinking questions (*a*) the
supposed simplicity and primitiveness of ostensively meaning
something – this is not in fact a situation in which meaning
something is somehow perfectly transparent and unproblematic; and (*b*) the idea that such mental proxies can ever confer
meaning. Now it may be that this rejected way of thinking has a
stronger hold when we come to consider sensation words: we
are perhaps more tempted to think of meaning a particular
kind of sensation as paradigmatically its actual presence to
consciousness, and accordingly to think of meaning an absent
sensation (say in another person or in one's own past) in terms
of an act of *imagining* that sensation – of having an image of it
before one's mind. We certainly do think of understanding
sensation words as intimately bound up with (at some time) experiencing what they stand for; and so it might seem that we only
really know what 'pain' or 'the sensation of red' mean when we
are actually having those experiences (I have in fact heard this
said in discussion). The thought would then be that talk of
absent sensations must, to be meaningful, approximate to the
ideal of the actual presence to consciousness of the sensation,
and this would be for something like an *image* of pain to come
before the mind. Moreover, it might be thought, the notion of
resemblance makes more sense for the case of sensations than
for the case of physical objects: an image of pain has more
chance of resembling a pain than an image of a chair has of
resembling a chair, since the former pair are at least both
experiences whereas the latter pair are dissimilar in this respect.
And insofar as we are tempted to bolster the way of thinking
under consideration with notions like resemblance we stand a
better chance of coherence in the sensation case than the
physical object case. In short, it may be more tempting to take
words *for* states of consciousness to be understood by being *in* a
state of consciousness than it is to hold this for other sorts of

words. Now if there is such a temptation, at least in the domain
of the 'philosophical unconscious',[50] then we will need to
make special efforts to combat the inner state model when we
come to consider sensation words: we need to see that just the
same sorts of considerations about meaning and rules apply in
this case as we saw to apply in the case of words for numbers or
physical objects. Viewed in this light, the discussion leading up
to 202 is indeed very relevant to the later treatment of sensation
language; for it serves to rule out a conception of meaning for
such language which, were it not for the earlier considerations,
would be especially tempting to us.[51] In particular, the
ostensive model of understanding sensation words needs to be
scrutinised with special care, since it provides the starting-
point for the way of thinking into which we are tempted to fall.
However, I must emphasise that this conjectured connexion
between the earlier and later discussion is more superimposed
on Wittgenstein's text than derived directly from it; I do not
claim that Wittgenstein himself is actually thinking in these
terms, however natural it may seem to descry the connexion I
have tried to bring out.

So far we have been considering Wittgenstein's treatment of
the notion of an *individual's* meaning something, following a
rule, understanding a sign; nothing has yet been said about his
view of what it is for a *number* of individuals to communicate or
to share a language. Between the sections dealing with what I
have called the epistemology of rule-following (roughly
208–239) and the beginning of the discussion of sensations and
private language (243f) Wittgenstein has three sections which,
in effect, deal with the *social* aspect of meaning – they comment
upon the idea of a linguistic community. I think these three
sections (240–242) are best seen as drawing *consequences* for
the idea of a shared language from the earlier conclusions
concerning what is involved in a given individual's meaning
something or following a rule. Let me now expound each of

[50] I got this phrase from Brian O'Shaughnessy, *The Will: A Dual Aspect Theory*
(Cambridge University Press, 1981), p. 74.
[51] If the charm of the inner state model is particularly strong for sensation language,
then we might be inclined, were it not for the earlier considerations, to find no
distinction between real and apparent rule-following in a putatively private language;
but it is the necessity for this distinction to exist in any language which for
Wittgenstein excludes the possibility of a private language.

these sections in the light of what has already been said about Wittgenstein's general position, beginning with 240:

> Disputes do not break out (among mathematicians, say) over the question whether a rule has been obeyed or not. People don't come to blows over it, for example. That is part of the framework on which the working of our language is based (for example, in giving descriptions).   (240)

Here the point is that mathematicians, for example, do not find themselves disagreeing over what is the correct use of a sign, i.e. over whether the rule associated with the sign has been followed: they do not, for example, engage in heated arguments about how '+2' is to be applied to a number. And that there is this kind of agreement is part of what makes a shared language possible: if people did constantly disagree about the correct use of signs, then those signs would not be suitable vehicles of communication. That we all go on in pretty much the same way with our signs is essential to our meaning the same thing by those signs, and hence to the possibility of inter-personal communication. This point about communication is readily seen to be a consequence of the idea that following a rule is a practice: for, if obeying a particular rule is applying the associated sign in a certain way over time, then obeying the *same* rule consists precisely in the *coincidence* of such temporally extended practice. It is not that meaning is something inherently independent of practice, so that people could radically diverge in their practices and yet still agree in their meanings; rather, agreement of meaning between people depends essentially upon agreement of practice. Hence certain sorts of linguistic dispute are precluded by the very fact that people speak the same language.

The next section takes up a natural objection to what Wittgenstein has just said:

> "So you are saying that human agreement decides what is true and what is false?"—It is what human beings *say* that is true and false; and they agree in the *language* they use. That is not agreement in opinions but in form of life.   (241)

The objection is that Wittgenstein is construing truth as (mere) inter-personal agreement; Wittgenstein's reply is, in effect, that his claim concerns the conditions for *meaningful* utterances, not the conditions for their truth. Of course if a sentence is to have a determinate truth-value it must be endowed with a determinate meaning, and having a shared meaning requires agreement of use between people; but it does not follow that this agreement is what makes sentences *true*, since that is something that goes beyond simply what the sentence means ('how the world is'). The last sentence of the section then clarifies what notion of agreement is being invoked: this is not agreement in 'opinions' but in 'form of life'. I take it that Wittgenstein is here (somewhat obliquely) recalling his earlier contention that applying a sign in a certain way is not based upon reasons but upon natural propensities: by an 'opinion' here he means something that results from ratiocination, something that is backed by reasons; by a 'form of life' he means that which forms part of our nature, that which determines how we spontaneously find ourselves reacting.[52] It is not that mathematicians have all come to the same considered opinion about how signs are to be used, so that a radically errant sign-user might be rationally persuaded to change his ways; it is rather that the existence of a common language depends upon an unreflective and natural set of shared propensities to behave in certain ways. Adapting an earlier phrase of Wittgenstein's, our confidence that we share a common language is 'blind' (see 219) in the sense that it is not something for which we could (or need to) provide a discursive justification; it rests upon the presumption of a common nature and not upon a common set of reasons for going on in a particular way.[53]

Section 242 can be usefully compared with a paragraph from the *Remarks*:

[52] See also 19, 23; *cf.* 454. When Wittgenstein says 'What has to be accepted, the given is – so one could say – *forms of life*' (p. 226) he is, I think, suggesting that forms of life should play the foundational role ascribed by empiricists to ungrounded but self-evident judgements or opinions; thus the basis of language is, in a certain sense, pre-judgemental for Wittgenstein. So the agreement of judgements that he goes on to say is necessary for communication is itself founded upon an agreement in form of life or 'way of living' (*RFM* p. 335).

[53] Wittgenstein uses 'opinion' in this way in another connexion, when he says: 'My attitude towards him is an attitude towards a soul. I am not of the *opinion* that he has a soul' (p. 178). His point in both passages is that the attitudes and propensities in question are too primordial to be aptly described as 'opinion'; both our use of language and our recognition of other persons occupy a level below that of reflection, and hence of justification.

If language is to be a means of communication there must be agreement not only in definitions but also (queer as this may sound) in judgments. This seems to abolish logic, but does not do so.—It is one thing to describe methods of measurement, and another to obtain and state results of measurement. But what we call "measuring" is partly determined by a certain constancy in results of measurement.   (242)

We say that, in order to communicate, people must agree with one another about the meanings of words. But the criterion for this agreement is not just agreement with reference to definitions, e.g., ostensive definitions – but *also* an agreement in judgments. It is essential for communication that we agree in a large number of judgements.   (*RFM* p. 343)

Wittgenstein is here addressing himself to the most natural rival account of what shared meaning consists in, namely that you and I mean the same by a word just if we agree in the *definition* we would give of it, either by using other words or ostensively. Wittgenstein does not dispute that communication sometimes requires agreement in definitions, but he thinks that this is not all there is to it; there must also be agreement in how words are applied to things, i.e. in judgements:

It is true that *anything* can be somehow justified. But the phenomenon of language is based on regularity, on agreement, in action.

Here it is of the greatest importance that all or the enormous majority of us agree in certain things. I can, e.g., be quite sure that the colour of this object will be called 'green' by far the most of the human beings who see it.   (*RFM* p. 342)

The reason for this is that definition by itself does not determine meaning: both verbal and ostensive definitions can be variously interpreted, and so there must be something else which fixes the meaning the definition is intended to fix – i.e. a background understanding of how the definition is to be taken. And this background consists in the application made of the signs figuring in the definition – how people use those signs in actual and potential judgements. If two people differ in the background of judgements in which the defining signs are applied, then they differ with respect to the meaning they attach to those signs; and verbal or ostensive definitions work only because there is this underlying agreement of use. It is to be noted that 'judgement' in 242 cannot mean the same as

'opinion' in 241, on pain of an outright inconsistency: the
apparent inconsistency is removed if we associate 'opinion'
with the idea of considered belief formed on the basis of
reasoning and evidence and 'judgement' with unreflective and
'blind' application of a sign, e.g. calling a green thing 'green'
simply as a matter of course. That is, what underlies such
unreflective judgements, in which meaning is displayed, is our
'form of life' (our natural propensities) and not a foundation of
reasons; this is why Wittgenstein contrasts opinion and
judgement in the way he does. The rest of 242 is, I think, a bit
more obscure, but I take it that he means to be saying that
logic, which is a matter of meaning alone, cannot be regarded as
wholly anterior to the activity of judging, as it has been thought
by some to be, since meaning is something *coeval* with the
activity of judging. It is not that logic is determined by meaning
in *advance* of employing the language to make judgements;
rather, logical relations between expressions are *established* by
the judgements in which those expressions are used. What
Wittgenstein wants to say in 242 is then that this conception of
meaning and logic does not 'abolish logic', i.e. collapse it into
ordinary judgements about the world. And he aims to show
this by making an analogy with measurement: logic is like the
method of measurement, whereas judgement is like the *result* of
measurement; but method and result are not totally independent because we will only regard an operation as a method of
measurement if it gives us a certain constancy of results. A foot
ruler is different from the results it gives when used to measure
length, but it serves as a measure of length only because of a
regularity in the results it gives. Analogously, Wittgenstein
wishes to say that meaning (logic) is what we take for granted
when we judge, but there is meaning only because people
exhibit a regularity in their judgements. Accordingly, communication depends upon a background of agreement in
judgements, as measurement depends upon a constancy of
results; even though there is room for a distinction between
people meaning something different by a word and their
applying it differently in certain cases (i.e. judging differently).

This completes my general exposition of Wittgenstein's
views on meaning. I have not, of course, discussed all of
Wittgenstein's views on meaning – I have not, for example,

discussed his emphasis upon the *diversity* of meaning, i.e. the important differences between the various language-games there are;[54] but I have, I think, laid out his basic ideas about meaning, understanding and rules. I have done this without entering into exegetical disputes with other expositors of Wittgenstein, in full knowledge that the interpretation I have offered would be resisted by others; and I have refrained from expressing my own views on the claims I have taken Wittgenstein to be making. In the next two chapters these restraints will be thrown off, first by comparing my interpretation with Kripke's and then by critically assessing Wittgenstein's views.

[54] See 24, 65, p. 224. Despite this emphasis on the variety of language-games and of words, I know of no passage in which Wittgenstein explicitly asserts that the notions of rule, meaning and understanding are themselves family-resemblance concepts; and it seems to me not an easy matter to determine what he *should* have said about this, given his general views.

2

Kripke's Interpretation of Wittgenstein: Paradox and Community

In this chapter I shall contrast Kripke's interpretation of Wittgenstein with the interpretation I put forward in Chapter 1; we shall see that these interpretations are very different. Kripke's expository procedure differs somewhat from that adopted in the previous chapter: he does not expound Wittgenstein by paying close attention to the text, supporting each attribution with an apposite citation; rather, he develops a systematic argument which he hopes will make sense of, and occasional contact with, Wittgenstein's text. Kripke's assumption is that this argument is what *underlies* Wittgenstein's actual text, and that we shall understand Wittgenstein better if we see his text as the surfacing of this systematic argument in different ways and contexts: it is not that Wittgenstein is to be found explicitly propounding this argument, but we can illuminatingly treat his text *as if* he were. And it is this feature of Kripke's exposition which causes him to qualify his attributions to Wittgenstein from time to time – to admit that his way of presenting Wittgenstein is somewhat alien to Wittgenstein's own conception of his views.[1] We should therefore take seriously Kripke's prefatory caveat: 'the present paper should be thought of as expounding neither "Wittgenstein's" argument nor "Kripke's": rather Wittgenstein's argument as it struck Kripke, as it presented a problem for him.'

---

[1] See Kripke, pp. 5, 67–71. These qualifications particularly concern the sceptical thesis Kripke attributes to Wittgenstein.

(p. 5) Kripke is here disarmingly aware that he is foisting onto Wittgenstein's text what is not to be found inscribed on its surface; and this is why he adopts the method of exposition he does adopt. My own procedure has been quite different: I have assumed that Wittgenstein can be satisfactorily interpreted without seeing his text as the occasional surfacing of an underlying systematic argument but rather by paying close (and perhaps somewhat pedantic) attention to what he actually *says*. I would not therefore think it appropriate to issue the sort of caveat Kripke does. This observation is not intended as a piece of self-congratulation on my part, but as a recognition of the procedural difference between Kripke and me. In fact I believe that the more substantive differences stem fundamentally from this difference in respect of exegetical method. For what Kripke has done is to produce an impressive and challenging argument which bears little affinity with Wittgenstein's own problems and claims: in an important sense Kripke and the real Wittgenstein are not even dealing with the same *issues* (they have a different 'problematic'). I shall begin by summarising Kripke's interpretation, assuming some familiarity with its outline, and then I shall explain why I think it goes wrong as an interpretation. This task should be facilitated by what has already been argued in Chapter 1; since I believe I there gave ample textual evidence for my interpretation, it will be necessary only to spell out the points of disagreement and give some diagnosis of how Kripke came to the wrong interpretation.

The general structure of Wittgenstein's argument, according to Kripke, is as follows. Wittgenstein focuses attention upon the normative notion of an application of a sign being (linguistically) correct, i.e. in accordance with its meaning. (This is not the notion of *factual* correctness, i.e. stating a truth about the world; it concerns the question *which word* is linguistically appropriate to the facts. Thus, for example, suppose I believe truly that this object is red; the question of linguistic correctness is then which word expresses this belief: is 'red' the word I ought to use to state the fact in which I believe?) We ordinarily think that some uses of words are correct and some are incorrect, some uses correctly express the fact we want to state and some do not: Wittgenstein's question is supposed to be what this distinction consists in. What makes it right to use words in one way rather than another? It is clear that this normative property of words depends upon their having a determinate meaning: for the notion of a *correct* use is well-defined only if words mean one thing rather than another – that is what *makes* it right to use one word rather than another to state a given fact. Therefore we need to make sense of the idea of a word meaning one thing rather than another if we are to give content to the notion of correct (or incorrect) use of language. To put it differently: any proposed candidate for the meaning of a word must be such as to sustain linguistic normativeness; we must be able to read off from any alleged meaning-constituting property of a word what is the correct use of that word. The normativeness of meaning thus functions as a condition of adequacy upon any account of what meaning is.[2] Now Kripke's claim is that Wittgenstein finds this notion of normativeness deeply problematic, and hence finds the whole notion of meaning correspondingly problematic. For nothing can be produced to *constitute* meaning that meets the normativeness requirement: there is no property of a word from which we can read off its correct use, and so there is nothing for meaning to be. This is what Kripke calls Wittgenstein's 'sceptical paradox' – the thesis that there is nothing, no fact, that could constitute meaning one thing rather than another. But Wittgenstein does not (according to Kripke) want to leave us helpless in the jaws of this paradox; he proposes a 'sceptical solution' to the paradox which, while conceding to the sceptic that no *fact* constitutes meaning, nevertheless preserves our ordinary talk of meaning and rules. The sceptical solution does this by persuading us that we do not *need* to supply the kind of account of meaning the sceptic shows to be unavailable; we can take a radically different view of the significance of statements about meaning, namely that such statements do not *purport* to state facts at all. Since ascriptions of meaning and rule-following do not set out to state facts, it is no disaster for them that we can discover no facts for them to state; we can provide a quite different account of their function. This, then, is the general shape of Wittgenstein's argument, as Kripke sees it; let us now fill the argument in a bit.

The sceptical paradox is initially presented by considering

---

[2] See Kripke, pp. 11, 23–4.

the meaning I attach to signs I used in the past. I normally and uncritically assume that my present use of (say) '+' accords with my past meaning, so that when I now give the *sum* of 67 and 58 in answer to the question '67 + 58?' I am interpreting '+' as I did in the past: that is, I assume that in the past I meant *addition* by '+' and so I conform with my past meaning (I use '+' *correctly*) if I now take questions containing '+' to require doing some addition. Kripke's sceptic questions whether this assumption is on reflection legitimate: perhaps in the past I meant by '+', not addition, but quaddition, a mathematical function whose value is 5 for the pair of arguments 67 and 58. What is it about my past history that makes me so sure that I meant addition and not quaddition, and hence so confident that my present linguistic response conforms with my previous meaning (the response of giving 125 in answer to '67 + 58?')? The sceptic's question is, in effect, what justifies my confidence that '+' has a constant meaning for me over time: what is it that *constitutes* this presumed constancy? To answer this question we need to be able to point to some feature of my past usage that establishes that I then meant addition; and the semantic sceptic claims that this cannot be done. (In fact, the sceptical paradox has two aspects, an epistemological aspect and a constitutive or metaphysical aspect: epistemologically, the claim is that nothing can now be cited to *justify* my assumption of semantic constancy; constitutively, the claim is that there is no *fact* about me which could constitute my meaning addition rather than quaddition. It is the second aspect which is the more important in Kripke's exposition of Wittgenstein; the epistemological challenge is regarded chiefly as a way into the constitutive challenge.[3])

The case for the sceptical paradox proceeds by exhausting the candidates. First, my actual computations involving '+' do not suffice to determine that I meant addition, since these are logically compatible with my having meant some other function which agrees with addition for just the numbers on which I have performed computations with '+' but diverges

---

[3] Kripke emphasises that his central problem is constitutive on p. 21, though he does initially state the problem more epistemologically (see p. 8). His use of the term 'sceptic' must therefore be understood in a slightly nonstandard way: Kripke's sceptic is not (primarily) interested in questions of certainty, knowledge or justification – his real interest is 'ontological' or 'metaphysical'.

thereafter. Actual use of '+', either externally or in my head, *underdetermines* which function is denoted; for there are indefinitely many functions distinct from addition which are compatible with the finitely many applications of '+' I have made. For any finite sequence of applications of a sign we can always envisage different ways of continuing to apply the sign which conform to different assignments of meaning. Second, my past inner states of consciousness cannot determine what I meant because they admit of various interpretations or applications: no experience I have can dictate what is the right way to use a sign, and whatever meaning is it must provide for such normativeness. Nor are there any 'magical' states of consciousness which are capable of doing what the mundane states cannot do. So there are no facts about consciousness which can furnish a reply to the sceptic. Third, Kripke considers the suggestion that my past meaning consisted in my having a certain sort of linguistic *disposition*: instead of looking to my *actual* use of '+' in the past, let us turn to how I was *disposed* to use '+' and read my past meaning off from that. The appeal of this suggestion is that it offers the hope that the underdetermination problem will be got round: for we can now cite the fact that in the past I was *disposed* to say '125' and not '5' in answer to '67 + 58?', even though this question never actually came up. Dispositions to use are thus supposed to mirror the *productivity* of meaning; their consequences extend beyond the actual history of a person's use of a sign. Kripke's reply to this dispositional suggestion consists in two observations: in the first place, dispositions to use are *finite*, since human beings are finite objects existing for a finite time, whereas addition is a function with infinitely many arithmetical consequences; in the second place, speakers are disposed to make *mistakes* in their use of signs, and so dispositions by themselves cannot properly account for normativeness. The dispositional suggestion just equates, Kripke says, competence with performance: but performance by itself cannot capture the infinity of meaning nor its normativeness. So meaning addition by '+' cannot *consist in* being disposed to give the sum of arbitrary pairs of numbers on demand: some numbers are simply too big, and we may have systematic tendencies to give something other than the sum because of errors of calculation. Kripke claims (on Wittgenstein's behalf) that these three replies to the semantic sceptic exhaust the possibilities, and so we must concede that there is nothing for my having meant addition to consist in. But once we concede this we admit that the same scepticism applies to my *present* use of '+': for the same sceptical question could be asked about my present meaning at some *future* time, and the same range of possible answers will be shown to be inadequate *then*. Indeed, if we ask directly what constitutes my *presently* meaning addition and not quaddition we shall be faced with the same difficulty: actual use, present states of consciousness and present dispositions to use will all fail to fix a unique meaning for my words. So there is likewise nothing about my present use of signs that makes that use right or wrong: the whole notion of meaning appears to collapse.[4] This, then, is the first, negative phase of Wittgenstein's discussion of meaning, as Kripke interprets him.

The second, positive phase consists in an effort to draw the sting from the sceptical paradox while not questioning its substance. The strategy, as I remarked, is to reject the sceptic's presupposition that ascriptions of meaning are in the business of stating facts; rather, we are to conceive of their significance in terms of (a) their assertibility conditions and (b) their role or utility or point in discourse. The effect of this move is to undercut the key assumption of the sceptic: we are to see that all along he was attacking a straw man, though a straw man with whom we naturally and naively identify. According to Kripke, the change of perspective needed to fend off the sceptic reflects Wittgenstein's shift from the philosophy of language espoused in the *Tractatus* to that put forward in the *Investigations*: the sceptic is presupposing the kind of fact-stating model of meaning advocated in the *Tractatus*, and the cure for this scepticism is to adopt the different conception of meaning we find in the *Investigations* – with its emphasis upon the role of criteria and the place of language in our lives. The sceptic *seems* to us to be striking at the very notion of meaning only because we are powerfully attracted to the conception of language articulated in the *Tractatus*: if we can free ourselves from that conception we shall no longer feel ourselves threatened by the

---

[4] 'It seems that the entire idea of meaning vanishes into thin air' (Kripke, p. 22); understandably, this gives Kripke 'an eerie feeling' (p. 21).

sceptic's arguments; but it is hard to free ourselves from it, so the threat feels real.[5]

Although Kripke does not himself say so, there are, I think, other areas of philosophy in which much the same strategy has been tried, and it will be useful to have these in mind when we enquire whether Wittgenstein really proceeds as Kripke suggests. Three parallels may be mentioned. First, certain sorts of noncognitivism in ethics can be viewed in an analogous way: the noncognitivist cannot find facts suitable for correspondence with ethical statements, and so he suggests that ethical utterances be conceived in a non-fact-stating way instead – as prescriptions to action or expressions of emotion, say. This type of view might be motivated by the incapacity of non-queer facts to add up to what we intuitively demand of ethical truth or by a conviction that what would add up to that is in some way metaphysically rebarbative.[6] Instead of abandoning ethical utterances as meaningless in the absence of ethical facts the noncognitivist reinterprets their purport – he proposes a different conception of meaning for such sentences. Thus emotivism (say) can be seen as a sceptical solution to a sceptical paradox – the paradox, namely, that there is nothing in the world that could constitute the value-fact we naively take ethical assertions to require; and the sceptical solution is that these 'assertions' serve rather to express the emotions of the speaker or some such thing.[7] Second, there is the doctrine of instrumentalism with respect to the theoretical sentences of science: the instrumentalist cannot (he thinks) find any genuine facts to correspond to such sentences, but he preserves their

[5] Kripke exploits this alleged contrast with the *Tractatus* to impose a structure on the *Investigations* according to which the early sections (1–137) are concerned to undermine the *Tractatus* truth-conditional conception of language, as a preliminary to solving the sceptical problem (see Kripke, pp. 78–9). Plainly, this architectonic suggestion can be correct only if Kripke is right to interpret Wittgenstein as solving a sceptical problem by means of a sceptical solution based upon assertibility conditions; and I do not think he is right so to interpret Wittgenstein.

[6] I am thinking here of J.L. Mackie's view that objective values would be metaphysically 'queer': see his *Ethics: Inventing Right and Wrong* (Penguin Books, 1977), chapter I.

[7] This type of view saves meaningful ethical utterances in the absence of ethical facts (truth) by reconstruing such utterances as (logically) non-assertoric: an ethical sentence is meaningful while lacking genuine truth conditions because it is really imperatival or exclamatory or hortatory or some such. And clearly a sentence can be meaningful in these ways without purporting to state a fact.

role in discourse by interpreting them in a different way – as useful devices for organising the real facts. Instead of reacting to the lack of suitable facts by declaring talk of unobservables void of significance, he gives up the fact-stating model and opts for a different account of meaning – in terms, perhaps, of assertibility conditions and organisational utility. Third, certain views of mathematical statements display this dialectical form: seeking facts to correspond to mathematical sentences we find ourselves discouraged either by the incapacity of mundane facts to do the job or by the seeming necessity to postulate 'queer' facts (platonism); so we abandon the fact-stating referential model altogether and put in its place a different account of meaning – e.g., that mathematical sentences get their significance from their empirical applications. This again would be aptly characterised as a sceptical solution to a sceptical paradox: one *agrees* with the sceptic that no mathematical facts can be found, but one averts his radical conclusion (mathematics is meaningless) by proposing an alternative account of meaning that makes the sceptical paradox irrelevant.[8] I think that these three issues exemplify the general pattern of argument Kripke attributes to Wittgenstein; we can see Kripke's dialectic as adding yet another kind of 'noncognitivism' to the list of more familiar doctrines of which I have given three examples.

So far I have only explained the sense in which Kripke's positive view of semantic statements is a sceptical solution; I have not said what form that positive view takes. The central idea, attributed to Wittgenstein, is that the assertibility conditions and point of ascriptions of meaning essentially involve the notion of a *community*. Thus to say that someone means addition by '+' is warranted just if (*a*) he *agrees* in his responses with '+' with the responses of some community who use '+' and (*b*) he can be trusted in his interactions with members of a community in situations involving '+'. That is to say, the notion of a rule is an essentially *social* one, involving

---

[8] One might see Paul Benacerraf, in 'Mathematical Truth', *Journal of Philosophy* LXX (1973), as posing a kind of sceptical problem, *viz.* how can mathematical propositions be true and known; and Hartry Field, in *Science Without Numbers* (Blackwell: Oxford, 1980), as offering a kind of sceptical solution, *viz.* mathematical sentences need not be regarded as possessing genuine truth conditions and so do not *call* for 'queer' facts to correspond to them.

inter-personal relations; so we cannot give an account of rule-following in *individualistic* terms.[9] We cannot, Kripke says, make sense of someone following a rule 'considered in isolation'. Kripke compares this result with Hume's positive account of causation: the relation of causation between a pair of events cannot be explicated solely by reference to those events, as we naively suppose; rather, when we speak of causal relations we are (tacitly) subsuming the pair of events in question under a generalisation involving *other events*. Thus the assertibility conditions of '*e* caused *f*' are inherently 'social': events can stand in causal relations only in virtue of their membership in a 'community' of events. Kripke puts this by saying that there cannot, on Hume's view, be 'private causation'; as there cannot be 'private', i.e. individualistic, rule-following, according to Wittgenstein. In sum, then, the 'sceptical solution' consists in two moves: first the replacement of truth conditions (correspondence to facts) by assertibility conditions, and second the introduction of the community into the notion of rule-following. These two moves are, of course, logically independent, but Kripke's claim is that both are necessary if the sceptical paradox is to be answered.[10]

What I have just given is a swift summary of a rich and detailed course of argument, intended to remind the reader of the salient points of Kripke's interpretation rather than substitute for it. Let us now ask whether this interpretation accords with what Wittgenstein says, beginning with the question whether Wittgenstein really advocates a sceptical paradox about meaning and rules. The central passages to consider here are 198 and 201 in which Kripke takes Wittgenstein to be stating his sceptical thesis that there are no facts for meaning to consist in. Kripke quotes the beginning of 201:

> This was our paradox: no course of action could be determined by a rule, because every course of action can be

[9] I am using 'individualistic' roughly in the sense Tyler Burge does in 'Individualism and the Mental', *Midwest Studies in Philosophy*, vol. IV, ed. P.A. French, T.E. Uehling and H.K. Wettstein (University of Minnesota Press, 1979): that is, a property of a person is individualistic just if the instantiation of that property can be explained without reference to the condition of any other person; a property is social just if this is not so.

[10] It is especially important to see that the introduction of the community pertains to assertibility conditions and not truth conditions; for essentially the same difficulties would afflict the attempt to find a social *fact* for meaning to consist in.

made out to accord with the rule. The answer was: if everything can be made out to accord with the rule, then it can also be made out to conflict with it. And so there would be neither accord nor conflict here.   (201)

But he signally fails to quote, or even to heed, what immediately follows this:

> It can be seen that there is a misunderstanding here from the mere fact that in the course of our argument we give one interpretation after another; as if each one contented us at least for a moment, until we thought of yet another standing behind it. What this shews is that there is a way of grasping a rule which is *not* an *interpretation*, but which is exhibited in what we call "obeying the rule" and "going against it" in actual cases.
>
> Hence there is an inclination to say: every action according to the rule is an interpretation. But we ought to restrict the term "interpretation" to the substitution of one expression of the rule for another.   (201)

There are two things to notice about this passage which give the lie to Kripke's interpretation.[11] First, Wittgenstein makes it clear immediately that the stated paradox arises from a 'misunderstanding', i.e. a false presupposition; so he cannot really be *endorsing* the paradox, as Hume embraces his own sceptical claims about causation. Second, when we ask what the misunderstanding is we are told that it is the mistake of assuming that grasping a rule is placing an *interpretation* upon a sign, i.e. associating it with another sign – an assumption which Wittgenstein thinks we are by no means compelled to make. In other words, Wittgenstein is putting forward the paradox as a *reductio ad absurdum* of the interpretational conception; it is the inevitable result of that particular misunderstanding about the nature of grasp of a rule. Wittgenstein no more endorses the stated paradox than does any philosopher who gives a *reductio* of his opponent's position. Wittgenstein does *not* say that the paradox arises from the misunderstanding that ascriptions of rules state facts

---

[11] It is significant that in other passages in which the interpretational conception is rejected, e.g. *BB* pp. 33–35, there is no mention of a paradox into which we are in imminent danger of falling; Wittgenstein's point in these passages is just that we should not think of meaning and understanding in terms of inner interpretations (i.e. symbols) – he is *not* saying that this is the *only* way we can think if we cleave to a 'factual' conception of these concepts.

or have truth conditions, nor does he suggest that the underlying mistake is to consider the rule-follower in social isolation; what he is objecting to is the specific conception of understanding as a mental operation of translation. If Kripke were right, Wittgenstein ought to be found saying, after his statement of the paradox: 'What this shows is that grasping a rule is not a fact about an individual considered in social isolation'; but this is *nothing like* what he actually does say. If there is one key oversight in Kripke's exposition of Wittgenstein, it is that of ignoring what Wittgenstein says in 201 straight after stating the paradox: for Wittgenstein here gives his most explicit diagnosis of the paradox and what he says is remote from Kripke's attribution. This is also made very clear in 198: the lesson of the paradox is said to be that interpretations do not determine meaning; it is not that meaning does not consist in individualistic facts. What Wittgenstein is saying is that *certain sorts* of facts fail to determine meaning, *viz.* substituting one sign for another, not that *no* facts do.[12]

Kripke's misinterpretation comes out clearly in his remarks about Wittgenstein's treatment of 'reading'. Reading is a kind of rule-following, and so Kripke takes Wittgenstein to be propounding his paradox for reading – reading is not an individualistic fact but is to be understood in terms of social assertibility conditions.[13] But when we consult the text we find that what Wittgenstein is opposing is a particular family of views about the sort of fact reading is – that it consists in an inner process: conscious, queer, or physical – and advising us to look to what the reader *does*:

> But in the case of the living reading-machine "reading" meant reacting to written signs in such-and-such ways. This concept was therefore quite independent of that of a mental or other mechanism.—Nor can the teacher here say of the pupil: "Perhaps he was already reading when he said that word". For there is no doubt about what he did.—The change when the pupil began to read was a change in his *behaviour*; and it makes no sense here to speak of 'a first word in his new state'.   (157)

[12] More specifically, Wittgenstein is asking what it is about a person that determines his future use of a sign: and his answer is that this is a matter of the technique of use of which he is master, not of what comes before his mind. If you like: the *fact* that gives signs life is a fact about use, not a fact about inner states.

[13] See Kripke, pp. 45–49.

There is no suggestion in these sections that we are under threat of the paradox that reading never occurs, that there is nothing for reading to consist in; rather, we are told to redirect our attention from supposed inner processes to the outer criteria we use for judging someone to be a reader. In fact these sections do not contain a statement of the paradox at all, yet Wittgenstein is considering a case of rule-following; so it can hardly be maintained that the paradox is Wittgenstein's central and recurrent theme.[14] I think the paradox is best seen as just one battle in a general campaign against the inner process model, not as the primary focus of Wittgenstein's whole discussion. Kripke says that the paradox is really the main problem of the *Investigations*, but its infrequent appearance belies this suggestion; and when it does appear it figures as one more nail in the coffin of the inner process model, to be hammered in along with a number of other nails.

So the passages upon which Kripke bases his interpretation fail to support it and suggest instead a quite different view of Wittgenstein's intentions; but can Kripke's interpretation find sustenance in more general considerations? This question has two parts, corresponding to the constitutive and epistemological versions of semantic scepticism. That Wittgenstein is advocating a constitutive scepticism certainly seems hard to square with the fact that he does offer an account of the sort of thing understanding is: it is mastery of a technique, possession of a capacity, participation in a custom. And it is notable that Kripke nowhere registers Wittgenstein's concern to connect understanding with the concept of *ability*, as an alternative to the conception of understanding as a condition of consciousness. Nor does Wittgenstein show any tendency to contest the *factuality* of ascriptions of ability; he merely protests against what he takes to be misunderstandings about the sort of thing

[14] Kripke says: 'The sceptical paradox is the fundamental problem of *Philosophical Investigations*' (p. 78). It might clarify Wittgenstein's attitude to this paradox to contrast it with Russell's attitude towards his class paradox. Wittgenstein sees his paradox as a problem for anyone who assumes that meaning is a matter of interpretation, but he thinks that this assumption is not at all compulsory or unavoidable; whereas Russell's paradox arises from assumptions that seem inescapable – there is no straightforward *mistake* in the premises that generate the contradiction. In a word, Wittgenstein's paradox is not a *problem for Wittgenstein*, as Russell's paradox is a problem for Russell.

an ability is (e.g. a configuration of one's 'mental apparatus').[15] It would be more accurate I think to say that Wittgenstein locates understanding in one kind of fact rather than another kind; but if we want to capture the true spirit of Wittgenstein's discussion we do better still to drop all play with the notion of *fact* and simply say that Wittgenstein is offering a description of the 'grammar' of the notion of understanding in terms of the notions of ability, technique, etc. I do not believe that Wittgenstein is thinking in terms of facts and non-facts at all here; certainly there is no hard textual evidence to support this sort of interpretation. Any resistance on Wittgenstein's part to saying that understanding *consists in*, or is *constituted by*, a capacity stems from a general distrust of the enterprise of philosophical analysis, not from a conviction that understanding is somehow not a fact.[16] Indeed, I think Wittgenstein would have regarded such an assertion, and such a debate, as quite empty, since there is no substantial philosophical mileage to be got out of the notions of fact, truth conditions and correspondence to conditions-in-the-world. Kripke himself shows some awareness of this kind of point, but he boldly brushes it aside in the expectation that he is conforming to the real spirit of Wittgenstein's position; but I think he should take more seriously Wittgenstein's deflationary remarks about truth and facts.[17] At any rate, if we want to talk in terms of facts it seems that Wittgenstein *does* suggest that understanding consists in a fact, the fact of having an ability to use signs.

[15] In particular, *BB* pp. 113–17, which deals at some length with the notion of ability, does not suggest that sentences containing 'can' and its cognates do not correspond to 'conditions-in-the-world'; the point there is rather that we should not construe abilities as special sorts of inner process or state which lie 'behind' what counts as the exercise of the ability.

[16] Remember that the form of Wittgenstein's account is to be the perspicuous connecting of concepts (see 122): he says that the 'grammar' of 'can' and 'is able to' is 'closely related' to that of 'understands' (150), not that we can actually *analyse* the latter in terms of the former. In fact, I think that the failure to provide necessary and sufficient conditions for the application of a concept would, for Wittgenstein, have no significance whatever for the question whether that concept could be interpreted in a 'fact-stating' way.

[17] Kripke notes that Wittgenstein subscribes to a redundancy theory of truth (so-called) in 136 (Kripke, p. 86), but he does not, I think, draw the right lesson from this: given that 'true' adds nothing to the content of an assertion, it cannot be that Wittgenstein really wishes to deny that semantic sentences have truth conditions – on pain of denying that they express propositions. Similarly for 'it is a fact that' or 'states a fact'.

It would also be wrong to interpret Wittgenstein as an epistemological sceptic. As I emphasised in Chapter 1, Wittgenstein's denial that our use of words is founded on reasons is not intended sceptically: the traditional sceptic makes an inappropriate and impossible demand on our epistemic concepts, and the right response to him is to question the need for what he says there isn't. To lack reasons is not to be in a predicament to which doubt is the proper response; for doubt can be removed (better pre-empted) by our natural and habitual reactions.[18] This epistemological position would prompt Wittgenstein to dismiss Kripke's sceptic with the remark that of course our reasons come to an end but this does not mean we are in any sort of epistemological trouble: that I cannot *prove* to a determined sceptic that my present use of '+' is correct does not show that I do not know how to apply it correctly or that I have anything less than a perfect right to proceed as I feel inclined. The author of *On Certainty* would surely not propound the kind of sceptical argument Kripke develops, resting as it does upon a conception of knowledge and epistemic right that he steadfastly resists. Wittgenstein's epistemology would stop Kripke's sceptic before he got going; so we cannot interpret Wittgenstein as *conceding* victory to Kripke's epistemological sceptic and then offering what is at best a salvage operation.

A crucial part of Kripke's constitutive paradox is his rejection of a dispositional conception of understanding; so we should expect, if Kripke has Wittgenstein right, that the same sort of argument be found in Wittgenstein, in view of its importance to the success of the sceptical thesis. What we find, however, when we scour Wittgenstein's text is a total lack of anything remotely resembling the sorts of considerations about dispositions advanced by Kripke. All Kripke can say to explain this disparity is that Wittgenstein is assuming the dispositional reply to the sceptic to be unattractive to the audience of his book at the time of writing – whereas the conscious state reply is taken to be the natural response to the

---

[18] *Cf.* '"But, if you are *certain*, isn't it that you are shutting your eyes in face of doubt?" – They are shut' (p. 224). He is saying that the question of doubt, in certain standard sorts of case, simply does not arise for us; so the sceptic can make no impact on our customary confidence by inventing a doubt (we should keep our eyes firmly shut).

sceptic for that audience. It is the change in the philosophical climate that explains the apparent difference between what Wittgenstein says and what Kripke argues.[19] I find this explanation unconvincing – for three reasons. First, it seems to me inconceivable that Wittgenstein would wholly neglect to consider what is probably the most natural reaction to the constitutive sceptic; surely the demolition of this idea is essential if the paradox is to be carried through. And the form of Kripke's demolition – the arguments from finiteness and mistakes – finds no echo in Wittgenstein's text: in particular, at the places where Wittgenstein states his paradox one would expect him to indicate that the paradox shows (*inter alia*) that understanding is not a disposition and is not to be explicated in terms of counterfactuals about use, instead of saying (as he does) that the paradox refutes the interpretational conception. Nowhere does Wittgenstein say, in parallel with his claim that interpretations do not determine meaning, that 'dispositions fail to determine meaning' and that 'what this shows is that there is a way of grasping a rule which is not a disposition'. We just do not find the kinds of remark about dispositions which Kripke's interpretation leads us to expect.

Second, and more probatively, in those rare places in which the notion of disposition is invoked Wittgenstein is clearly making a quite different point from Kripke. Thus consider 149, the only passage in the relevant sections of the *Investigations* in which the notion of disposition is explicitly invoked:

> If one says that knowing the ABC is a state of the mind, one is thinking of a state of a mental apparatus (perhaps of the brain) by means of which we explain the *manifestations* of that knowledge. Such a state is called a disposition. But there are objections to speaking of a state of the mind here, inasmuch as there ought to be two different criteria for such a state: a knowledge of the construction of the apparatus, quite apart

---

[19] See Kripke, p. 43. In fact, this explanation of the disparity does not fit the historical facts very well, since behaviourism was enjoying a considerable vogue at the time Wittgenstein was writing what became the *Investigations*, and dispositional accounts of psychological concepts were widely advocated. Russell, in particular, was strongly influenced by behaviourism, as Kripke himself notes (Kripke, p. 25): see Russell's *My Philosophical Development* (George Allen and Unwin: London, 1959), esp. chapters 11–13. In view of the prevalence of such doctrines at the time of his writing, one might have thought Wittgenstein would take their refutation as a first *priority*, if Kripke's interpretation were on the right lines.

from what it does. (Nothing would be more confusing here than to use the words "conscious" and "unconscious" for the contrast between states of consciousness and dispositions. For this pair of terms covers up a grammatical difference.) (149)

Here Wittgenstein's objection seems to be that talk of dispositions is likely to be accompanied by the idea that knowledge is a state of mind; and he thinks that this way of conceiving of knowledge leads to the mistaken idea that there are two independent ways of telling whether someone (e.g.) knows the ABC – by examining his mental apparatus or by seeing what he does. Wittgenstein's purpose is, as usual, to discourage the inner state model of concepts such as knowledge, and he is warning us that talk of dispositions is apt to go along with this model; instead we should attend to what the person does. If Kripke's interpretation were correct, Wittgenstein would have to be saying that what a person is disposed *to do* does not fix what he knows when he knows the ABC; but this is not what Wittgenstein says and indeed he seems to be suggesting just the contrary.[20]

Third, Wittgenstein makes remarks that actually *support* the kind of dispositional suggestion Kripke pits himself against: that is, Wittgenstein can be found explaining meaning in terms of counterfactuals about use. Thus consider this passage:

> What is essential is to see that the same thing can come before our minds when we hear the word and the application still be different. Has it the *same* meaning both times? I think we shall say not. (140)

That is, if two speakers differ in their application of a sign then we should say that they mean something different, despite the identity of their conscious states: use determines meaning, not what transpires within. This thought of Wittgenstein's hardly fits with Kripke's claim that differences of dispositions to use do *not* suffice to establish differences of meaning, on account of

---

[20] That is, Wittgenstein is objecting to the notion of disposition if this notion is understood independently of behaviour, i.e. as an internal state that is explanatory of behaviour; but Kripke's objections to the dispositional suggestion construe dispositions precisely in terms of counterfactuals about *behaviour*: so Wittgenstein and Kripke mean quite different things by 'disposition', and hence are making quite different objections to the invocation of this notion. (This explains why Wittgenstein objects to talk of dispositions, but commends the use of counterfactuals to elucidate meaning and knowledge.)

the possibility of systematic mistake: Wittgenstein's remark from 140 shows no sign of acknowledgement of this kind of point, which would be amazing if he were really arguing in the way Kripke suggests. What Wittgenstein is doing here is drawing a *contrast* between application and what presents itself to the mind, holding that identity of meaning between people depends upon identity in respect of the former not the latter; but Kripke's interpretation would have Wittgenstein insisting upon the *parity* of the two sorts of circumstance, not upon the contrast between them. On Kripke's view, both conscious states and application fail to fix meaning, and so equally make no progress against the sceptic; but Wittgenstein himself evidently believes that there is an important *difference* between these with respect to the determination of meaning. (This is not to say that Wittgenstein has some answer to Kripke's point about mistakes; it is just that Wittgenstein shows himself to be unconcerned about such issues in the passage quoted – so it cannot be that he has on his mind what Kripke has on his.) A second passage of some significance for the present issue is this:

> "But I already knew, at the time when I gave the order, that he ought write 1002 after 1000"—Certainly; and you can also say you *meant* it then; only you should not let yourself be misled by the grammar of the words "know" and "mean". For you don't want to say that you thought of the step from 1000 to 1002 at that time—and even if you did think of this step, still you did not think of other ones. When you said "I already knew at the time . . ." that meant something like: "If I had then been asked what number should be written after 1000, I should have replied '1002'." And that I don't doubt. This assumption is rather of the same kind as: "If he had fallen into the water then, I should have jumped in after him".—Now, what was wrong with your idea? (187)

What is notable about this passage is Wittgenstein's willingness to employ a counterfactual about what someone would have said in explication of that person's having meant something. Applied to Kripke's favourite example, Wittgenstein's suggestion would run as follows: for me to have meant by '+' that '125' is the right answer to '67+58?' (assuming that this is a computation I had not come across or thought about) is for it to be true of me that *had* I been faced with that question in the past I *would* have given that answer. Wittgenstein is com-

paring the case of meaning (or knowing) with the case of a trait
of character such as bravery: to say I was brave yesterday is to
assume that there are true counterfactuals such as 'If he had
fallen into the water, I would have jumped in'; it is not to
assume that I had somehow mentally rehearsed the brave
action of saving a potential drowner. Similarly, to mean
something at a given time is not to have it before one's mind at
that time, so that every step of the series '+2' has already
occurred to one; it is rather to be *disposed* to give the right
answer, i.e. for the kinds of behavioural counterfactuals
Wittgenstein cites to be true of one.[21] It is surely incredible that
Wittgenstein could have written this if his attitude to
counterfactuals concerning use were as Kripke suggests; for
Wittgenstein is in effect saying in 187 exactly what Kripke
supposes him to reject. It is true that Wittgenstein does not
claim that the counterfactuals provide a reductive *analysis* of
the notion of meaning something – he says only that the latter
'means something like' the former – but this is to be seen as a
reflection of his suspicion of the whole idea of conceptual
analysis; it is not prompted by an unstated recognition of the
kinds of argument Kripke gives against explicating meaning in
terms of counterfactuals. What Wittgenstein is suggesting is
that we can capture enough of the grammar of the notion of
meaning by invoking counterfactuals to point us in the right
philosophical direction (or away from the wrong direction); he
cannot therefore be taken to be conducting a sceptical
campaign in which the employment of counterfactuals is a
defensive manoeuvre to be blocked and repulsed. What
Wittgenstein ought to be saying, on Kripke's interpretation, is
that ascriptions of meaning are not tantamount to (mean
nothing like) the assertion of counterfactuals about use; but this
is the exact opposite of what he does say in 187. In this passage,
as in 140, Wittgenstein is *contrasting* what happens in one's

---

[21] This, then, is Wittgenstein's answer to the question that ends 187, and to the puzzle
originally raised in 138: when one suddenly comes to understand a word, or hears it
with understanding, or knows the meaning of a word, what is true of one is that certain
counterfactuals hold, which correspond to the possession of an ability; it is not that one
performs a remarkable mental act in which the whole of future and possible use comes
before one's mind as a condensed seies of thoughts or images or some such (see 188). A
man's entire life may flash before his mind when he believes he is about to die, but his
temporally extended use of a word does not similarly flash before his mind when he
means it in a certain way.

mind when something is meant with what is true of one's behaviour, including counterfactuals about one's behaviour; he is not treating both as *sharing* an incapacity to supply the sort of fact Kripke's sceptic is demanding.

For these reasons, then, I doubt that Kripke is right to interpret Wittgenstein as advocating a sceptical paradox designed to show that there is no 'fact of the matter' about what we mean. So nothing in Wittgenstein's discussion suggests the sort of negative first stage characteristic of the analogous doctrines I mentioned earlier; we are not being prepared for the kind of sceptical solution proffered by the likes of emotivism and instrumentalism. There is not a distinguishing of truth conditions and assertibility conditions accounts of meaning and then a purported demonstration that semantic statements have no determinate truth conditions; rather, there is an opposition between two different conceptions of the sort of thing meaning is – roughly speaking, conceptions which locate meaning in the inner and in the outer.[22] And if this is the correct interpretation, we will not be able to construe Wittgenstein as proposing anything that deserves to be called a 'sceptical solution': his positive view simply has the status of a correct account of the concepts at issue, though it is an account which for various reasons it is hard to see ourselves clear to accepting as adequate and complete. Nevertheless, we can still ask whether Kripke is right to ascribe to Wittgenstein a community conception of rule-following, independently of whether this is intended as a sceptical solution to a sceptical paradox. I shall maintain that this ascription is also mistaken.

The community enters, according to Kripke, by way of the normativeness of meaning and of rules generally: when we say that someone is using a word wrongly we mean that his use of that word disagrees with the use made of it by members of a linguistic community; and right use is agreement of use. If we

---

[22] As I observed in chapter 1, Wittgenstein's treatment of the concept of meaning takes its place along with a like treatment of a wide range of other psychological concepts; and his general aim is to resist driving these psychological phenomena inward. If Kripke were right about Wittgenstein's treatment of meaning, then he would have to take a parallel line about the whole range of psychological concepts treated by Wittgenstein: he would have to say that Wittgenstein is advocating a sceptical paradox about believing, recognising, remembering, comparing, willing, etc., and proposing a community-based sceptical solution. Or if he did not, he would have to explain why Wittgenstein himself treats all these concepts in a similar way.

consider the individual in isolation all we can say is that it *seems* to him that he is using words correctly; but if we broaden our gaze to take in his community we can make sense of the indispensable idea that this seeming may be delusive, that he is not *really* using words correctly at all. Thus the correct assertibility condition for "he means addition by '+'" is that his responses with '+' agree with mine or those of his community, and these latter persons are primitively entitled to take themselves to mean addition by '+'. On this interpretation, Wittgenstein builds the notion of community right into the notion of rule, in such a way that rule-following cannot be individualistically conceived – to say someone is following a rule is necessarily to advert to *other* rule-followers. Thus the notion of rule-following turns out to be a social notion in somewhat the way the notions of a conformist or a club member or a fashionable dresser are social notions: none of these properties can be possessed by individuals 'considered in isolation'. Now is there any textual support for this interpretation of Wittgenstein?[23]

Let us re-examine 198–202 in which Wittgenstein is putting forward his positive view and opposing it to the view he rejects. The most glaring feature of these sections in the present connexion is that the words 'custom', 'practice' and 'use' are never qualified with 'social' or 'community' – and 'social custom/practice' is not *pleonastic*. Surely Wittgenstein would have inserted these qualifying adjectives if he really meant to maintain a social conception of rule-following, especially in view of the fact that the introduction of the community is taken to be a surprising result of signal importance – as sharply conflicting with what we antecedently expect. And if we look for a gloss on the use of 'custom' etc. we find, as I stressed in Chapter 1, the insistence that rules must be followed on more than one *occasion* – i.e. the existence of rules depends upon 'regular use'. Wittgenstein does use 'custom' and 'practice' to suggest the idea of a multiplicity, but it is a multiplicity of *instances* of rule-following not of *persons* who follow the rules.

---

[23] Kripke is, of course, not the first to propose a broadly community interpretation of Wittgenstein's discussion of following a rule; an early exponent of this interpretation is Peter Winch, in *The Idea of a Social Science* (Routledge and Kegan Paul: London, 1958), esp. pp. 24–39. And this general interpretation has been endorsed by a great many, perhaps the majority, of commentators since then.

And this is part and parcel of Wittgenstein's general thesis that meaning is use: a sign has meaning only in virtue of being (repeatedly) used in a certain way. *This thesis does not in itself carry any suggestion that meaning is inconceivable in social isolation.* But is there anything *else* in these sections which might be supposed to encourage the community interpretation? Two points may be mentioned here.

The first concerns the use of 'privately' in 202. Kripke takes this word to be intended to contrast with 'social', so that it has roughly the sense 'private' has in 'private property', i.e. relating to a single individual; I suggested in Chapter 1 that it contrasts rather with 'public' or 'overt', i.e. relates to what transpires covertly within consciousness. On Kripke's understanding of the intended notion of privacy a person's *overt behaviour*, say in following a sign-post, is to be considered 'private', at least if it is described individualistically; and so we could quite properly claim that all non-rule-governed behaviour (e.g. pain behaviour) can and does take place 'privately', since its description does not require reference to other people. It is thus possible to wave your arm 'privately' but not possible to follow the addition rule 'privately', according to Kripke's construal of 'privately' in 202. What is *public* can be 'private' in this sense – knowability by others is therefore not sufficient for non-privacy. We can even say that (non-relational) properties of material objects, e.g. being cubical or weighing a stone, are possessed 'privately' in Kripke's sense, since their ascription does not make essential reference to *other* objects and their condition. Now it seems to me that this would be a very odd way for Wittgenstein to intend his use of 'privately' in 202: in general he opposes 'private' to 'public' or 'overt', as in 'private sensations'.[24] Kripke takes Wittgenstein to be saying in 202 that if rule-following were private in the sense that it involved

---

[24] Wittgenstein does not, perhaps, use 'private' and 'privately' in an entirely uniform way; but its central meaning for him is, I think, twofold: he uses it to suggest a condition of consciousness, and he uses it to suggest unknowability by another (see 251, 272, 294). When states of consciousness are conceived in an erroneous way, their (admitted) 'privacy' becomes a kind of unknowability, instead of a harmless truth about them ('The proposition "Sensations are private" is comparable to "One plays patience by oneself"' (248), i.e. this is a 'grammatical remark'). I think both of these connotations are present in Wittgenstein's use of 'privately' in 202. I do not know of any passage in which Wittgenstein clearly uses 'private' in the sense Kripke gives to it in 202, i.e. as meaning 'making no reference to other people'.

just the individual rule-follower, then rules could not be normative – correct rule-following would collapse into *apparently* correct rule-following; whereas I take the claim of 202 to be that if rule-following were private in the sense of being a condition or process of consciousness, then self-ascriptions of rule-following would be infallible. Aside from the overall plausibility of the interpretation I prefer, I think that my interpretation makes better sense of Wittgenstein's use of 'privately' in 202 – it conforms better with Wittgenstein's general use of the notion of privacy. At the very least it should be agreed that the use of 'privately' in 202 cannot be cited to *establish* the correctness of the community interpretation.

The second point concerns Wittgenstein's mention of 'one man' in 199:

> Is what we call "obeying a rule" something that it would be possible for only *one* man to do, and to do only *once* in his life?—This is of course a note on the grammar of the expression "to obey a rule".   (199)

Wittgenstein's reply to this question is: 'It is not possible that there should have been only one occasion on which someone obeyed a rule.' What is *prima facie* puzzling here is why Wittgenstein should *raise* the question whether it is possible for one *man* to follow a rule and answer it by saying that it is not possible for there to be a single *occasion* of rule-following.[25] His reply, let it be noted, is *not* that it is not possible for one man to obey a rule: why then does he appear to ask a question to which he gives no answer (or half an answer)? Since Wittgenstein does not *answer* his question by saying rule-following requires more than one man, 199 cannot be cited as evidence that Wittgenstein endorses a community conception of rules; but the passage certainly seems to raise the *issue* of whether rule-following is individual or social. What is going on here? The

---

[25] The question is also raised in *RFM* p. 349: 'Could there be only one human being that calculated? Could there be only one that followed a rule?' It is not, however, answered negatively. Elsewhere we read: 'But what about this consensus – doesn't it mean that *one* human being by himself could not calculate? Well, *one* human being could at any rate not calculate just *once* in his life' (*RFM* p. 193). These remarks seem best explained as I explain the passage from the *Investigations* cited in the text: Wittgenstein's underlying point is that we need a plurality of *occasions*, and it is a question to be raised whether one man provides enough of these. Wittgenstein's implication appears to be that he does, so long as he calculates more than once.

explanation that seems to me the most plausible is this: Wittgenstein's central contention in these passages, *viz.* that rules require many occasions of manifestation, is ambiguous as stated, between (*a*) the claim that *each* individual who grasps a rule must obey it on more than one occasion and (*b*) the weaker claim that there must be many occasions of rule-following *possible distributed over several individuals*. The latter claim would allow as possible the circumstance that each of many people obey a given rule only once, since this would be enough for the rule to be followed on many *occasions*. Now Wittgenstein's actual words in 199 commit him only to the weaker thesis, and so are compatible with the possibility that *each* person follows a rule only once; what they are not compatible with is the possibility that *one* man follows a rule just *once* – exactly the question he raises. The point being made, then, is that if there is just one man then *he* must follow his rules more than once, but if there are many men it can be enough that *each* follows his rules just once (or possibly not at all). I think this reading of 199 is consonant with the gist of other passages in which the question of how many occasions of rule-following are necessary is raised and answered; for example:

> In the same way it cannot be said either that just once in the history of mankind did someone follow a sign-post. Whereas it can be said that just once in the history of mankind did someone walk parallel with a board. And that first impossibility is again not a psychological one. (*RFM* p. 346)

There is no suggestion here that solitary rule-following is impossible; for this is not ruled out by the claim that sign-posts have to be obeyed more than once. The reason Wittgenstein broaches the question of solitary rule-following in 199 is that he wants to make allowance for the possibility that the occasions are spread over many individuals when he claims that many occasions are required. It is not, I think, that he is greatly attracted to the idea of spreading the many occasions over equally many individuals – one occasion each, so to speak – but he feels the need to acknowledge that this is logically compatible with his fundamental contention, *viz.* the multiple application thesis. As we saw in Chapter 1, he is anxious not to over-state this thesis, requiring only that there be *some* rules which are multiply obeyed and not that *all* should be; I surmise that in 199 he is again guarding against exaggerating a thesis which he thinks his readers may find it hard to accept even in its weakest form. So I conclude that 199 cannot be cited to establish the community interpretation either, once it is seen in context and read carefully. And besides, would it not be astonishing if Wittgenstein had put forward his major positive thesis in such an oblique and laconic remark?[26]

Perhaps I should make it clear that I am not suggesting that in these disputed passages Wittgenstein is consciously opting for an individualistic as opposed to a social conception of rule-following: that is, my interpretation is not that Wittgenstein is centrally exercised with this question and is taking a definite stand on it. Rather, my view is that this whole issue is foreign to his true concerns: it is simply not a question with which he is wrestling. So when I say that his positive view is individualistic I am imposing a classification upon his position which is imported from outside: if he had been asked where he stood on this issue, he would have said on the individualistic side, but I do not think he would have reckoned this to be especially relevant to the problems with which he was centrally occupied. This general lack of concern with the kind of question Kripke sets up seems to me to indicate how fundamentally Kripke's interpretation misrepresents what Wittgenstein is really up to. Not only does Wittgenstein not advocate a community conception of rules; this is not even a considered position in the space of philosophical views within which he is operating. So the individualism I claim to discern in Wittgenstein's stated views is not to be seen as a doctrine he is keen to promote; it is rather a claim about what his positive view in fact comes to, irrespective of his own main intentions.

So far I have been addressing myself to detailed textual considerations; I now want to object to the community interpretation on a more general or thematic ground, namely

---

[26] Kripke never so much as mentions what I have argued to be Wittgenstein's main point in these passages about rules and customs, *viz.* the multiple application thesis. Since it seems beyond question that this is at least *one* thing Wittgenstein is saying, Kripke must hold that Wittgenstein is making the community claim in the same breath as he is propounding the multiple application thesis. However, in view of the *toto caelo* difference between these two claims, it would seem at best highly confusing for Wittgenstein to be running them together so carelessly. Better to attribute only one of them to him; and there seems no question but that he held the multiple application thesis.

its relation to Wittgenstein's thesis that we follow rules 'blindly'. For I think that the kind of epistemology of rule-following Wittgenstein advocates is inconsistent with Kripke's suggestion that right rule-following consists in agreement with the community. As we saw in Chapter 1, Wittgenstein's view is that our natural inclination to follow rules as we do is not something we can justify, nor are we required to justify it – we obey rules 'blindly', without guidance. So if someone challenges me to justify an application of a sign, all I can ultimately reply is 'This is simply what I do' (217); nothing *demonstrates* that my application is correct.[27] But on Kripke's community interpretation this will not be the epistemological situation: for agreement with others *does* provide a court of appeal in case of such a challenge. Suppose someone claims that it only strikes me that my present application of '+' is correct (accords with its past meaning) and that in fact I am now using '+' wrongly; then Kripke's sceptical solution offers me an answer, namely that my present use is correct *because* it agrees with the use made of that sign by others. That is to say, the community view allows me to get beyond, or beneath, my natural sign-using propensities to something that can be cited to give these propensities a justification, since correctness, on Kripke's view, is precisely a matter of community concordance in use: the community, in short, provides the kind of *guidance* that Wittgenstein explicitly says there isn't.[28] Kripke's conception makes rule-following like being in fashion in this respect: if someone challenges my belief that I am in fashion, I can rebut him by pointing out that my mode of dress agrees with that of (certain) members of my community – I am not reduced to saying that this is a belief for which a justification is neither

[27] Cf. 'The danger here, I believe, is one of giving a justification of our procedure where there is no such thing as a justification and we ought simply to have said: *that's how we do it*' (*RFM* p. 199). But this does not imply any epistemic defect, since 'To use the word without a justification does not mean to use it wrongfully' (*RFM* p. 406). Essentially the same point could be put by saying that I have (and need) no *criterion* for applying a word as I do, i.e. for supposing that I am using it in a rule-governed way.

[28] Thus 'we look to the rule for instruction and *do something*, without appealing to anything else for guidance' (228): that is, when I naturally react in a certain way to a rule (expression of a rule) I cannot check that this reaction is right by looking to the community for guidance. What prompts this appeal to community guidance is what also prompts the appeal to a voice of intuition, namely the feeling that we must be able to provide some *reason* for what we do when we follow rules.

possible nor required. Note that Wittgenstein does *not* say that the *community* considered as a whole follows rules blindly, i.e. proceeds upon the basis of a collective human nature; his claim is that *I* do. So it would not be faithful to Wittgenstein's words to transpose his claim about the absence of rational foundations to the level of the community; and neither is it correct to interpret him as trying to alleviate the epistemological discomfort we may feel about *my* lack of reasons by equipping me with the test of community conformity.[29] In fact, it is precisely the thirst for the kind of rational basis Wittgenstein denies that causes Kripke to introduce the community; but of course this goes right against the thrust of Wittgenstein's position – it is trying to find reasons for what does not (and need not) rest upon reasons. To put it in a nutshell, Kripke's interpretation misses, or underestimates, Wittgenstein's epistemological *naturalism.*

This point leads into the question, crucial for Kripke's interpretation, of Wittgenstein's attitude toward the normativeness of meaning – what he took its nature and ground to be. Kripke represents Wittgenstein as preoccupied in the *Investigations* with the question what makes a present use of a sign correct, i.e. in accordance with our previous linguistic intentions; and Wittgenstein's answer is supposed to be that this is to be explained in terms of agreement with the community. However, I think that an unprejudiced examination of the passages with which we are concerned (138–242) reveals notably little that can be construed as a concern with this question: that is, we just do not find Wittgenstein fretting over the question whether my present inclinations to apply a sign really conform with my past meaning. It seems to me, in fact, that Wittgenstein's attitude towards this kind of question

[29] In *Z* 319 Wittgenstein says something very relevant to this, which seems to me of considerable significance for community interpretations of Wittgenstein's thought about rule-following. After saying, 'I cannot describe how (in general) to employ rules, except by *teaching* you, *training* you to employ rules' (*Z* 318), he goes on: 'I may now e.g. make a talkie of such instruction. The teacher will sometimes say "That's right". If the pupil should ask him "Why?" – he will answer nothing, or at any rate nothing relevant, not even: "Well, because we all do it like that"; that will not be the reason.' It is very hard to see how this passage could be squared with the idea that, for Wittgenstein, correctness in following a rule is a matter of agreement with the reactions of the community – either in respect of truth conditions or assertibility conditions.

verges on the dismissive.[30] His view is that what underlies (if
that is the word) our practices and customs with signs is our
human nature in interaction with our training: this is what
explains our unreflectively going on as we do. Different kinds
of being, endowed with a different 'form of life', could
naturally go on in different ways given the same training:

> Now we get the pupil to continue a series (say + 2) beyond
> 1000—and he writes, 1000, 1004, 1008, 1012.
> We say to him: "Look what you've done!"—He doesn't
> understand. We say: "You were meant to add *two*: look how
> you began the series!"—He answers: "Yes, isn't it right? I
> thought that was how I was *meant* to do it."——Or suppose he
> pointed to the series and said: "But I went on in the same
> way."—It would now be no use to say: "But can't you
> see. . . .?"—and repeat the old examples and explanations.—In
> such a case we might say, perhaps: It comes natural to this
> person to understand our order with our explanations as *we*
> should understand the order: "Add 2 up to 1000, 4 up to 2000, 6
> up to 3000 and so on."
> Such a case would present similarities with one in which a
> person naturally reacted to the gesture of pointing with the
> hand by looking in the direction of the line from finger-tip to
> wrist, not from wrist to finger-tip.   (185)

It is our nature that (partly) determines what we mean by our
words and which plays an ineliminable role in our learning
language. Given that this is so, Wittgenstein sees no real
substance to the question whether what we are *naturally*
inclined to do *really* conforms with the meaning of our signs:
such a question must be futile, since what we are by nature

---

[30] The question of correctness in the application of a rule is the question what counts
as a *mistake* in applying the rule. Wittgenstein does not in fact make heavy weather of
this question, as witness this passage: 'But how does the observer distinguish in this
case between players' mistakes and correct play? – There are characteristic signs of it in
the players' behaviour. Think of the behaviour characteristic of correcting a slip of the
tongue. It would be possible to recognize that someone was doing so even without
knowing his language' (54); see also 143, in which mistaking the order of a series is said
to be simply a matter of 'frequency'. That is, Wittgenstein takes there to be readily
recognisable criteria for making a mistake; he is not supposing there to be a deep and
perplexing problem about what the distinction of correct and incorrect application
consists in (for the case of language about public objects). Rather, he typically *assumes*
a given pattern of possible future use to be correct and is then exercised with the
question how this relates to what I *now* mean.

inclined to do is what it is that *constitutes* what we mean.[31] What we are inclined to do by nature and what we mean cannot come apart in the way the question assumes. There is, for Wittgenstein, not the sort of gap that Kripke's sceptic trades on between meaning and naturally determined use. Reading a little into what Wittgenstein says, I think his response to Kripke's question of what determines normativeness would be that this question erroneously assumes that our meanings are not fixed (in part) by our natural propensities but by something logically independent of these propensities, since it envisages the possibility that we should by nature treat a pattern of use as linguistically correct and yet that pattern be incorrect; but the thought of this possibility involves the mistaken supposition that once the natural facts about us are exhausted there remains somewhere else to look for what determines meaning. What has to be recognised is that at some level meaning is fixed by our nature: meaning something is not an achievement of a transcendent mind divorced from our 'form of life'. The basis of the normative is the natural.[32]

A comparison of Wittgenstein with Hume may help to clarify Wittgenstein's position. Suppose someone were to put the question 'What makes causal judgements *correct* on Hume's view?' Granted that our minds are so constituted that we form causal beliefs upon exposure to constantly conjoined events, what is it for a belief so formed to be true or false: might not our minds lead us to form a causal belief in the way Hume describes and yet that belief be false? It is clear what Hume would reply to this question: he would say that there is not the sort of gap between belief and truth that the question presupposes, since causation involves nothing over and above constant conjunctions and the mind's natural propensity to form expectations – there is, in particular, nothing independent of our minds (i.e. objective) to constitute 'necessary connexion'. On Hume's view, then, correctness in a causal judgement ultimately rests upon our (mental) nature; so it cannot be that we naturally form causal judgements on the basis of observed

[31] Here we might think of very simple language-games in which training produces fairly uniform and mechanical reactions; or even of the 'language' of bees.

[32] On this point I am in agreement with Barry Stroud, 'Wittgenstein and Logical Necessity', *Philosophical Review* LXXIV (1965). This interpretation contrasts with the idea that Wittgenstein is some kind of 'conventionalist'.

constant conjunctions which are (objectively) false, at least ultimately. Only if one rejects Hume's 'projectivist' account of causation could one press the question whether our natural propensities lead us to have *true* causal beliefs upon exposure to constant conjunctions. The respect in which Wittgenstein's position on rules resembles Hume's on causation is that both locate the source of correctness in our given nature, not in some aspect of reality quite independent of us and our natural propensities.[33] The main difference between them (as I remarked in Chapter 1) is that Hume takes his view to be 'sceptical', whereas Wittgenstein takes his to be non-sceptical once we attain a right epistemology. And it would, of course, be radically contrary to the whole spirit of Hume's position on causation to locate correctness in the conformity of one's causal judgements with those of one's community: that is, Hume would not want to say that the distinction between seemingly true causal beliefs and really true ones is to be explained in terms of whether your judgements agree with others' judgements. This would just be a doomed attempt to postpone the sceptical conclusion that our causal judgements correspond to no objective or external feature of reality. I think that Kripke's community interpretation of Wittgenstein makes a similar mistake as this community interpretation of Hume in respect of what constitutes the correctness of a causal belief: Kripke is in effect jibbing at one of Wittgenstein's main theses – that there is *nowhere* I can turn to underpin or bolster how I naturally proceed in my application of signs, not even to other people. Kripke is trying to locate what I mean, and hence linguistic correctness, in something external to my nature as a language-user, i.e. in my relations to a community; but this would be to refuse to accept Wittgenstein's claim that my judgements of linguistic correctness are not based upon reasons. Wittgenstein's position is simply this: what I mean is

[33] There is even in Wittgenstein some analogue of Hume's projectivist 'error theory': when we reflect philosophically upon our following of rules we are irresistably tempted to suppose that our natural propensities have some foundation in what is 'out there', and hence we get the idea of 'rails invisibly laid to infinity' (218) and of 'something which only needs the addition of "and so on", in order to reach to infinity' (229). These illusions result from a kind of 'externalization' of the compulsion we are under when we follow a rule – rather as Hume thought that we 'externalize' necessary connexion in our thought about causation. (Of course this analogy should not be pressed too far; there are also plenty of differences between Hume and Wittgenstein in this regard.)

determined by my natural use of words, so that we cannot
sensibly ask whether my use really conforms to what my words
mean.[34] (Compare Hume: the causal truths are determined by
regularities acting upon our minds to produce expectations, so
that we cannot sensibly ask whether the expectations thereby
produced are really correct, i.e. lead us to form true causal
beliefs.) This is not, of course, to say that our application of
words can *never* be mistaken, that every use is self-certifyingly
correct; but it is to say that judgements of linguistic correctness
always rest *in the end* upon natural propensities to apply words
in a certain way: we do sometimes make judgements of
linguistic mistake, but these judgements have their ultimate
source in our natural sense of what is right – they do not involve
prescinding altogether from our natural propensities to apply
signs. So, on Wittgenstein's view, linguistic mistake is necessarily *local*; we cannot make real sense of the idea that our
natural ways of using signs are *globally* mistaken, since that
would be to assume that our meaning is fixed by something
external to us.[35] In a sense, then, Wittgenstein dismisses as
incoherent the kind of scepticism that lies behind Kripke's
sceptical paradox: I mean the general scepticism that questions
whether my use of signs has *ever* conformed with their meaning
– for their meaning cannot in this way come apart from the use
I make of them. It is for these reasons that I say that
Wittgenstein would not have pursued and pressed the question
of normativeness in the way Kripke does; and, as I remarked,
he does not in point of fact make a great deal of the question of
normativeness in these sections of the *Investigations*.

My rejection of the community interpretation is not yet
complete. Someone wedded to this interpretation might allow
that 198–202 fail on their own to establish that Wittgenstein
held a social conception of rules but urge that these sections

[34] It is important here that my use of language is interwoven with various kinds of
non-linguistic activity in such a way as to fix what my words mean; so correctness of
use will (partially) consist in how my linguistic actions fit in with my non-linguistic
actions.

[35] 'Philosophers very often talk about investigating, analysing, the meaning of
words. But let's not forget that a word hasn't got a meaning given to it, as it were, by a
power independent of us, so that there could be a kind of scientific investigation into
what the word *really* means. A word has the meaning someone has given to it' (*BB* pp.
27–8). So it could not turn out that a word has a meaning different from that which I
(we) give to it by dint of my (our) use of the word.

should themselves not be considered in isolation: and when we place them in the context of other passages we will see that they should be read as embodying the social conception; that is, 198–202 leave implicit what other passages make explicit. I need, then, to consider what other passages might be thought to lend themselves to a community interpretation and show that they have a different purport. The section I have most often heard cited as displaying Wittgenstein's commitment to the social conception is 242:

> If language is to be a means of communication there must be agreement not only in definitions but also (queer as this may sound) in judgments. This seems to abolish logic, but does not do so.—It is one thing to describe methods of measurement, and another to obtain and state results of measurement. But what we call "measuring" is partly determined by a certain constancy in results of measurement.   (242)

The claim is that Wittgenstein is here building the notion of agreement into the notion of meaning. This interpretation ignores, what I stressed in Chapter 1, that Wittgenstein is in this passage making a claim about the necessary conditions of *communication*: his claim is that for two or more people to share a language – to mean the same by their words – they must agree in their judgements. This claim expressly concerns a social concept, *viz.* that of a linguistic community, and so naturally it is formulated in social terms, *viz.* agreement *between* members of that community. What Wittgenstein does not say, and what fails to follow from what he does say, is that for there to be meaning *at all* there has to be inter-personal agreement. He is certainly not saying in this section that the idea of an idiolect makes no sense: he is not ruling out the possibility that I might employ words with different meanings from those of other people. His point is that *if* we are to use words with the same meanings then we must agree in their use. Indeed, the interpretation I am rejecting would have Wittgenstein claiming, absurdly, that I cannot mean by a word what no-one else means by it, since meaning requires inter-personal agreement of use. In general, the relation between agreement and rules, as Wittgenstein sees it, concerns the notion of two or more people following the *same* rules; agreement is not supposed to be a necessary condition of an *individual's* following a rule – that requires, rather, a multiplicity of *occasions* of application.

What may also mislead is that Wittgenstein speaks typically of communal languages, e.g. English and German, and so formulates his claims in terms of these shared languages; but it is not to be inferred from this that he rejects the very notion of a language confined to a single individual. Since most actual rules are in fact shared, including the semantic rules of natural languages, it is only to be expected that Wittgenstein's examples should be of this kind; but this should not be taken to exclude the very possibility of rules followed by only one person – and Wittgenstein says nothing to suggest that he intends to exclude this possibility. It is not, as I remarked earlier, that he is especially anxious to insist on the coherence of solitary rule-following and to contest a community conception; the truth is that he is simply unconcerned with this kind of question. His citation of communal signs thus does not betoken a commitment to the *essentially* communal employment of signs; rather, he is, for his purposes, indifferent to the question.

Much the same should be said of Wittgenstein's emphasis upon the notion of *training* in his account of language and rules. Training is, of course, a social concept – it involves an inter-personal relation – and training in the use of a sign may be said to aim at agreement between the trainee's behaviour and that of the trainer. Does this commit Wittgenstein to a community conception of what it is to grasp a rule? Clearly not, since nothing so far said implies that in order to explicate the concept of the learner's grasping a rule we must make *essential* reference to the behaviour of the trainer – any more so than for any skill acquired by means of training, e.g. kicking a ball. Wittgenstein emphasises training not because he thinks all rules are necessarily social but because it helps to remind us of what really goes on when someone achieves understanding: it acts as a prophylactic against myth-making.[36] (I should say

---

[36] See esp. 208–10, in which it is emphasised that in teaching someone a rule I do not communicate less than I myself know. This claim of Wittgenstein's bears certain similarities to W. V. Quine's position on radical translation in *Word and Object* (MIT Press: Cambridge, Mass, 1960), chap. 2; and to Michael Dummett's insistence upon the exhaustive manifestability of linguistic understanding in 'What is a Theory of Meaning? (II)', in *Truth and Meaning*, ed. G. Evans and J. McDowell (Clarendon Press: Oxford, 1976).

that Kripke himself shows no tendency to rest his community interpretation on either of the last two considerations; I mention them because I have heard them cited by others in support of a community interpretation.)

I am not, in rejecting the community interpretation, saying that Wittgenstein thinks the notion of a linguistic community is 'unimportant' or totally irrelevant to a proper account of meaning; nor am I denying that when a language is communal others may legitimately correct one's use of words; I am not even denying that what others mean by words can determine their meaning on the lips of a given speaker. I am saying only that Wittgenstein does not hold that the very notion of a rule of language must needs be explicated in social terms – that we cannot make *sense* of rule-following on the part of a given individual unless we relate that individual's behaviour to the behaviour of some community of rule-followers. Wittgenstein no more holds this view about understanding a rule than he holds a parallel view about being in pain or remembering something. And, as I shall argue in Chapter 4, it is well that Wittgenstein did not hold such a view, because it is clearly wrong.

The divergence between Kripke's interpretation and mine shows up sharply in our different views of the way 202 relates to the later sections dealing (explicitly) with private language (243f). Kripke's view is that by 202 the argument against the possibility of a private language is essentially *complete* – Wittgenstein has already shown that there must always be public criteria for the correctness of linguistic use. This result has already been established because rule-following *in general* depends upon communal agreement of response: for an individual to be following *any* rule he must exhibit behaviour which others can use to correct his sincere avowal that he is following a rule, since this is what the normativeness of rule comes to. The notion of correct rule-following is explicated in terms of assertibility conditions which are available to members of one's linguistic community, and so there is no possibility of following a rule which others cannot know one is following correctly or incorrectly.[37] This view of what is going on in 202 obviously depends upon the community interpret-

---

[37] See Kripke, pp. 3, 98–113.

ation, i.e. upon building agreement of response into the notion of rule-following. On the interpretation I have put forward, there is not this direct link between 202 and the private language argument: 202 sets the stage for that argument without actually completing it; more argumentative work has to be done before the possibility of a private language can be excluded. What is left open by 202 is the possibility of a 'private technique', i.e. a capacity to apply a sign in a regular way which is not checkable by others. In the case of public objects the technique of use will be checkable by others because the objects themselves are accessible to others and hence regularity of use is verifiable; but if the objects are private, as sensations have often been supposed to be, then there will be no telling whether the speaker is referring to the same (kind of) sensation on different occasions of use. I think my interpretation of the relation between 202 and the later material on private language better fits Wittgenstein's procedure in those later sections, for he speaks as if new considerations were being advanced and not simply a specific consequence of earlier conclusions being drawn.[38] Kripke, in fact, claims that Wittgenstein anticipates his sceptical paradox and its solution as early as the very first section of the *Investigations*, in which case the possibility of a private language would have been excluded right at the beginning: this seems implausible in itself, and inspection of section 1 discloses only an emphasis upon *acting* as against 'explanations' – there is no essential mention there of the community. My conclusion is then that the more traditional view of where the private language argument occurs (after 243) is to be preferred to Kripke's. It would, perhaps, be pleasant if Kripke's view of the overall structure of the *Investigations* were correct, but it does not seem to me that it is. And the reason Wittgenstein's book does not have the *structure* Kripke attributes to it is that it does not have the *content* he attributes to it.

---

[38] He does not anywhere say or imply that a private language has already been excluded by his earlier considerations, and that it is necessary for him now only to bring out how those considerations apply to the special case of words for sensations. In fact, I think he writes as if the earlier conclusion – that understanding is mastery of a practice – leaves open the possibility of a private language. Hence the need to show that we have to impose further conditions on what it takes for a genuine practice (rule) to exist, notably third-person criteria of correctness.

3

Critical Evaluation of Wittgenstein's Views

I have confined myself hitherto to purely exegetical questions, suppressing any interest in whether the views I have attributed to Wittgenstein are correct; I believe that this detached procedure has resulted in a more accurate representation of Wittgenstein's views than the more typical method of mixing textual interpretation with one's own philosophical position. Now that we have before us an account of what Wittgenstein is really saying we can proceed to ask whether his views are acceptable, confident that we are at least addressing ourselves to the right questions. I shall not in this chapter be able to offer a complete and definitive critique of Wittgenstein's views, but I hope I can at least identify the sorts of considerations that are relevant to deciding whether Wittgenstein's position is defensible. I shall proceed by discussing each of the four theses I attributed to Wittgenstein in Chapter 1 in turn.

Thesis (i) is that understanding is not an inner state or process. This thesis divides into two logically independent subtheses, corresponding to two different notions of the inner: the inner as a condition of consciousness, and the inner as some kind of non-conscious state or mechanism. Wittgenstein spends more time on the former idea – in particular, upon the idea that understanding consists in some item 'coming before the mind'. He rejects the conception of understanding as a kind of experiencing or imagining, and insists that we acknowledge a different category of 'psychological concepts' of which understanding is one central example – others are intention, belief, knowledge, attention, remembering, etc. His view is that we are prone to assimilate the two sorts of concept, taking the experiential concepts as our paradigm; we thus tend to construe every psychological concept as standing for some sort of feeling. Thus he says: 'when we do philosophy, we should like to hypostatize feelings where there are none' (598); and our proneness to assimilate all psychological concepts to concepts of consciousness leads us to *invent* experiences to correspond to the concepts we have erroneously assimilated – hence a sort of introspective mythology arises.[1] Now in order for this diagnosis of the source of (some) philosophical error to carry conviction we need to be sure that there is the kind of distinction of psychological concepts Wittgenstein suggests: and what would fill this need would be a criterion for drawing the distinction. What exactly distinguishes the concepts of consciousness from those others that must on no account be assimilated with them? To this rather natural question it is hard to find any explicit or articulated reply in the *Investigations*: Wittgenstein tends to proceed by offering piecemeal contrasts without addressing himself to what general principle lies behind these contrasts. This is unsatisfactory, given his reliance upon a quite general diagnostic thesis about our tendency to assimilate one sort of concept with another. But Wittgenstein was by no means unaware of the question and in *Remarks on the Philosophy of Psychology* he suggests an answer to it:

> I want to talk about a 'state of consciousness', and to use this expression to refer to the seeing of a certain picture, the hearing of a tone, a sensation of pain or of taste, etc. I want to say that believing, understanding, knowing, intending, and others, are not states of consciousness. If for the moment I call these latter 'dispositions', then an important difference between dispositions and states of consciousness consists in the fact that a disposition is not interrupted by a break in consciousness or a shift in attention. (*RPP* vol. II, 45)

What Wittgenstein is giving us is a mark of those psychological concepts that stand for 'states of consciousness', so that we have a firmer grip upon what this phrase comes to and hence

[1] See, e.g., 36, 153, 166, 171, 173.

upon what the difference is between these states and what he calls 'dispositions'.[2] Here we have, what is notably absent from the *Investigations*, a more or less explicit division of psychological concepts into two exclusive and exhaustive categories, and some attempt to provide a test for whether a given concept falls into one or the other category. I think that Wittgenstein is right to draw this distinction and that the mark he offers is indeed adequate as a rough criterion: understanding differs from pain, for example, in that you do not cease to understand a word when you go to sleep or concentrate upon some other word, whereas the sensation of pain does not survive these sorts of change. This is simply because the persistence of a condition *of* consciousness depends upon changes *in* one's consciousness, such as sleep (unconsciousness) or the redirection of attention; whereas what is *not* a condition of consciousness is *independent* of these sorts of change in one's consciousness. (Note that this is not intended as a *definition* of consciousness; it merely connects the notion of a 'state of consciousness' with the notion of a *change* in consciousness.) Using this criterion we can sharpen Wittgenstein's first negative thesis as follows: understanding is not the sort of mental state[3] that can be interrupted by a cessation of consciousness or by a redirection of attention, i.e. by a change in consciousness. This reformulation now supplies a ready 'proof' that understanding does not consist in something coming before the mind; for such a state of mind surely *is* interrupted by a break in consciousness or a shift in attention. In (dreamless) sleep I have no images of red though I do not cease to understand 'red', and if I lose an image of red by being distracted by a loud noise I still retain my understanding of the word. (It is hard to see how Hume, for instance, could accommodate these facts about understanding and changes of consciousness into his view that understanding is imaging.[4])

---

[2] *Cf.* 'The general differentiation of all states of consciousness from dispositions seems to me to be that one cannot ascertain by spot-check whether they are still going on' (*Z* 72). Presumably one cannot tell by spot-check because such a check is sensitive only to whether there has been a change *in* one's consciousness.

[3] I use the phrase 'mental state' provisionally and *in propria persona*; as we will see, Wittgenstein himself objects to the phrase.

[4] See Hume, *A Treatise of Human Nature*, ed. L.A. Selby-Bigge (Clarendon Press: Oxford, 1978), esp. Part 1. What happens to Hume's 'faint images' when he goes to sleep?

No doubt more could be said about the nature of the distinction Wittgenstein is drawing, but I want to agree with him that the distinction exists and that he has a workable way of drawing it. What is less clear to me is whether neglect of the distinction has quite the status Wittgenstein appears to think it has: that is, whether the kind of assimilation he resists is endemic to the philosophical mind or is just a transitory philosophical tendency originating in seventeenth century empiricism. Certainly philosophers today do not *seem* to be in the grip of this mistake – if anything they tend to make the opposite assimilation, viewing *all* psychological concepts as 'dispositional'.[5] Perhaps this is because Wittgenstein's lessons have been learned and inwardly digested by now, so that imaging no longer seems to us the right model for understanding; but still I doubt that philosophical thinking about the mind is *constitutionally* prone to construe everything on the model of experience. It is true enough that people are constitutionally prone to overlook distinctions, but this is a general fault due to intellectual laziness or ineptitude; it is not that we are somehow especially blind to distinctions in the mental realm. In fact it seems to me that once Wittgenstein makes the distinction we have no great difficulty acknowledging it; there is no residual temptation with which we need to do battle that prevents us seeing that (e.g.) knowledge is just not the same *kind* of phenomenon as pain. This is not to say that there are no *other* endemic sources of error about the concepts of meaning and understanding; it is just that recognising two categories of psychological concept does not seem to me to call for any special effort to ward off 'misleading pictures'.[6]

Wittgenstein is surely right to reject the idea that understanding consists in the presence to consciousness of some sort of 'intentional object',[7] on the ground that such a mental act is

---

[5] I am thinking of functionalism as a general theory of mind: according to this theory, all mental states are 'dispositional'.

[6] To my knowledge, Wittgenstein nowhere explains *why* we are so prone to this kind of assimilation, nor why the assimilation is always in the direction he identifies. It seems insufficient here to appeal to his general account of philosophical error, namely the error of allowing our thought to be dominated by the surface forms of language (90, 111, 112).

[7] I use this phrase in the following sense: an object is 'intentional' if it is *considered as* the object of a mental act, so that a material object can be said to be an 'intentional object' if it is perceived or thought about. I do not imply that an 'intentional object', in this sense, lacks existence, or is in some other way ontologically peculiar.

neither necessary nor sufficient for meaning a sign in a particular way. Not necessary because (a) introspection does not always deliver up an appropriate experience and (b) because having an ability does not in general require any particular condition of consciousness. And not sufficient because of the following dilemma: either the conscious content is quotidian, in which case its connexion with correct use is merely contingent; or it is queer (a 'superlative fact'[8]), in which case it is chimerical – no conscious content can 'contain' all of future and counterfactual use in the magical way envisaged (by it all coming before one's mind in an instant). I think Wittgenstein's argument here can be strengthened: not only is meaning not determined by what *actually* passes before the mind – it is not determined even by one's *dispositions* or *abilities* to bring items before one's mind. That is, two people could use a sign and the same *counterfactuals* be true of their states of consciousness and yet they mean something different by the sign: meaning is not supervenient upon dispositions to have things come before one's mind (not even in conjunction with one's conscious history). Neither does adding a course of training to these facts about consciousness enable us to reach meaning, since that too is susceptible of alternative interpretations. In view of this strong non-supervenience, we can say, as Wittgenstein does, that if God could look into our consciousness, including its future and its dispositions, he would not see there what we mean.[9] Strengthening Wittgenstein's claim

---

[8] See 192. What is the relation between the 'queer' and the 'superlative' in Wittgenstein? Roughly this: all superlative facts are queer, but not necessarily conversely. We are prone to postulate superlative facts when we have a misplaced ideal which the mundane facts fail to live up to (*cf.* 97–8): such alleged facts will always be in some way odd, queer, peculiar. But queer facts are not always the result of trying (vainly) to fulfil such an ideal; they may be introduced simply in order to sustain a mistaken theory, as that reading is a particular kind of experience. Both sorts of fact are characteristically conceived as 'hidden'.

[9] His own words are: 'If God had looked into our minds he would not have been able to see there whom we were speaking of' (p. 217). I think that here Wittgenstein is using 'mind' in the restricted sense that he often gives to this word and its cognates, *viz.* as connoting what is inner, in particular what goes on inwardly in consciousness. This is made clear by consulting a parallel passage: 'One would like to ask: "Would someone who could look into your mind have been able to see that you *meant* to say *that?*"' (*Z* 36). As the context of this remark makes plain, Wittgenstein is concerned with whether what the person meant to say had 'swum into view before his mind' (*Z* 38), i.e. had been readable off from his introspectible state of consciousness.

in this way seems necessary if we are to rebut a diehard empiricist who accepts that our *actual* states of consciousness as we use a word do not determine its meaning but insists that meaning is determined by our dispositions to entertain (say) images. The right reply to this weaker form of empiricist view is to point out (*a*) that it seems that a person could understand words, as shown in his use of them, and yet lack the sort of disposition in question, and (*b*) that the dispositional empiricist proposal does not get over the crucial point that images can always be variously applied – adding dispositions to have images (etc.) does not meet this point. The independence of understanding and conditions of consciousness is not, I think, very surprising once one takes to heart the idea that understanding is an ability to use words; for it is not true of ability concepts generally that their application conditions can be stated in terms of properties of consciousness: this is obvious for motor abilities like the ability to swim, but it is also true of more intellectual abilities, e.g. the ability to do arithmetical calculations. As Wittgenstein says:

> How should we counter someone who told us that with *him* understanding was an inner process?——How should we counter him if he said that with him knowing how to play chess was an inner process?—We should say that when we want to know if he can play chess we aren't interested in anything that goes on inside him.—And if he replies that this is in fact just what we are interested in, that is, we are interested in whether he can play chess—then we shall have to draw his attention to the criteria which would demonstrate his capacity, and on the other hand to the criteria for the 'inner states'.
>
> Even if someone had a particular capacity only when, and only as long as, he had a particular feeling, the feeling would not be the capacity.   (p. 181)

It seems to me that Wittgenstein's critique of the 'intentional object' conception of grasp of meaning can be extended in a direction he does not himself explicitly consider: I mean to the Fregean idea that understanding a word consists in a mental act directed onto a mind-independent abstract entity, *viz.* a sense.[10] According to Frege, you succeed in referring to or

[10] The nearest Wittgenstein gets to making this point is in this passage: 'In attacking the formalist conception of arithmetic, Frege says more or less this: these petty explanations of the signs are idle once we *understand* the signs. Understanding would

thinking of something by virtue of standing in a relation of 'grasping' to a sense, which determines some entity as reference. The character of this mental act is notoriously under-explained by Frege, but we may suppose it to be akin to those acts of 'mathematical intuition' by which platonists conceive us to be cognitively related to numbers: a kind of mental act in which a certain sort of entity comes before the mind, though an entity that is neither mental nor concrete.[11] The structure of this mental act is presumably to be conceived on the model of other sorts of mental act in which items come before the mind; so the Fregean conception, as just outlined, does not differ in *this* respect from the empiricist conception – both locate understanding in the apprehension by consciousness of some 'intentional object'. Now let us pretend that we know what all this means: let us suppose that 'grasping a sense' is thus analogous to having an image before one's mind, in respect at least of the structure of mental act involved. Then we can ask whether the Fregean theory is not open to essentially the same objections as Wittgenstein brings against the empiricist theory. And I think we must answer that it is: for how can an entity that comes before one's mind at a particular time determine a pattern of use over time? The would-be understander has an abstract sense in his mental sights and his problem is to go from this to a particular pattern of application of the associated sign: how is this to be done? It appears that we are faced with the same kind of dilemma the image theory faced: either we construe the sense in some quotidian way, in which case it will not dictate a use; or we invest it with suitable magical properties, but then we are engaged in what Wittgenstein would condemn as hocus-pocus. In the case of Fregean senses it seems that it must be the magical conception we have in mind, since senses are by their nature not familiar

---

be something like seeing a picture from which all the rules followed, or a picture that makes them all clear. But Frege does not seem to see that such a picture would itself be another sign, or a calculus to explain the written one to us' (*PG* p. 40). This passage seems to me of some importance in understanding the relationship between Frege's and Wittgenstein's conception of meaning.

[11] See Frege, 'On Sense and Reference', in *Translations from the Philosophical Writings of Gottlob Frege*, ed. P. Geach and M. Black (Blackwell: Oxford, 1952), esp. pp. 59–60. See also Dummett, *Frege: Philosophy of Language* (Duckworth: London, 1973), pp. 153–9.

introspectively discoverable items: we must be thinking of senses as somehow *containing* use, as miraculously condensing all of use into something that can come before the mind in an instant. What could be a better example of a 'superlative fact' invented to sustain a philosophical misconception? In fact, it is hard to see how the Fregean conception can be *au fond* anything other than a manifestation of the idea that understanding consists in an association of signs: for what is a sense but an 'interpretation' of the sign whose sense it is? Tacitly we are being offered a 'rule for interpreting a rule': but a sense can be no more *intrinsically* related to use than any other sign-like item can. We are tempted to think otherwise because we have the picture of directions for use being somehow inscribed in (or on) the sense, but of course this just is the old interpretational conception in another guise. It is not surprising, then, that we can press essentially the same kinds of questions against the Fregean model as Wittgenstein does against the empiricist model. Could not two people have the same senses before their minds and yet use their signs differently, thus demonstrating a difference of meaning (*cf*. 140)? Why should someone not be able to use a sign in the usual way and yet suffer from 'sense-blindness': he lacks the capacity to perform that peculiar mental act of getting senses before his inner eye? Moreover, should not an interruption of consciousness put an end to understanding on the Fregean view: do you apprehend senses in your sleep, or when you are attending to something other than words? Is grasping a sense a *conscious* mental act at all? We were encouraged to think it was, but this seems not to be compatible with the persistence conditions of understanding. And if understanding is having a sense before one's mind should not it be capable of existing for brief isolated periods, as entertaining an image can? But this conflicts with Wittgenstein's plausible thesis that whether and what someone understands at a given time is not independent of what is true of him at other times. It should be possible on the Fregean view to envisage a two-minute England in which the semantic facts are as determinate as they are in reality – we need only suppose that in two-minute England the people have the right senses before their minds.[12] Connectedly, ought not understanding to

---

[12] For the two-minute England, see *RFM* p. 336

have sharp temporal boundaries on the Fregean model – a person comes to understand just at the precise moment at which he gets a sense in his sights? In sum, all the difficulties Wittgenstein finds with the image theory seem to arise for the Fregean theory; and this is because the two theories are fundamentally the same in holding that understanding is a matter of an interpretation that comes before one's mind.[13]

It might be replied to these criticisms that I am tendentiously assimilating the Fregean conception to the empiricist conception: why, it might be asked, should the mental act of grasping a sense be compared with other sorts of mental act in which we speak of what comes before the mind instead of being taken as *sui generis*? I think the right response to this retort is that it is taking refuge in obscurity: it wishes to construe understanding as a cognitive relation to an 'intentional object', but it jibs at taking this construal with full seriousness and literalness. Talk of 'grasping a sense' sounds all very well until the picture being presupposed is brought to light; once we appreciate what is really being suggested it begins to look highly problematic. At bottom the Fregean model represents understanding as a relation of apprehension between the mind and some sort of entity, and it is this basic picture that invites the kinds of objections we have taken over from Wittgenstein: for meaning cannot be *any* kind of entity that comes before the mind.[14] The parallel, in this respect, between the empiricist theory and the Fregean theory is, of course, somewhat ironic for Frege: he replaced subjective images with objective senses in order to secure the communicability of

[13] Dummett, *op. cit.* pp. 158–9, makes the point, against the empiricist image theory, that the use or application of the image needs to be determined, and he credits to Frege the recognition that images will not serve as meanings; but he does not show any awareness that a parallel question about the application of a *sense* might also be pressed by Wittgenstein. Nor does this question get a grip only when senses are conceived as abstract mind-independent entities; it also makes trouble for the more psychologically loaded notion of a 'mode of presentation', if this is conceived in a quasi-perceptual way.

[14] *Cf.* 'Studying the grammar of the expression "explanation of meaning" will teach you something about the grammar of the word "meaning" and will cure you of the temptation to look about you for some object which you might call "the meaning"' (*BB* p. 1). If there were such an object, then it would come (or be brought) before the mind in such a way as to confer understanding; but understanding can *never* be conferred in this way.

meaning, but he retained the empiricist idea that meaning consists in some sort of 'intentional object' onto which one's mind gets directed; and so he becomes vulnerable to Wittgenstein's critique of this *type* of theory. The basic problem is suitably to connect what comes before the mind with a pattern of use: Frege was anxious to secure a relation of determination between sense and *reference*, but he neglects what Wittgenstein takes to be the essential thing – the determination of *use* by meaning. Had Frege been sensitive to this requirement he might have seen that his senses cannot really do the job – any more than references could. That this is so is perhaps best seen by recalling one of Frege's very few efforts to explain what kind of thing a sense is, namely his comparison of senses with the image projected onto the lens of a telescope.[15] His point is that a sense, like an optical image, is accessible to many people; but he does not enquire how such an image, or anything analogous to this, might serve to determine a use: could we not interpret an optical image in indefinitely many ways, as we can a picture, so that no specific application is derivable from the image? In fact Frege's optical analogy strongly suggests the kind of 'picture theory' of understanding Wittgenstein is at pains to refute, for an optical image of something just is a kind of picture of it: if senses are really to be compared with such an image, then they will be inherently incapable of fixing a determinate pattern of application. To put it another way: consciously apprehending a sense does not confer an *ability* to use the corresponding sign.[16]

We have agreed with Wittgenstein that understanding is not a state of consciousness directed onto an 'intentional object'; but he sometimes makes a stronger claim than this – namely that understanding is not a 'mental state' or 'mental process' of *any* kind. We need to be careful about exactly what it is that

---

[15] See Frege, *op. cit.* p. 60.

[16] Frege would have been unhappy with Wittgenstein's account of meaning in terms of techniques of use, because each person has his own technique of use, as he has his own 'ideas'; so the materials Wittgenstein appeals to would be rejected by Frege as 'subjective'. However, Frege's desideratum of the communicability of meaning can be met otherwise than by the postulation of 'objective senses': it is enough that meaning should be 'public', as techniques of use are. The real objection to 'ideas' as meanings is not their 'subjectivity' but their logical independence from use; but *this* objection seems to apply equally to 'objective senses'.

Wittgenstein wishes to deny here. Consider first his denial that understanding is a 'mental process':

> Try not to think of understanding as a 'mental process' at all.—For *that* is the expression which confuses you. But ask yourself: in what sort of case, in what kind of circumstances, do we say, "Now I know how to go on," when, that is, the formula *has* occurred to me?—
>
> In the sense in which there are processes (including mental processes) which are characteristic of understanding, understanding is not a mental process.
>
> (A pain's growing more and less; the hearing of a tune or a sentence: these are mental processes.)   (154)

We can interpret this advice in two ways, an interesting way and an uninteresting way. The uninteresting claim that Wittgenstein might be making is simply that 'understand' is not a 'process verb' but a 'state verb': it does not signify a kind of happening or activity but rather an abiding condition. When Wittgenstein gives examples of what he takes to be genuine mental processes, e.g. a pain's growing more or less, he seems to be assuming that mental processes are (or involve) *events*; so *being in pain* is not a 'mental process' in this sense either. Now this claim is surely correct, indeed so obvious as hardly to need urging. I doubt that this anodyne point is what Wittgenstein really has in mind; for we have seen that elsewhere he wishes to *contrast* understanding with being in pain. I think he is making the more interesting claim that *coming* to understand is not a mental process: that is, when we use 'understand' in descriptions of changes or events we are not describing what should be called a 'mental process'.[17] So even when there is a superficial grammatical similarity between reports of changes of understanding and reports of changes in one's sensations, this should not lead us to speak of both sorts of reports as descriptions of 'mental processes'. This reading of 154 is encouraged by his initial formulation of the question in terms of phrases that signify the *onset* of understanding:

> But wait—if "Now I understand the principle" does not mean the same as "The formula . . . . occurs to me" (or "I say the formula", "I write it down", etc.)—does it follow from this

---

[17] Though Wittgenstein can be found denying that understanding is a mental process, state or activity, he does not, so far as I know, ever explicitly deny that it is a mental *event*; it seems clear, however, that he would deny this.

that I employ the sentence "Now I understand . . . . ." or "Now I can go on" as a description of a process occurring behind or side by side with that of saying the formula?   (154)

Here he is saying that when, as we say, a person *comes* to understand, this should not be thought of as a mental process that accompanies uttering the formula. Now Wittgenstein is very cautious in this passage about the form of his claim: he warns us not to think of understanding as a mental process, and he distinguishes understanding from the processes that accompany it. Neither of these sayings actually *entails* the outright denial that coming to understand is a mental process; his advice is just that we should not *think* of understanding as a mental process because this will lead us into mistaken assimilations. But if his reason for giving this advice is that he thinks it *false* to call understanding a 'mental process', then I think he is wrong. For surely coming to understand a sign is some kind of change in the condition of one's mind, as the onset of a pain is too; and changes in what is true of one's mind have every right to be described as 'mental events/processes'. Indeed, it would seem more in conformity with ordinary usage to call coming to understand a 'mental process' than to call the onset of pain by that phrase; for pain is ordinarily conceived as *bodily*, whereas understanding is the province of 'the mind/intellect'. Similarly, I myself would have no hesitation in calling the acquisition of a belief by means of reasoning a 'mental process': for it is both process-like (not state-like) and mental (not physical). In the *Blue Book* Wittgenstein even asserts that *thinking* is not a 'mental activity', or at least that it is misleading to think of it so;[18] but again, it seems to me that this phrase is entirely proper, since thinking is certainly something mental and is surely some kind of activity. So as remarks about 'ordinary language' I think these claims of Wittgenstein are mistaken. But it might be suggested that this is the wrong way to take what he says: Wittgenstein's real point is that it is wrong to assimilate what happens when someone comes to understand to what happens when (e.g.) he starts to feel a pain or hear a tune – and calling both 'mental processes' encourages this assimilation. With this point I do not wish to

---

[18] 'It is misleading then to talk of thinking as of a "mental activity"' (*BB* p. 6).

quarrel, but I think that Wittgenstein is (at best) exaggerating this correct observation when he recommends that we not call understanding a 'mental process' at all: he is in effect conflating what it is literally *false* to say with what it is potentially *misleading* to say; and I myself would hold that it can never be good advice to tell someone to disbelieve what is true in the interests of getting him to avoid believing what is false. At this point it might be suggested that, strictly speaking, all Wittgenstein *says* is that understanding is not a mental process in the *same sense* that hearing a tune is: that is, 'mental process' is *ambiguous* between the two cases. I doubt that this can be all Wittgenstein means to assert in view of (*inter alia*) the last sentence of 154, but I would also dispute that even this is exactly correct: for it does not obviously follow from the admission that there are two different *sorts* of mental process that 'mental process' is literally *ambiguous*. I would say that it has the same *sense* when applied to the two different sorts of mental process, despite the important differences between these sorts. On balance I think it is most reasonable to interpret Wittgenstein as holding only that it is potentially *misleading* to call understanding a 'mental process', a claim with which we can agree; but unfortunately he exaggerates this legitimate point into the unacceptable claim that it is false or improper so to describe understanding.

Much the same should be said of his opposition to describing understanding as a 'mental state' or a 'state of mind', as in these passages:

> Has he got the system, if he continues the series correctly so far?—Perhaps you will say here: to have got the system (or, again, to understand it) can't consist in continuing the series up to *this* or *that* number: *that* is only applying one's understanding. The understanding itself is a state which is the *source* of the correct use.
>
> What is one really thinking of here? Isn't one thinking of the derivation of a series from its algebraic formula? Or at least of something analogous?—But this is where we were before. The point is, we can think of more than *one* application of an algebraic formula; and every type of application can in turn be formulated algebraically; but naturally this does not get us any further.—The application is still a criterion of understanding.
>
> (146)

> If one says that knowing the ABC is a state of the mind, one is thinking of a state of a mental apparatus (perhaps of the brain) by means of which we explain the *manifestations* of that knowledge. Such a state is called a disposition. But there are objections to speaking of a state of the mind here, inasmuch as there ought to be two different criteria for such a state: a knowledge of the construction of the apparatus, quite apart from what it does.   (149)[19]

It is not perhaps immediately clear exactly what Wittgenstein finds objectionable here. We might initially suppose that he objects to calling understanding a 'state', on the ground that this encourages misleading analogies and assimilations; but there are other passages that conflict with this interpretation:

> Expectation is, grammatically, a state; like: being of an opinion, hoping for something, knowing something, being able to do something. But in order to understand the grammar of these states it is necessary to ask: "What counts as a criterion for anyone's being in such a state?" (States of hardness, of weight, of fitting.)   (572)

> To have an opinion is a state.—A state of what? Of the soul? Of the mind? Well, of what object does one say that it has an opinion? Of Mr N.N. for example. And that is the correct answer.
> One should not expect to be enlightened by the answer to *that* question. Others go deeper: What, in particular cases, do we regard as criteria for someone's being of such-and-such an opinion? When do we say: he reached this opinion at that time? When: he has altered his opinion? And so on. The picture which the answers to these questions give us shews *what* gets treated grammatically as a *state* here. (573)

So Wittgenstein has no real objection to the *word* 'state' for such phenomena as are mentioned here, and there seems no reason to suppose that he would make an exception of understanding.[20] His objection is rather to the idea that belief

---

[19] *Cf. Z* 21, 26, 78, 669; *BB* pp. 5, 20, 32, 78, 143.

[20] It would be wrong to object that understanding differs from these other concepts in being an ability, and that Wittgenstein denies that abilities may be called 'states'. For consider this passage: 'States: "Being able to climb a mountain" may be called a state of my body. I say "I can climb it – I mean I am strong enough." Compare with this the following condition of being able. "Yes, I can go there" – I mean I have enough time' (*Z* 675). Wittgenstein's point here is that the 'can' of ability does ascribe a state, whereas the 'can' of mere possibility does not (*cf. BB* pp. 100–1).

and understanding are states of the *mind* and not of the *person*:
he wants us to stick with the commonsense practice of
ascribing such states to the individuals who have them and not
invent another entity – the mind or soul – which is the proper
metaphysical subject of these states.[21] So, as with his discussion
of 'mental process', Wittgenstein's objection is not to 'state'
but to 'mental'; and this is just as well, since there can be no
grammatical objection to classifying 'understands' as a state-
word, nor to the truth and propriety of saying 'understanding
is a state (of the person)'. Understanding is to be classified with
belief and intention in this respect: and to call these 'states' is to
do little more than record the fact that they are not events but
abiding conditions.[22] That it is calling understanding a *mental*
state that worries Wittgenstein is confirmed by this passage:

> (a) "Understanding a word": a state. But a *mental* state?—
> Depression, excitement, pain, are called mental states. Carry
> out a grammatical investigation as follows: we say
> "He was depressed the whole day".
> "He was in great excitement the whole day".
> "He has been in continuous pain since yesterday".—
> We also say "Since yesterday I have understood this word".
> "Continuously", though?—To be sure, one can speak of an
> interruption of understanding. But in what cases? Compare:
> "When did your pains get less?" and "When did you stop
> understanding that word?" (p. 59)

Wittgenstein's position here parallels his resistance to calling
coming to understand a 'mental process': being in pain is
properly described as a 'mental state', but understanding is not
to be assimilated to this kind of state, so we had better not
describe understanding as a 'mental state'. And I think
our reaction to this claim should parallel our reaction to

---

[21] Here there is an affinity with P. F. Strawson's thesis of the primitiveness of the
concept of a person as the subject of mental predications: see his *Individuals* (Methuen:
London, 1959), chap. 3.

[22] *Cf.* 'Saying something is an activity, being inclined to say something is a *state*' (*Z*
671). Of course, Wittgenstein would warn that calling this (and like phenomena) a
'state' is merely a 'grammatical remark' from which no substantive philosophical
claims can be derived; also that we should not be tempted to assimilate all that is
correctly described as a 'state'. Still, he clearly does not think it *false* to describe
understanding and the rest as states. This goes against a major exegetical thesis of P.
Hacker and G. Baker in *Wittgenstein: Understanding and Meaning* (Blackwell: Oxford,
1980): see esp. pp. 282f.

Wittgenstein's claim about 'mental process': it is true enough that calling pain and understanding both 'mental states' may tempt us into supposing that there is no important ('categorial') difference between them, but it does not follow that it is not *true* so to describe them. Calling understanding a 'mental state' obviously does not *entail* that it is experiential in nature, so the phrase itself is innocent of the assimilation to be resisted: what has to be recognised I think is just that there are two different sorts or categories of mental state. Indeed, as a point of ordinary usage it is more natural to reserve 'mental state' for the likes of belief and intention and understanding – pain (as I remarked earlier) is commonly thought of as a *bodily* state. We want to speak of the physical states or properties of a person – his weight, height, etc. – and we want to be able to distinguish these from states a person has in virtue of having a mind: talk of 'mental states' need reflect no more than the recording of this broad distinction of properties or predicates. The heterogeneity of what is thus classified as 'mental' should not disturb us if we remember Wittgenstein's discussion of the word 'game': indeed, it seems to me that Wittgenstein is here forgetting his own point about family resemblance words – that they can be unambiguous and yet have heterogeneous extensions.[23] If Wittgenstein had held that 'mental' is a family resemblance word, he could have avoided what looks like misplaced linguistic legislation: he could have insisted on the important differences between pain and understanding without committing himself to the implausible thesis that 'mental' is not correctly applicable to the latter state. I rather suspect that Wittgenstein would not, if pressed, have disagreed with describing understanding as a 'mental state', so long as he was convinced that no illicit assimilation was thereby intended; but I think he is led in these sections to say strictly unacceptable things by his desire to prevent us from falling into error.

Wittgenstein makes a further claim about how we should conceive the state of understanding which also seems to me

[23] See 65–71. (In a certain respect, I think Wittgenstein's way of introducing his notion of a family resemblance concept is unfortunate, since members of the same family are in fact unified by underlying genetic overlap; whereas nothing comparable holds for games. The idea of a biological natural kind, determined by an unobservable empirical essence, seems not to have been contemplated by Wittgenstein – no doubt because such an essence would not feature (criterially) in the language-game of classifying objects by the predicate in question.)

questionable: this is his suggestion in 146 that understanding should not be thought of as the *source* of correct use. Here again we need to distinguish the potentially misleading from the strictly and literally false. Wittgenstein's interlocutor maintains (surely correctly) that understanding is not continuing a series up to a certain point; in *some* sense that is just the *application* of one's understanding, not the understanding itself – which he thinks is rightly described as the 'source' of application. Now Wittgenstein objects to this by imputing to his interlocutor the tacit assumption that understanding is having a formula before one's mind from which one derives the series; and he repeats his incontrovertible point that this conception is inadequate. But I think it is by no means obvious that talk of understanding as the source of use *must* involve the interpretational conception, still less that this just *is* that conception in other words. It may indeed be true that the idea of understanding as the source of use can lead one into the interpretational conception, but this is not to say that the idea *itself* is thus mistaken or suspect. So let us ask what could be meant by 'source of use' which does not commit us to the interpretational conception. I think there are two things that might be meant, both of which seem to me legitimate: that understanding is the *causal* source of use, and that it is the *normative* source of use. Whether Wittgenstein would disagree with these claims as I intend them is hard to determine, since he says nothing in 146 that directly bears on them, but it is worth seeing that they need not be found objectionable and do provide clear senses in which understanding is a source of correct application.[24]

There can, presumably, be no denying the truth and propriety of sentences of the form 'he applies S thus-and-so *because* he means by S such-and-such': for example, 'he applies "red" to red objects because he means *red* by "red"'. This type of 'because' sentence belongs with sentences of the form 'he acted thus-and-so *because* he desired such-and-such and believed so-and-so' – that is, sentences which give a person's

---

[24] It is true that Wittgenstein resists the idea of 'a mental state from which all our acts spring as from a reservoir' (*BB* p. 143); but it is by no means clear that the idea of a mental state as a cause of behaviour needs to be committed to that idea: acknowledging, for example, that pain causes movements of withdrawal does not involve us in the strange idea that the movement somehow flows out from the pain – as if it was already there and merely changed its location, in the way water flows from the reservoir to the tap. The cause does not need to *contain* its effect in order to be its cause.

reason for acting in a certain way. Understanding can be cited to explain linguistic behaviour as beliefs and desires can be cited to explain other sorts of behaviour: in explaining or making sense of a particular linguistic act it is necessary to specify how the speaker understands the sign used, and to affirm that it is *because* of this understanding that he used the sign as he did. Now for familiar reasons, which I shall not rehearse here, it is plausible (indeed mandatory) to take this 'because' as (at least in part) *causal*, so that part of what is being said is that the mental state of understanding was a causal factor in the speaker's use of the sign – as beliefs and desires are causal factors in the production of intentional action generally.[25] Accordingly, we can say that these 'because' sentences give (partly) causal explanations of use; and this is I think one good sense we can give to the phrase 'source of use'. The analogy with the rationalization of action also helps us to see that understanding may be regarded as a normative source of use. For the 'correctness' of an action depends upon the beliefs and desires of the agent: an action is rational (a normative concept, this) when it is appropriately related to the agent's set of propositional attitudes. Similarly, we explain why a piece of linguistic use is correct by saying that it accords with the speaker's understanding of the word (what he means by it): my use of 'red' in application to a fire-engine was correct because by 'red' I mean *red*.[26] As the agent's beliefs and desires are the yardstick by which the rationality of his action is measured, so the speaker's understanding of his words is what makes a particular use correct: these 'attitudes' are thus rightly characterised as the 'source' of correctness. And I take this to be a harmless and uncontroversial gloss on our use of the 'because' sentences in question: in particular, nothing I have said here involves us in the interpretational conception. I therefore think that Wittgenstein is not, in 146, objecting to exactly what I have maintained; but he does write *as if* any talk of understanding as a source of use is suspect because of a tacit

---

[25] See D. Davidson, 'Actions, Reasons and Causes', *Journal of Philosophy* LX. (1963).

[26] Similarly, we can explain why a given use of a word was mistaken by citing its meaning: it is wrong to ascribe 'red' to non-red things *because* 'red' means *red* and not (say) *blue*. Such normative claims can hardly be supposed *false* – however easy it may be to misconstrue their purport.

commitment to the idea of an inner formula – and in this I think that he is wrong.

There is another strand to Wittgenstein's thinking on the idea that understanding is a state of mind which is the source of use, and it concerns the relation between understanding and the criteria for understanding. In 149 and elsewhere Wittgenstein is anxious to stress that application is the authoritative criterion for understanding; any conception of understanding which involved demoting application from this sovereign position would therefore be in error. I would agree with Wittgenstein on this point, both with respect to first- and third-person ascriptions of understanding: if the use criterion is adequately met then nothing could rationally persuade us that this was not a case of understanding; and if it is not met then we shall not be persuaded that understanding is nevertheless present (*a fortiori* if the criteria in use for *not* understanding are met). But it does not follow, as 149 appears to suggest, that understanding cannot be conceived as a state of mind which explains the manifestations of understanding. For this conception does not in itself imply that there exist (possibly competing) criteria for understanding in 'the construction of the apparatus'; it does not imply, more specifically, that there could be rival criteria to be read off the condition of the nervous system or the condition of consciousness. Compare belief and intention: we should likewise agree, I think, that the behavioural criteria (at least in the third-person case) are authoritative and irreplaceable, but this admission does not force us to deny that these are states of mind that cause behaviour. Only if we impose a particular *picture* of what a 'state of mind' is will it seem that there ought to be non-behavioural criteria, but nothing in this phrase by itself compels us to think this way: again, the dangerousness of a conception or locution is not a good reason for alleging its erroneousness. It seems to me best to say that understanding is a state of mind which is *essentially* ascribed on the basis of criteria in use, and I see nothing inconsistent or untoward in saying this.[27]

---

[27] For some discussion of this, see my 'Mental States, Natural Kinds and Psychophysical Laws', *Proceedings of the Aristotelian Society*, Supp. Vol. LII. (1978). In the terms of that paper, the point in the text may be restated by saying that we can regard understanding as a mental state without supposing that it has the features characteristic of natural kinds (*cf.* 308).

In 149 Wittgenstein tells us that 'If one says that knowing the ABC is a state of the mind, one is thinking of a state of a mental apparatus (perhaps of the brain) by means of which we explain the *manifestations* of that knowledge': that is, talk of states of mind is prompted by the idea that knowledge (or understanding) is really a condition of some underlying mental mechanism such as the nervous system. And, as we saw in Chapter 1, Wittgenstein is opposed to conceiving psychological concepts in terms of physical states of the body – though his opposition to this takes up a relatively small part of his discussion. He seems to think indeed that if a philosophical tendency can be diagnosed to arise from this sort of conception that is enough in itself to show it to be wrong. His fullest treatment of 'psycho-physiological correspondence', in *Zettel* 608-10, asserts that there is no good *a priori* reason to believe that for every mental state there is a corresponding physical state, and states of the nervous system could play no role in constraining our application of psychological concepts to people – such states play no part in the language-game of describing people psychologically. He even suggests that for all we know our behaviour could proceed from internal physical chaos, and that psychological and behavioural differences between people need not correlate with any underlying physical differences: in short, psychological phenomena may turn out to have no physical explanation. The upshot of this view of the relation (or lack of it) between the mental and the physical is thus that it would be quite wrong to think of understanding as necessarily grounded in, or realised by, states of the brain – or to cash out 'states of mind' talk in terms of such physical states. A materialist might argue that understanding *must* be a state of mind that is the (causal) source of use because understanding is a state of the brain and brain states causally explain behaviour; Wittgenstein's position on 'psycho-physiological correspondence' would pre-empt this kind of view of understanding. Now it does seem to me that *if* states of understanding had physical realisations or embodiments then this would provide a clear sense in which understanding is the source of use; and if this were a conceptual or *a priori* truth then the *concept* of understanding would be the concept of a state which had this kind of physical basis and causal role. So the question is whether Wittgenstein is right to take the view he does of the relation between mind and body; for if he is right, then this will have repercussions for our general conception of the sort of thing understanding is. And it seems to me that Wittgenstein is *not* right about this: his position has some very unpalatable consequences for anyone of even moderately physicalist tendencies. For Wittgenstein's position permits the following as a conceptual possibility: two people could be just alike physically (both being, say, in a state of internal chaos) and yet one of them understands a sign the other does not understand or understands it differently, i.e. understanding is not *supervenient* on a person's (internal) physical properties. This may not seem so alarming (except to a committed physicalist) until we remember that for Wittgenstein meaning is use: if two people differ in their understanding of a sign, then they differ in their use of it. But use is a kind of *behaviour* which can be described physically; so the two people must also differ with respect to the physical descriptions true of their behaviour. It follows that there are events which differ physically but which have no differentiating physical explanation. For example, one person follows (i.e. walks in the direction of) the point of an arrow while the other follows its tail, though they are internally physically indiscernible: nothing about their internal physical state (nor their past physical history) explains this difference. This is tantamount to the admission or claim that some physical events have no physical explanation, *viz.* those that issue from psychological differences which correspond to no physiological differences. As some sort of physicalist I find this consequence intolerable (though I confess I would find it hard to *prove* to someone that it is). Those of my readers who share this degree of physicalism will accordingly feel bound to dissent from Wittgenstein's general stance on the mind-body relation, and will want to say that there *is* some state of the brain corresponding to each state of understanding which is the causal source of linguistic behaviour. We need not claim anything so strong as that each state of understanding is *identical* with, or *reducible* to, a brain state, i.e. be type-type identity theorists; but we will want to claim that each state of understanding has *some* physical realisation, and that the causal powers of the former are in some way grounded in those of the latter.[28]

[28] It is worth stressing that it is not just mental concepts for which Wittgenstein takes the view he does; he also supposes (in effect) that there could be botanical differences

It cannot be said that Wittgenstein gives any real arguments for his radical anti-physicalist thesis, but it is possible to discern a certain sort of consideration that weighs with him. This consideration turns out to rest upon an equivocation to which we have recently become sensitive. As we have seen Wittgenstein is insistent that behaviour furnishes us with our ultimate criterion for understanding: if someone meets this criterion it does not matter how he is arranged in the interior of his body. We can even say that if someone turned out to have a head full of sawdust at his *post mortem* that would not (or should not) make us conclude that, contrary to our earlier belief, he never meant or understood anything – as the discovery of internal 'chaos' would not cause us to revise our judgement that this man is or was an understander. In this sense our certification of someone as understanding signs is *independent* of what happens physically inside him. But it does not I think follow from this that someone *really could* have a head full of sawdust or a chaotic nervous system and yet understand words: we cannot infer from the proposition 'if it turned out that p, it would be rational (or even true) to say such-and-such' the proposition 'it is really (metaphysically) possible that p'; for it is compatible with the truth of the former counterfactual that 'p' states a 'metaphysical necessity'. As Kripke has made clear, it might *turn out* that water is not H_2O, but (given that water *is* H_2O) it is *necessary* that water is H_2O.[29] So when we admit that if it were to turn out that other people had heads full of sawdust we would still say that they understood, we are not thereby committed to allowing that this is a real metaphysical possibility: we are in effect considering what would be the case on an impossible supposition. That is to say, in making a (correct) point about the final authority of behavioural criteria we consider what is in fact a metaphysical impossibility; and this is why it is consistent to add 'but of course no such thing *is* possible'. The point is that there are two senses of 'independent'

---

which are ungrounded in chemical differences (see *Z* 608, on the seeds). Indeed, his general principles recommend the claim that there could be distinct substances, with different gross dispositions, which did not differ in their intrinsic physical nature. So his claim about psycho-physiological correspondence reflects a more general thesis about causation and explanation, and does not derive from the specific character of psychological concepts.

[29] See Kripke, *Naming and Necessity* (Blackwell: Oxford, 1980), esp. Lecture III.

to distinguish when it is asserted that mental states are 'independent of brain states'; and the truth is that they can be independent in the epistemic sense without being independent in the metaphysical sense. Thus when Wittgenstein says in 157 that the concept of reading is 'independent of that of a mental or other mechanism' we need to ask which of these two senses is intended: I think he is right in the epistemic or criterial sense, but it is a *non-sequitur* to infer that a person could read and yet his nervous system really be just any old way. I suspect that Wittgenstein's view of what is really possible as to psycho-physiological correspondence stems at least in part from blurring over this distinction: he thinks, in short, that one's nervous system really could be just any way because its condition does not figure in our criteria for ascribing understanding.[30]

It might be replied, on Wittgenstein's behalf, that the idea of a systematic psycho-physiological correspondence introduces the *possibility* of a non-behavioural criterion for understanding, *viz.* the condition of the speaker's nervous system. We saw that this does not follow simply from the assertion that understanding is a state of mind; but would not a physical realisation of this state of mind provide an independent way of telling whether and what someone understands? That this is not so can I think be seen by considering an analogous question: does insisting upon a physical grounding for colour properties imply that how a thing looks is not the ultimate criterion for what colour it is? Let us agree that colour is a dispositional property (a secondary quality) and that nothing could override the criterion of visual appearance in determining an object's colour: does this prohibit us from supposing that there must be *some* physical basis in the object which (in part) explains the experiences produced by the object? It had better not; and it doesn't. For a physical property of the object can be certified as grounding its colour only in so far as that property figures appropriately in the explanation of the perceiver's colour experience; so we could never (*ab initio*) determine an object's

[30] Just as whether a seed is disposed to develop into a certain kind of plant is tested by seeing whether it does so develop: but it does not follow from this that it is really possible to develop into a plant of that kind no matter what the intrinsic physical structure of the seed. There are necessities in nature that are fixed independently of the criteria we use for applying a concept.

colour by discovering its physical properties independently of ascertaining its visual appearance. The physical basis cannot, that is, function as an *autonomous* criterion for colour ascription; it is essentially parasitic on the experiential criterion. For this reason, also, we can say that no matter what the physical properties of red-looking objects turned out to be (sawdust or chaos at the object's surface) we would still count them as red – while adding that of course there are constraints of real metaphysical possibility on the physical nature of a red object's surface.[31] The case of understanding is analogous in that what qualifies a state of the nervous system as the physical basis of understanding (e.g.) 'cube' can only be that it (that state) figures appropriately in the explanation of the speaker's use of 'cube': psycho-physiological correlations can thus be established only on the basis of behavioural criteria – a person can be ascribed a given mental state only if he displays the right sort of behaviour, and a brain state realises this mental state only if it is causally responsible for that behaviour. So we could not (*ab initio*) determine someone's condition of understanding by examining his nervous system independently of ascertaining what he does with his words: there is thus no prospect of *replacing* the use criterion of understanding by a physical criterion – this would be to put the criterial cart before the horse.[32] In rejecting Wittgenstein's view of the relation between the mental and the physical, by insisting upon the existence of some kind of psycho-physiological correspondence, we are therefore not committing ourselves to the admittedly unacceptable claim that facts about a person's nervous system might take on a criterial life of their own. And so we can preserve what is importantly true in Wittgenstein's conception of understanding – that use is the ultimate arbiter of meaning – without following him into his radically anti-physicalist position. And maintaining this degree of physicalism provides us with a further sense in which understanding

---

[31] For the conception of colour and other secondary qualities here presupposed, see my *The Subjective View* (Clarendon Press: Oxford, 1983), esp. chap. 2.

[32] The '*ab initio*' qualification is inserted in order to allow for the possibility of a *derivative* use of brain states as evidence of mental states: that is, once we have a behaviourally based ascription of mental states to a person, we may then establish what are the corresponding brain states and subsequently rely upon these independently of behaviour. This would, however, be necessarily derivative and always answerable to the original behavioural criteria.

may be described as a state which is the source of use.[33]

This concludes my critical discussion of thesis (i). If there is a general point that emerges from it, it is this: we should sharply distinguish two different versions of the idea that understanding is a 'state of mind', one right and the other wrong. The wrong idea is that understanding is a state of consciousness in which some item comes before the mind: Wittgenstein convincingly demolishes this idea. The right idea recognises that there are other states of mind than the kind which understanding is not: we do not have to assimilate understanding to the experiential to find it natural and correct to call it a 'state of mind' – indeed this phrase commits us to very little in the way of a substantive conception of understanding. Wittgenstein objects on a number of grounds to this other use of 'state of mind'; but I have argued that his objections are unpersuasive, resting as they do (in the main) upon misplaced linguistic legislation in the interests of philosophical prophylaxis.

Let us turn now to thesis (ii): that understanding a sign is not placing an interpretation upon it. About this thesis we can be briefer; for I think it is the kind of point which once seen can only be acceded to. To interpret a sign, in Wittgenstein's sense, is simply to *translate* it into another sign; and translation cannot by itself determine meaning or understanding, since the sign into which the translation is made must itself be understood or meant in a particular way. At some point understanding must break out of the circle of signs – no matter what sort of sign we consider. This kind of point has, indeed, been made recently in connexion with the form of a meaning-theory for a language, though apparently quite independently of Wittgenstein's discussion: thus we find both David Lewis and Donald Davidson urging that a theory of meaning (understanding) cannot take the form of a translation manual – we do not capture what knowledge of meaning consists in by

[33] Note that if the source is conceived in terms of underlying physical states, then the same state of understanding may be realized by different physical causes, given that mental states may be multiply realized in physical states. For this reason, I think we should preserve the idea that understanding *per se* is a causal source of use: this allows us to speak of two people who mean the same by their words as using these words as a result of the same causal source, despite the possible difference in the realizing physical states. Also, we do not want to pull apart the causal and normative bases of use: what causes use should also be what makes it correct.

representing the speaker as associating one sign with another
(be it in Markerese or Mentalese).[34] The idea of a canonical
language into which translation is made when words of one's
natural language are understood is, in fact, the same kind of
conception of understanding presupposed by Wittgenstein in
the *Tractatus*; recent philosophy has thus in this respect
recapitulated Wittgenstein's own philosophical development.
(It must be said, though, that the positive views recently put
forward in opposition to the translational conception bear
little resemblance to Wittgenstein's own positive suggestions
about the nature of understanding.[35]) What is more surprising
and challenging about Wittgenstein's critique of the interpretational conception is its application to the idea of *mental* signs,
signs whose medium is not marks and sounds but the mind
itself. For it seems that there is a standing temptation to endow
such alleged mental signs with the power of generating their own
meanings – to think of them as 'self-interpreting'. The old
imagist theory of meaning labours under this misconception by
failing to acknowledge that images do not determine their own
application, but there is also a more recent trend which seems
to suffer from essentially the same problem: I refer to the
doctrine that there is a 'language of thought' which determines
linguistic comprehension.[36] It is hard to see this particular
theory of understanding as anything other than the idea that
there are privileged signs which *terminate* questions of meaning
– special signs which are such that if translation is made into
them then meaning is determined. Wittgenstein's question
about such a system of signs would be how *it* acquires a
meaning, seeing that syntax alone cannot add up to semantics;
and he would suggest that it can only be the *use* made of these
signs. But then why not apply the use conception directly to the

[34] See Lewis, 'General Semantics', in *Semantics of Natural Language*, ed. D.
Davidson and G. Harman (Reidel: Dordrecht, Holland, 1972), pp. 169–70; Davidson,
'Radical Interpretation', in *Inquiries into Truth and Interpretation* (Clarendon Press:
Oxford, 1984), p. 129.

[35] Fundamentally, what is opposed to translational semantics is a semantic
theory that specifies truth conditions by using, not mentioning, appropriate
sentences; whereas Wittgenstein's alternative is the idea of a practice of use. (Worries
that the truth condition conception does not really avoid the circularity of the
translational conception do not appear to have any basis in respect of Wittgenstein's
own view.)

[36] See J.A. Fodor, *The Language of Thought* (Harvester Press: Sussex, 1975).

natural language and cut out the intermediate step? The language of thought theorist appears to be making the same sort of mistake as Wittgenstein ascribes to Augustine in 32:

> Someone coming into a strange country will sometimes learn the language of the inhabitants from ostensive definitions that they give him; and he will often have to *guess* the meaning of these definitions; and will guess sometimes right, sometimes wrong.
>
> And now, I think, we can say: Augustine describes the learning of human language as if the child came into a strange country and did not understand the language of the country; that is, as if it already had a language, only not this one. Or again: as if the child could already *think*, only not yet speak. And "think" would here mean something like "talk to itself". (32)

The point here is not that all languages must be learned, i.e. cannot be innate; Wittgenstein's point is the logical one that meaning cannot be got from syntax – that in which a person's understanding of a sign consists cannot amount to no more than associating that sign with some other. The traditional empiricist supposes, in effect, that the child comes to a natural language equipped with a repertoire of mental images which are somehow intrinsically meaningful, and that words come to have meaning for the child by being linked to these images; the language of thought theorist in effect replaces images with syntactically characterised symbols in a mental medium and regards the task of the child as that of linking these mental symbols with the spoken symbols to which he is exposed: both types of view assume, mistakenly, that meaning and understanding can be determined by what are after all only (logically) *further signs*.[37] In respect of this point, I think that Wittgenstein is entirely correct and of continuing relevance.

I suggested in Chapter 1 that thesis (ii) has a further aspect, namely that understanding a sign is not forming a hypothesis: like seeing-as, following a rule is automatic, spontaneous and unreflective. When we see something *as* a so-and-so it is our

---

[37] In fact Fodor cites Wittgenstein's passage about Augustine (*op. cit.*, p. 64), declaring his adherence to the Augustinian conception; but he does not, so far as I can see, provide any convincing answer to Wittgenstein's criticism. He contents himself with saying that language learning *has* to be as Augustine describes it.

experience that embodies the aspect; when we grasp a rule it is our *behaviour* that embodies that grasp (recall 201): in neither case is it a matter of bringing a hypothesis to bear. When someone I fear orders me to do something I act immediately; I do not form a *hypothesis* about what he means me to do.[38] In other words, Wittgenstein is saying that seeing-as and rule-following are in a certain sense not *ratiocinative*: they belong with more primitive and instinctual parts of our nature: one simply finds oneself obeying a rule in a certain way or seeing something in a certain way without the necessity to take thought. So thesis (ii) is in part an expression of Wittgenstein's 'anti-intellectualism' (for want of a better word) about mastery of a language. Construed as a 'phenomenological' point this aspect of thesis (ii) seems to me right: one's use of language is habitual, unreflective, taken for granted; it is not a perpetual guessing game in which hypotheses about correctness of use are constantly reviewed and selected. What the significance of this 'phenomenological' point is for epistemological questions about following linguistic rules is I think less easy to determine – in particular, whether Wittgenstein's 'naturalism' affords a satisfactory response to traditional sceptical worries as they might be applied to our use of language.

This question brings us onto thesis (iii): the thesis that rule-following is not founded upon reasons. Let us then take up the question whether Wittgenstein's epistemology of rule-following is adequate.

As I noted in Chapter 1, Wittgenstein's position on rule-following is echoed in his treatment of induction: he regards both as natural and inevitable; he thinks that doubt does not come into the picture, except in exceptional cases; he takes the traditional sceptic to be imposing inappropriate standards of epistemic warrant. In short, though it is true that our reasons quickly run out, this is not in itself a cause for epistemological concern, since we are not dealing with an area of human activity which *needs* the kind of epistemological foundation traditionally sought (perhaps there are *no* such areas). I might bring out Wittgenstein's idea as follows: when we train a dog to

---

[38] So in both cases Wittgenstein is rejecting the idea of an intermediary, something interpolated between word and use or between visual stimulus and how it is seen; accordingly, we do not have *reasons* for our use of signs or the way we see things.

give a paw on demand we do not supply the dog with *reasons* to give a paw whenever we say 'paw!', yet the dog comes through training reliably to do what is the 'right' thing. The lack of reasons does not paralyse the dog with doubt whenever we say 'paw!', nor does this lack prevent us from undertaking successful training: we and the dog rely upon presumed natural propensities and we are not troubled by the absence of reasons.[39] Now if we think of a child learning a language in this kind of way, we shall likewise not be concerned that the training we give the child is not proof against traditional scepticism, and the child himself is not inhibited in his learning by his lack of conclusive reasons. The question now is whether these observations constitute a satisfactory reply to someone who is convinced that our rule-following practice is *irrational* because not properly justifiable in terms of reasons for going on as we do. In order to set about answering this question, we should need to take a stand on the question of whether Wittgenstein has a good answer to scepticism in general; this is not a question I can hope to settle here (or indeed elsewhere), but some remarks may serve at least to indicate the relevant considerations. The basic issue is whether there is a legitimate notion of justification which transcends what people routinely *take* as justification in the various language-games that make up our linguistic practice, i.e. a notion which can be brought to bear to decide whether cases in which people generally *take* themselves to be warranted are cases in which they really *are* warranted. Wittgenstein's view of our practice of induction is that our success is itself an adequate ground for inductive certainty (see 324), and that the proper standards for inductive justification are *internal* to our inductive practice (see 325). The standard objection to this kind of view is that it seems to prevent any rational *revision* of our epistemic standards; it seems to leave us helpless in the face of an institutionalised practice of accepting palpably inadequate reasons for belief.[40] Thus there arises the well-known controversy about whether Wittgenstein's epistemology leads to the epistemic autonomy of religious discourse: do we have to say that what a religious

[39] See *BB* pp. 89–90. This analogy is not intended to suggest that the dog is genuinely following rules (as opposed to conforming to rules).

[40] For a general discussion of this, see Stanley Cavell, *The Claim of Reason* (Oxford University Press, 1979).

person accepts as a reason for belief in God just *is* a good reason for this belief? I personally would find this consequence of Wittgenstein's epistemology unacceptable: for it seems to me to lead to an unhealthy and misguided epistemological conservatism. But it is not in fact totally obvious to me that Wittgenstein's view does have this undesirable consequence, because it is not clear what counts as a *single* epistemic practice and hence what counts as exceeding one's legitimate sphere of epistemic influence. Analogous questions arise about Wittgenstein's epistemology of rule-following, though here his position seems to me more secure. In Chapter 4 we shall have occasion to consider a well-articulated scepticism about rules, and we will then be in a better position to decide what should be said about this form of scepticism; for now let it suffice to have raised the question.

What now of Wittgenstein's positive thesis: that grasp of a rule is mastery of a practice, the capacity to engage in a custom? We saw in Chapter 1 that this thesis has a number of aspects and implications which can be usefully separated out; let us start with those sub-theses which should be accepted. What certainly seems acceptable is the construal of understanding as a practical capacity: to know the meaning of a word is to be able to use it; linguistic knowledge is a kind of knowing-how. This thesis has, indeed, become something of a truism in recent philosophy of language, no doubt partly under Wittgenstein's influence.[41] Putting it in terms of rules, it is the claim that grasping a rule essentially involves knowing how to follow it; so there is a direct conceptual connexion between the concept of understanding and concepts of action, in particular linguistic action. This general thesis seems to me hard to deny in the schematic form in which it has been formulated; controversy is apt to begin only when we enquire how such capacities are to be characterised: what *is* a capacity, and what precisely is grasp of a linguistic rule the capacity to do? One issue that is raised by this latter question, recently broached by Dummett, is whether the equation (or association) of understanding with a practical capacity has any verificationist consequences, and hence any

---

[41] See, notably, Dummett, 'What is a Theory of Meaning? (II)', in *Truth and Meaning*, ed. G. Evans and J. McDowell (Clarendon Press: Oxford, 1976), esp. pp. 69f.

anti-realist or finitist consequences: if understanding is the capacity to apply or employ words, does this imply (as the positivists thought) that we cannot understand sentences which we cannot verify?[42] How, for example, are we to reconcile the infinitary character of the meaning (reference) of '+' with the idea that to understand '+' is to be able to use or apply it? Is this not a case in which our grasp of meaning goes beyond what we are able to do with the understood word? To answer these questions we need to be clearer about what the supposed practical capacity consists in, what it is a capacity to do. If we insist upon conceiving the capacity as 'recognitional' in a sense modelled upon the case of observation, then indeed there will be a problem about our understanding of words which we have not the ability to apply to each member of their extension: we cannot, for example, apply '+' to each of the pairs of numbers for which the addition function determines a unique value.[43] So we cannot conceive of *understanding* such a word on the model of being able to apply it to arbitrary pairs of numbers: some sentences containing '+' will be 'verification-transcendent', i.e. we lack the capacity to verify them. But it is by no means obvious that we are compelled to conceive of linguistic abilities in this simple 'recognitional' way, and I know of nothing in the passages of the *Investigations* with which we are concerned which entails such a restricted conception of use. Wittgenstein's position is descriptive not revisionary; and a full specification of the use of a word, if there could be such a thing, would take in all features of what we do with it – the specification would be a total description of a language-game in all its complexity. The purpose of giving such a description, or of having the *idea* of such a description, is primarily to dissolve philosophical mistakes – in particular, the mistakes Wittgenstein takes to be associated with the 'inner process' model – not to provide anything deserving of the name 'theory of meaning'. This would allow, to be more specific, the

---

[42] Or that an understanding of undecidable sentences consists in how we *would* respond to evidence were any to come our way (in contrast to being able actually to gather evidence that verifies or falsifies the statement).

[43] Kripke's discussion of the dispositional view of understanding is relevant here (see Kripke, pp. 26f): we do not *have* a disposition to give the sum of *arbitrary* pairs of numbers in suitable circumstances, because (*inter alia*) of our finiteness and the infinitary character of the addition function. As Dummett might put it, there are undecidable (for us) addition problems.

use of words in reasoning or inference, and so their interaction with logical laws (e.g. excluded middle).[44] Or again, the bare idea that understanding is a practical capacity is not inconsistent with the claim (right or wrong) that there is no account of such a capacity which does not employ the very concepts expressed by the understood sentence – as with the suggestion that to understand a sentence '*p*' is to have the capacity to say or communicate *that p*.[45] It is true that Wittgenstein himself sometimes exhibits what can only be described as verificationist tendencies (e.g. in the private language argument) and that he commonly characterises use in terms of the application of words on the basis of criteria (ways of telling); but it is not at all obvious that his capacity view of understanding commits him to a full-scale verificationist account of meaning – in view of the elasticity of the schematic notion of a capacity-for-use.[46] My own position would be that understanding is (or essentially involves) a practical capacity but that this admission is by itself quite neutral and untendentious with respect to general verificationism; we can derive nothing substantive about the form of a 'theory of meaning' (what its central concept should be, to put it Dummett's way) from Wittgenstein's positive thesis – and I think that Wittgenstein would be the first to agree with this. So we can readily agree with thesis (iv) because, by itself, it has little positive content – at least by the standards of current approaches to questions of 'realism' and 'verificationism'.

We can also agree I think that (*a*) understanding is a

---

[44] If we conceive of such an holistic description of a language-game as aimed at dissolving philosophical perplexity about meaning, instead of as a *theory* of what grasp of meaning 'consists in', then (some of) the standard objections to holism become irrelevant: therapeutic holism (as it might be called) does not claim that a speaker's grasp of an individual sentence is *constituted* by his appreciation of how that sentence relates to all (most, many) of the sentences of the language. (I am not here endorsing this view of meaning, or of philosophy.)

[45] This is what Dummett calls a *modest* theory of meaning, i.e. a theory that does not seek to explicate what it is to possess the concepts implicated in understanding sentences: see his 'What is a Theory of Meaning?', in *Mind and Language*, ed. S. Guttenplan (Clarendon Press: Oxford, 1975)

[46] Nor do I think that Wittgenstein's emphasis upon criteria betokens an inchoate 'criterial semantics', in the sense of G. Baker, 'Criteria: a New Foundation for Semantics', *Ratio* XVI (1974). We must always remember that Wittgenstein is not concerned to put forward a 'theory of meaning'; rather, emphasising criteria is intended to remind us of our ordinary use of language, so that we may avoid falling into philosophical error. Indeed, I doubt whether the notion of a criterion is used in any technical or special sense in the *Investigations*: it simply means 'way of telling'.

condition with respect to which first-person ascriptions are fallible and (*b*) this can be explained by invoking the capacity idea. Understanding resembles knowledge in being a kind of cognitive achievement about which one may be mistaken: in the case of knowledge the achievement consists in having a *true* belief (and perhaps more, depending on your analysis of knowledge) and one can be wrong about the truth; in the case of understanding the achievement has more to do with what one is equipped to *do* – hence Wittgenstein's constant association of understanding with 'going on the right way'. If we view coming to understand as the acquisition of an ability, then it is easy to appreciate why we are fallible in our self-ascriptions of understanding: it is because possessing abilities *generally* is not something about which we are infallible. To have an ability involves, trivially, being able to *do* something; and whether you *can* do something can be determined, ultimately, only by actually doing it – it is no good assiduously consulting the contents of your consciousness. There can, of course, be signs or symptoms in one's consciousness of having acquired an ability (e.g. a feeling of confidence when placed in the water and told to exercise the ability to swim), but these can always in principle be misleading. Acknowledging this point about understanding is, as we have seen, an important part of Wittgenstein's case against the 'state of consciousness' view of understanding; and it seems to me that on this point he is entirely in the right.[47]

Wittgenstein does not, however, confine himself to these relatively uncontroversial claims; he has some specific views about the requirements for having the capacity to follow a rule which are I think very far from truistic. I have already criticised his treatment of the 'state of mind' view of understanding, but I have not yet discussed his claim that rules can be grasped only if they (or some of them) are actually obeyed on more than one occasion (see 199, 204–5; *RFM* pp. 334–6, 346). It is noteworthy that despite his steadfast adherence to this claim (what I called in Chapter 1 the 'multiple application thesis') Wittgenstein

[47] The fallibility of self-ascriptions of bodily or motor skills is obvious enough; Wittgenstein's point is that the case is no different with 'mental' skills, since the criterion for possessing skills in general is whether one actually succeeds when one tries to do something. In contrast, having a pain (say) is not a skill, and so there is not this reason for regarding self-ascriptions of pain as fallible.

recognises that it will not strike his readers as obviously true:

> In order to describe the phenomenon of language, one must describe a practice, not something that happens once, *no matter of what kind.*
> It is very hard to realize this.   (*RFM* pp. 335–6)

My own suspicion is that the reason it is hard is that the thesis is not in fact true. Let us recall what precisely the thesis is: it is not the very strong thesis that *each* rule someone grasps must by obeyed by him on more than one occasion; nor is it the weaker claim that there are *some* rules such that *they* must be multiply obeyed (as it might be, the primitive or foundational rules which spawn the potentially idle rules). It is, rather, the comparatively weak thesis that there must be *some* rules which are multiply obeyed if a person is to grasp *any* (not necessarily the *same* set of rules for each person). The application must, however, be overt:

> I may give a new rule today, which has never been applied, and yet is understood. But would that be possible, if no rule had *ever* actually been applied?
> And if it is now said: "Isn't it enough for there to be an imaginary application?" the answer is: No. (Possibility of a private language.)   (*RFM* p. 334)

It is not enough that I imagine myself applying a word on more than one occasion, even if what I imagine perfectly represents what I would do were the application overt; no, I must actually overtly apply the word (or some word) if I am to be supposed really to understand it. This claim is not, of course, merely epistemological; it is a thesis rather about the conditions for the *possibility* of meaning anything at all, of grasping any rules at all. How should we react to this constitutive thesis? The immediate problem is that Wittgenstein himself gives no real guidance as to *why* his thesis should be accepted: what sorts of considerations lead him to suppose it true? It is clear enough that he takes the requirement of multiple application to reflect something about the notion of a *rule* in particular; he does not enunciate parallel multiple manifestation theses in respect of other psychological concepts: he does not say, for example, that *sensations* are possible (as opposed to *concepts* of sensations) only if *some* sensations are multiply manifested. In fact, he clearly believes that there is in this respect a *contrast* to be drawn with other psychological concepts, those that do not involve the notion of a rule. So it cannot be that he is simply converting an admittedly correct point about the criteria for rule ascription into a constitutive claim, or else we would expect to find him making the more general claim about the instantiation of psychological concepts. For the same reason we cannot diagnose the claim about rules as issuing from general behaviourist or verificationist tendencies in Wittgenstein – for this again does not account for the specificity of his claim. Quite possibly the general emphasis upon the criteria for applying a concept in giving an account of the content of the concept is not far in the background, but we need to discover what it is about rules in particular that makes Wittgenstein introduce their criteria so directly and emphatically.[48] The following stray remark might seem to provide a clue: 'concepts are not for use on a single occasion' (Z 568). The natural suggestion, unpacking this remark, is that concepts are inherently general – they are 'universals' – and so must be capable of instantiation by many objects; rules likewise have this generality because they are the sorts of things that can be applied repeatedly in different situations.[49] This is certainly a correct observation about the notions of concept and rule, but it neither explains Wittgenstein's official thesis nor provides an adequate justification for it. It does not explain why Wittgenstein says what he does about rules because it is an observation applicable to *all* concepts and rules, whereas Wittgenstein restricts himself to the claim that only *some* rules have to be multiply obeyed. And it is an inadequate justification because

[48] When Wittgenstein is considering the possibility of a private language, he does make the existence of third-person criteria necessary for the existence of semantic rules, and so one might think that he is making the same kind of point when he insists upon multiple occasions of use for expressions generally. Moreover, it is reasonable to suppose that he would require more than *one* occurrence of the behavioural criterion in order for an observer to judge that a genuine semantic rule is being followed when a sensation word is self-ascribed. However, though this may lie somewhere in the background of Wittgenstein's multiple application thesis, it is not clear that there is any straightforward logical connexion between this thesis and the requirement of third-person criteria; for, strictly speaking, the private language argument requires only that third-person criteria be *available* or *possible*, not that they be actualised (on more than one occasion), since this ensures the know*ability* (if not the actual knowledge) of correct rule-following. So in a clear sense the multiple application thesis is stronger than the conclusion of the private language argument.

[49] *Cf.* 'Roughly speaking, it characterizes what we call a rule to be applied repeatedly, in an indefinite number of instances' (*BB* p. 96).

the inherent generality of a rule or concept does not in itself
imply that one who grasps the rule or concept must *make* many
applications of it: why should the fact that a concept is
necessarily multiply instantiated (at least potentially) imply
that it cannot be *grasped* unless the grasper actually multiply
applies it? It is, indeed, part of the point or nature of a rule to be
applicable on more than one occasion, but why should
someone be unable to appreciate this property of rules unless
he actually puts it into practice? We need to look elsewhere for
a plausible reconstruction of what was moving Wittgenstein.

I think the following conjecture has some plausibility.
Wittgenstein has denied that understanding is an inner state or
process of any kind – conscious, unconscious, physical or
ethereal; understanding thus contrasts with what he thinks of as
mental states and processes proper (e.g. seeing red) in that it
has no introspectible phenomenal quality. But then what does
understanding *consist in* – what *is* it? It may seem to us that we
have exhausted all the candidates, so that there is nothing left
for understanding to *be*; yet it is surely *something* – it is not a
myth. This threat of evaporation does not loom when we have
available actual occasions of use; for these occasions can serve
to endow understanding with the requisite 'concreteness'. If for
sensations to be is to be *felt*, then for understanding to be is to
be *manifested*: the being of a rule can only consist in its being
obeyed. We have some conception of a state of consciousness
such as pain existing independently of all behaviour, because of
its felt quality; but we have no such behaviour-independent
handle on what is not a state of consciousness – as grasping a
rule is not. It can therefore seem that we are driven to adopt a
quasi-behaviourist view of understanding in the absence of any
other way of conceiving what understanding is: when we
subtract behaviour from conscious experiences we have a
conception of what is left over, but subtracting rule-following
behaviour from rule-grasping appears to leave us with
nothing.[50] This line of thought thus leads to the *sort* of position
we find Wittgenstein occupying: the conjecture then is that he

[50] I mean here to be recalling the question of 621: 'what is left over if I subtract the
fact that my arm goes up from the fact that I raise my arm?' Wittgenstein's claim is that
nothing is left over (or at any rate 'not a something'): not kinaesthetic sensations
because these are not identifiable with my willing, and not a trying because I do not
always try when I act. Somewhat similarly, I think, Wittgenstein is resisting the idea

is unwilling to allow rule-grasping without overt rule-following behaviour because to do so would be to rob the ascription of rules to people of any substantial content – we would have no idea *what* we were ascribing. I offer this as a conjectural reconstruction of at least part of what is motivating Wittgenstein to advance his multiple application thesis – it makes sense of what otherwise seems a puzzling claim. There are, however, at least two *prima facie* difficulties with this exegetical suggestion. The first is that on the face of it the suggestion requires multiple application for *all* rules grasped, since the being of *each* can only consist in being obeyed, whereas Wittgenstein's actual thesis is weaker than this. We might try to reply to this point by suggesting that Wittgenstein is under conflicting pressures here and opts for a view which best reconciles them: there is the pressure to find something for understanding to be, and there is the pressure to avoid what is manifestly unacceptable, *viz.* that *no* rule can be grasped and not be overtly followed. The reconciling position is that once we find something for *some* rules to be we can then suppose that the other rules are somehow 'ontologically parasitic' on those unproblematic rules – the unfollowed rules exist by virtue of being somehow *connected* with the followed rules.[51] This reply is, admittedly, somewhat lame, but it does at least offer some sort of explanation of how adherence to the weak multiple application thesis could be combined with the motivation for that thesis which I sketched. The second difficulty is that it is not easy to see why, given such a motivation, Wittgenstein should insist, as he does, that rules have to be followed *more than* once: would not a *single* occasion of rule-following suffice to endow the rule-grasping with the required reality? Why is there such a significant difference between one and two occasions of rule-following? This thesis of Wittgenstein's is anyhow puzzling, and the puzzle is only compounded when we motivate his thesis as I

---

that there is anything left over when my rule-following behaviour has been (wholly) subtracted – certainly there is nothing left over by way of a state of consciousness that is my grasping the rule. (As Wittgenstein said, his investigations go 'criss-cross in every direction' (p. vii)). Wittgenstein's mistake in both cases, I think, is an unduly restrictive view of the kind of thing that might be left over.

[51] It may be, for instance, that the unfollowed rules are of the same *type* as the followed rules, as the rules of chess are of the same type as the rules of draughts; or it may be that the concept of *winning* a game by deft following of its rules can be transferred from a played game to games that are never played.

tried to. It may be, however, that the puzzle can be partially resolved by getting away from considerations of literal cardinality and seeing his claim as an overly precise statement of an essentially loose idea. Perhaps the thought is that in practice we find a single occasion of use an altogether too exiguous basis on which to ascribe a particular rule – it radically underdetermines which rule is being followed, even by commonsense criteria; or again, a single occasion is compatible with what we would ordinarily regard as a fluke (a child getting one sum right by chance). Our usual criteria involve seeing whether the rule can be successfully followed on *other* occasions: normally we allow that if the rule is followed correctly 'two or three times' that is enough. So we might suppose that Wittgenstein is trying to capture this aspect of our actual practice of rule-ascription: he is saying that we *do* treat several occasions of application as providing a sufficient foothold for rule-ascription, whereas one occasion is not so treated (especially in the whole history of mankind).[52] Again, this reply limps somewhat, but it seems a possible way of understanding what may lie behind Wittgenstein's claim: it makes some kind of sense of what is otherwise hard to fathom.

But should we accept the multiple application thesis motivated thus? I think not, because (*a*) we should not accept the suggested motivation and (*b*) the thesis itself is intrinsically implausible. The conjectured motivation cannot be ours because we have earlier disagreed with Wittgenstein about whether understanding is a state of mind that is the source of application: we said that understanding may be regarded as a (*sui generis*) state of mind which causally explains use, and that this mental state has of necessity a physical realisation in states of the brain. So for us there *is* something left when actual use is subtracted, namely that state which is the causal basis of use. That is, we have not permitted the mental state of understanding to collapse into actual use, and so we have made room for the thought that there can be understanding which is not manifested in use (not *actually* manifested, that is). Putting it in terms of the notion of ability, we have allowed for abilities

---

[52] Compare my use of 'pain' in application to myself: unless I apply this word on a number of occasions on which others may judge whether I am using it with sufficient regularity, I cannot be said by them to be following a semantic rule; one occasion is not enough for others to decide whether my use is random or rule-governed.

which are not *actually* exercised, while agreeing that an ability is precisely an ability to *do* something – *potentially* though. Wittgenstein's denial that understanding is the source of use and a *bona fide* mental state (with a physical basis) renders him unable to detach understanding from actual use (according to the conjecture), but once we question this denial we are not compelled to accept the multiple application thesis. And it seems to me that this is just as well, since it is hard to see how that thesis can be defended against some rather natural objections.

Perhaps the most obvious line of objection stems from what we might call 'the subtraction argument'. Suppose we start with a subject who grasps rules $R_1 \ldots R_n$ and who overtly follows a sub-class of these rules – all but R_i let us say. Now consider subtracting from this subject the application he makes of the 'active' rules, i.e. consider a possible situation in which the actually followed rules are not obeyed. Imagine we carry out this thought-experiment one rule at a time gradually whittling the applications away. Wittgenstein in effect allows that we can carry out this procedure very extensively: in fact, the thought-experiment is deemed coherent until we get to the final rule grasped by the subject, R_j let us say, at which point, he thinks, we must call a halt to our supposings. We can also, he allows, remove large segments of the actual application made of R_j; but we must leave intact at least *two* applications of this rule if we are not to remove R_j and consequently $R_1 \ldots R_n$ altogether. The problem is to see why what seems such a small change in the actual situation could have such momentous consequences: Wittgenstein thinks that all the rules can be supposed preserved while subtracting their application save that we have to leave at least one that is applied more than once; but why should removing *its* application altogether (or reducing it to one occasion) suddenly obliterate all that had hitherto been preserved? Surely, one wants to say, we cannot so abruptly lapse into incoherence: why should not the final stage of the subtraction go as smoothly as the rest, leaving us with a *totally* idle set of grasped rules?[53] Of course we are not entitled

---

[53] Or again, consider the claim that we could be born grasping certain rules (as Chomsky suggests for the case of some grammatical rules): is it really plausible to declare such claims *a priori* impossible because of the absence of actual occasions of rule-following in the neonate? This seems too short a way with the suggestion that some rules may be innate.

to infer 'it is possible to subtract all applications' from 'for each application we can subtract it' – that would be a simple modal fallacy – but we are entitled to ask what conceptual barrier prevents us from pushing the subtraction operation through to its conclusion: how *could* there be the sort of lower limit the weak multiple application thesis commits itself to? Note that since that thesis does not claim that there is a privileged set of rules such that *they* must be applied more than once, it is not open to the defender of the thesis to suggest that some rules are inherently or intrinsically necessarily applied if they are grasped; for any rule *could* be one of those whose application has been thought away, so there is nothing about any *given* rule that compels *it* to be multiply applied. This should make it seem all the more odd to claim that some rules have to be applied more than once if any are to be grasped: for R_j could have been some *other* rule had we done the subtraction operation differently. So far as I can see understanding is comparable with other mental states in the present respect: we can, it seems, subtract the manifestations of pain (for instance) and be left with pain, as when we imagine extreme stoicism; and, similarly, we can think away the actions that manifest a (standing) intention without *eo ipso* thinking away the intention. Nor does Wittgenstein say anything explicitly to deny these possibilities, as he does with grasping a rule. As we can imagine a totally stoical pain-feeler, so I think we can imagine a totally indolent rule-grasper. Consider the rules of games: Wittgenstein allows that I could invent a game which no one plays, but he denies that this could be true of all games:

> As things are I can, for example, invent a game that is never played by anyone. —But would the following be possible too: mankind has never played any games; once, however, someone invented a game—which no one ever played?   (204)

> What surrounding is needed for someone to be able to invent, say, chess?
> Of course I might invent a board-game today, which would never actually be played. I should simply describe it. But that is possible only because there already exist similar games, that is because such games *are played*.   (*RFM* p. 334)

But he says nothing to persuade us that what seems *prima facie* to be possible is not really possible, *viz.* a person or community who or which knows the rules of various games but refrains from *ever* playing any of them (perhaps the games are described to children but there is a strict taboo on playing any of them). Would not the *imaginary* playing of games still be possible in these circumstances?[54] I have no objection to saying that mastery of games consists in possessing an ability to play them and hence is conceptually connected to concepts of action; what I fail to see is why such abilities must actually be manifested in order to be possessed at all. Nor am I denying that it may be in some sense 'psychologically impossible' for human beings to master a set of rules and never apply them – this would require a degree of indolence that most of us would find intolerable; what I am resisting is the multiple application thesis considered as a *conceptual* truth. (That Wittgenstein does not intend his thesis merely as some sort of psychological law is clear from *RFM*, p. 346: after asserting that 'it means nothing' to suggest that once in the history of mankind a game was invented but was never played, he says: 'Not because it contradicts psychological laws'.) I therefore think that Wittgenstein is right to describe rule-following as a practice or custom only in the sense that necessarily rules are things that *can* be followed on repeated occasions, not that necessarily they *are* repeatedly followed: grasping a rule is a mental state which is *potentially* multiply manifested, but the potentiality need not, at least as a matter of conceptual necessity, be actualised.[55]

It may now be suggested by someone that light can be thrown on the multiple application thesis by recalling a certain remark of Wittgenstein's about the nature of continuing a series in a particular way. He is considering the question what it is for an action to be in accordance with the rule 'add 2' and he remarks: 'It would almost be more correct to say, not that an intuition was needed at every stage, but that a new decision was needed at every stage' (186). The suggestion might be that here

[54] After all, there are plenty of scenes enacted in the imagination which a person would not dream of translating into overt action!

[55] There are two separable claims at issue here, with both of which I am disagreeing: (a) that to *grasp* a rule some rule must be overtly *followed*, and (b) a rule can be *followed* only if it (or perhaps some other rule) is followed more than *once*. My position is that grasp of rule is mastery of a practice only in the sense that it is (so to say) an *undertaking* to follow a rule in a certain way on indefinitely many occasions, should those occasions present themselves; and they may not present themselves.

Wittgenstein is committing himself to the idea that 'meaning is *created* by use': that is, the meaning of a word is progressively constituted or created by its use over time – determinate meaning is the final *result* of temporally extended use.[56] It is not, according to this suggestion, that meaning produces (is the source of) use; rather, use produces (is the source of) meaning. So when Wittgenstein says that a new *decision* is needed at each stage he is, on this interpretation, suggesting that each occasion of use is *undetermined* by prior meaning and functions as one phase in what is in fact the *construction* of a meaning: the meaning of a word is thus in some way indeterminate until the sum-total of its use has been reckoned with. Let us call this somewhat obscure and heady claim the *creative thesis*. The relevance of the creative thesis to the multiple application thesis is then supposed to be this: since no entity whose essence it is to be created can exist until the requisite acts of creation have been carried out, meaning (rules) cannot exist unless and until the creative acts of linguistic use have been performed. For how could I grasp rules I never overtly follow if my grasping them is essentially the created *result* of my following them? Moreover, the applications must be extensive enough to ensure that the construction operation has brought into being something recognisable as a specific rule – which a single application could not plausibly do. Now this is an ingenious line of thought, but I do not believe that it correctly interprets Wittgenstein's remark in 186; and I think that when that remark is correctly interpreted it lends no support to the multiple application thesis. Nor do I think that the creative thesis itself is at all credible.

To hold the creative thesis is to hold that what I mean at a given time is not determined (or determinate) until the rest of my (temporally extended) use has been taken into account, so that what I now mean cannot normatively constrain how I subsequently use the word in question. But this idea is directly inconsistent with Wittgenstein's explicit claim that future use *is* determined by present meaning, as in this passage:

[56] This idea is reminiscent of the existentialist conception of a person: it is the free action of an agent that *constitutes* what he is; it is not that action springs from an antecedently constituted self (see J-P. Sartre, *Being and Nothingness*, trans. Hazel E. Barnes (Methuen: London, 1957)). The 'existentialist conception of meaning' is thus the thesis that linguistic behaviour is free and unconstrained, and that we can speak of determinate meaning only as the *upshot* of such behaviour.

"But I don't mean that what I do now (in grasping a sense) determines the future use *causally* and as a matter of experience, but that in a *queer* way, the use itself is in some sense present."—But of course it is, 'in *some* sense'! Really the only thing wrong with what you say is the expression "in a queer way". The rest is all right; and the sentence only seems queer when one imagines a different language-game for it from the one in which we actually use it. (Someone once told me that as a child he had been surprised that a tailor could 'sew a dress'—he thought this meant that a dress was produced by sewing alone, by sewing one thread on to another.) (195)

And in earlier sections, notably 187–8, Wittgenstein makes it clear that what he is opposed to is only a particular *model* of future determination – the magical model of the present somehow containing the future 'in a queer way'.[57] He is not against saying such things as 'what you are now doing with that word is in accordance with (faithful to) your past meaning', so long as these remarks are properly understood (ultimately in terms of our natural ways of going on as these interact with our training). But the creative thesis cannot permit the legitimacy of such remarks: it simply has not the materials to make them come out true – indeed they must be taken as just false if the creative thesis is true. The creative thesis has no place for the commonsense idea that if my subsequent use of words is to be correct then it needs to accord with, or be faithful to, what I now mean. So what *is* Wittgenstein saying in 186 when he speaks of 'a new decision'? The first thing to remember here is what he says in 219, namely that when I obey a rule 'I do not choose'; for we do not want to find Wittgenstein saying contradictory things in these two sections. So when he says 'a new decision' is needed at each stage he cannot mean to imply that at each stage a *choice* is necessary: he cannot therefore be saying in 186 that I am (normatively) *free* to go on in different ways, so far as fidelity to my past meaning is concerned. Wittgenstein's position is that my rule-following behaviour is automatic and natural; it therefore does not require a decision in the sense of a deliberate exercise of will unconstrained by anything either

[57] That is to say, by the whole of future and possible use coming before the person's mind in an instant. A better model of future determination, according to 187, is the way a character trait, such as bravery, fixes which counterfactuals are true of one and thus allows for prediction of one's future behaviour.

antecedent or concomitant.[58] The clue to removing the
apparent tension between the two passages is to take seriously
the *comparative* form of Wittgenstein's claim in 186: what he
says there is that it would be *more* correct to speak of decision
than of intuition – and of course this is quite consistent with the
claim that it would be strictly *in*correct to speak of decision
absolutely.[59] Turning to the later remarks about intuition and
rule-following (notably 213) we find the point that if intuition
is conceived as an inner voice (and how else are we to think of
it?) then it is simply a variant of the interpretational conception
and so cannot settle questions of rightness. So in 186
Wittgenstein is suggesting that we would do better (which is
not to say that we would do *well*) to think of rule-following on
the model of decision than on the model of the inner voice that
guides our behaviour by means of something like internal
imperatives; and this is better because it prevents us from
thinking that there must be some consultable authority on how
our rules are to be followed – some body of reasons – which is
independent of how things naturally strike us, i.e. of our
natural propensities.[60] Nothing *tells us* how to go on in
applying a sign, and so the model of free autonomous decision
is more suitable than the model of the inner voice of intuition;
but this should not be taken literally and absolutely as implying

[58] We can distinguish two issues here: whether following a rule on a particular
occasion involves a *decision*, and whether it involves a *new* decision. I think
Wittgenstein rejects both of these ideas: he rejects the idea of a *new* decision because he
does believe in the future determination of use by meaning, when this determination is
properly understood; and he rejects the idea of a *decision* because he thinks that rule-
following is misdescribed by speaking of *choice* – it is unreflective and automatic in a
way that this description gets wrong. To use an analogy I have used before: when the
dog responds to an order on a new occasion he does not have to make a 'new decision'
about what action is now called for – he simply *does something* (cf. 217, 228).

[59] This is made clear by the following remark: 'It is no act of insight, intuition, which
makes us use the rule as we do at the particular point of the series. It would be less
confusing to call it an act of decision, though this too is misleading, for nothing like an
act of decision must take place, but possibly just an act of writing or speaking' (*BB* p.
143). This is closely followed by the assertion, '*We need have no reason to follow the rule
as we do*' (Wittgenstein's italics).

[60] Rejecting the idea of an inner voice, or an exercise of insight, is part of
Wittgenstein's attack upon the empiricist doctrine that the basis of our language-
games is a kind of *seeing*, i.e. a quasi-sensory apprehension of some species of truth; in
the case of rules what is thus seen are 'rails' projected to indefinitely many new cases
(see 218–19). Wittgenstein opposes to this the idea that *acting*, not seeing, is the right
model for the basis of our judgements; and this is why he says that decision is a *better*
model than insight, despite its misleadingness in other respects.

that we somehow *create* rules as we apply them, without any constraint from our given nature. Our nature and our training do combine to endow our signs with meaning, and future use must be faithful to this meaning if it is to be correct; but this conception is incompatible with the creative thesis. We cannot, then, interpret Wittgenstein as advancing his multiple application thesis because of adherence to the creative thesis. I think his position on understanding is analogous to the following position on physical dispositions such as solubility: although solubility is a property substances have in advance of particular manifestations of that disposition, there is (it might be thought) something suspect about the idea that there could be soluble substances which *never* manifested solubility: solubility is not of course *created* by its manifestations, but its manifestations are so integral to the language-game of ascribing the disposition that we cannot conceive of what it would be for that disposition to exist in a totally 'idle' form.[61] (I do not say Wittgenstein held this view of dispositions in general; it is intended only as an analogy to bring out the relation (or lack of it) between the creative thesis and the multiple application thesis.)

And it is good that Wittgenstein does not advance the creative thesis, since that thesis is surely radically revisionary of our ordinary commonsense ways of thinking about meaning: it undermines the whole idea that words can be wrongly used – indeed it undermines the distinction of truth and falsity as applied to sentences.[62] For, if every application of a word contributes to fixing its meaning by virtue of what it is applied to, then no use could be deemed incorrect (not be in accordance with the word's meaning): instead of saying that my application of 'cube' to a cylinder is incorrect we should have to say that 'cube' has a meaning such that cylinders (as well as cubes) can

[61] Remember Wittgenstein's analogy between meaning and bravery (187): he clearly does not wish to advocate a creative thesis with respect to the latter notion. Rather, by rejecting the inner state conception of bravery and proposing an explication in terms of counterfactuals, he is thinking of the trait through its characteristic manifestations, and hence will require the existence of enough in the way of manifestation if bravery is to be judged present. That, at any rate, seems to be Wittgenstein's thought.

[62] Crispin Wright, in *Wittgenstein on the Foundations of Mathematics* (Duckworth: London, 1980), chap. II, seems to accept what I am calling the creative thesis as an interpretation of Wittgenstein (see esp. pp. 36–8). I think he underestimates the role of our *nature* in determining how we go on, according to Wittgenstein.

be correctly described as 'cubes'. In general, the creative thesis, taken literally, permits me to apply my words in any arbitrary fashion with complete linguistic impunity; nothing in my present understanding can rule out *any* application I may care to make. Clearly the linguistic anarchy that results from the creative thesis fails to correspond with how we commonsensically think of the meanings of our words, and just as clearly Wittgenstein himself has no wish to commend such anarchy. (The case here is again analogous with physical dispositions like solubility in that we do not want an account of dispositions to have the consequence that just *anything* counts as a manifestation of solubility.[63]) What should be opposed is not the very idea of future determination, either for meaning or for dispositions, but rather mythical conceptions of what this determination consists in – notably the idea that in some queer way the future manifestations are *already present* in the meaning or disposition but in a shadowy form. Wittgenstein's fundamental thesis, as I have interpreted him – that meaning rests ultimately upon the bedrock of our natural propensities – can be seen as a position which avoids the normative anarchy of the creative thesis while not falling into the trap of making meaning magically *contain* all of future and counterfactual use. It seems to me that this is a desirable, indeed a mandatory, objective, and that Wittgenstein's positive view succeeds in achieving that objective. Those theses of Wittgenstein's we have found questionable can I think be detached without damage to this basic contention.[64]

[63] It is of course true that solubility is not normative in the way that meaning is, but this does not undermine the intended analogy, which concerns the constraints we recognise between meaning and solubility on the one hand, and use and physical events on the other. In the same way, Wittgenstein suggests such a constraint between bravery and behaviour, and compares this to meaning and use – despite the non-normative character of the former kind of constraint.

[64] Probably this contention is the most difficult of Wittgenstein's theses to see one's way clear to accepting. For there is a constant temptation to oscillate between thinking of meaning and use as magically connected and thinking of them as quite unconnected (linguistic anarchy). The thought that these unacceptable extremes can be avoided by way of the natural ways of reacting which constitute our 'form of life' has to fight with the empiricist-intellectualist conviction that we must have *some* justification for going on as we do, else our linguistic practice is irrational at root. This is indeed why it is so important for Wittgenstein's general position that there can be legitimate epistemic warrant which is not founded on reasons. If, as I think, Wittgenstein is fundamentally right about the dilemma, and about the right way to escape being impaled on it, then it seems that a basic plank of his epistemological position must be accepted, and traditional empiricist foundationalism rejected.

4

Assessment of Kripke's Arguments

In Chapter 2 I criticised Kripke's arguments taken as correct exegesis of Wittgenstein's views, contending that these arguments bear little relation to Wittgenstein's real position. In the present chapter I shall be concerned with these arguments in their own right: irrespective of whether Wittgenstein has such arguments in mind, are Kripke's arguments cogent in themselves? And I shall argue that, despite their great interest, these arguments are not as powerful as Kripke represents them as being; I think there are plausible replies to them that Kripke either overlooks or underestimates. Seeing why these arguments do not work will help us to come to a clearer view of meaning and of how we must think about it. I should perhaps stress that Kripke does not himself officially endorse the arguments he attributes to Wittgenstein: these arguments were prompted by reading Wittgenstein, he says, and should not be taken, in strictness, either as his or Wittgenstein's.[1] So when I speak in this chapter simply of 'Kripke's arguments' this should be regarded as an ellipsis for 'the arguments that occurred to Kripke while reading Wittgenstein'. Nevertheless, I think it is plain from Kripke's presentation that he takes the arguments to be more compelling than seems to me to be proper; so we can safely assume that he would not make the kinds of criticisms of these arguments that I shall be making. First I shall consider the sceptical paradox.

[1] Kripke, p. 5.

The sceptical paradox says that there is no kind of *fact* for meaning something by a word to consist in; the sentences we use to ascribe meaning, understanding and rules correspond to no 'condition-in-the-world'. Kripke's argument for this 'anti-factual' thesis about semantic statements proceeds by (as he thinks) exhausting the possibilities – when we try to discover an appropriate constitutive fact from among the natural candidates we find that nothing suitable can be produced. Initially, the paradox is presented as a problem about how present use might accord with past meaning; the question at this stage is what *past* fact makes it the case that (e.g.) '+' should now be used in a certain way, if my present use is to conform with (be faithful to) my past 'linguistic intentions'. This question is intimately connected with the question of what grounds the *normativeness* of meaning – its capacity to render uses of words correct or incorrect. Kripke's argument takes the form of showing (or trying to show) that no past facts can ground a judgement of present correctness or incorrectness: nothing shows that present use is *justified* by facts about past meaning. The basic difficulty, as Kripke sees it, is that all the facts that offer themselves as candidates for what my past meaning consists in are logically compatible with *indefinitely many* present uses I might make of my words, e.g. giving '5' as the answer to '67 + 58 = ?'. But now if there is no fact about my *past* to constitute my having meant one thing rather than another, then there can be nothing about my *present* condition which constitutes determinate meaning either, since the same argument could be given with respect to the present time at some later date; and furthermore, if we ask directly for a present fact to constitute present meaning, we will come up just as empty-handed as we did when our question concerned the past. So when I ascribe a meaning to myself or to another there is no fact about me or him that makes true or false that ascription; there is in short no 'fact of the matter' about what someone means. The candidate facts Kripke considers fall into three broad categories: actual applications of the sign in question, either overtly or in one's head (imagination), e.g. computations performed with '+'; introspectible qualitative states of consciousness enjoyed while using the sign, e.g. images and feelings had when performing computations with '+'; and dispositions to apply the sign, i.e. counterfactuals about how one would use the sign in respect of its extension, e.g. dispositions to give the right answer to any question of the form '$n + m = ?$', for all numbers n and m. The reasons Kripke gives for rejecting each of these candidates are, summarily stated, as follows: actual applications underdetermine meaning since alternative meanings (e.g. quaddition) are consistent with the applications that have so far been made of the sign; states of consciousness are (a) not always forthcoming and (b) can always be variously interpreted and applied; and dispositions are inadequate to determine meaning because (a) they are finite whereas the meaning of '+' has an infinitary character and (b) people can be disposed to make mistakes, so that there can be a systematic divergence between what one means and the answers one is disposed to give. Kripke's contention is that these candidates exhaust the field, and so there is nothing for meaning to consist in.

What I want to question in this argument for the anti-factual thesis is the claim that these three categories exhaust the possibilities; I think we can point to other sorts of fact which will do what those Kripke considers admittedly fail to do. But before I develop this line of objection it will be helpful to clarify the nature of Kripke's argument; for I think that when it is reformulated its weaknesses will become more apparent. There are three points of clarification or amplification that seem to me worth bringing out.

The first point to notice is that, although Kripke concentrates in the main on mathematical examples, secondarily extending his argument to predicates of material objects and sensations, the argument can and must be applied to words of *all* semantic categories (as doubtless Kripke is aware, though he does not explicitly say as much). The argument must be generalised in this way if it is to have the scope Kripke claims for it, i.e. as showing that the whole notion of meaning is threatened with evaporation; and it would be very odd indeed if the argument could establish the non-factual character of ascriptions of meaning to *predicates* (or function symbols) but not to other categories of expression. Fortunately for Kripke, however, it seems that we can get the sceptical argument going for other categories of expressions, e.g. proper names and sentence connectives, as follows. Consider the name 'Kripke' and my use of this name heretofore: I have used this name only finitely many times in a circumscribed range of circumstances (in particular, only up to the present time); yet we ordinarily think that the meaning of this name entitles me to use it in a certain way in other circumstances or at other times, e.g. if I see Kripke at a conference tomorrow I will be able to say correctly 'that's Kripke'. But suppose I encounter a bizarre sceptic who questions my right to apply 'Kripke' to Kripke at some future time: this sceptic says that the correct use of 'Kripke', determined by my past understanding of that name, is to apply it to *Putnam* after some future time *t*. That is, the sceptical hypothesis about 'Kripke' is that it refers to *Kripnam*, where Kripnam is either Kripke if seen before *t* or Putnam if seen after *t*: on this hypothesis, then, my past meaning for 'Kripke' dictates that it is correct to apply that name to Putnam after *t* and to Kripke before *t*; so if I call Kripke 'Kripke' tomorrow (let us say) I shall be using that word *wrongly*, i.e. not in accordance with its original meaning.

What could we say to refute this sceptic? Past use will not refute him since it is logically compatible with the sceptical hypothesis; neither will the states of consciousness I had in the past when I used 'Kripke', for the usual sorts of reasons; nor, it seems, will my linguistic dispositions do the job, since I might mean Kripke by 'Kripke' and yet be disposed to *mistake* Putnam for Kripke on occasions after *t*. What we have done in this example is to mimic the structure of the Kripke-Goodman examples for predicates in respect of names: we just find a possible occasion of use for the name which has not been actualised and then define a nonstandard meaning with respect to that occasion. The same Goodmanian trick can be applied to sentence connectives: I take my word 'and' to mean the truth-function of conjunction as defined by a truth-table which specifies its value for arbitrary arguments, i.e. I take it that if you join *any* two sentences with 'and' the resulting sentence is true just if both of the joined sentences are true. But suppose a semantic sceptic questions this ordinary assumption: he asks me to produce some fact about my past use of 'and' which shows that this word does not mean *quand*, where quand is a truth-function that agrees in its truth-table with conjunction only with respect to sentences of fewer than one hundred words and thereafter agrees with *dis*junction. Suppose I have never formed or heard any 'and' sentences of this length before, so that nothing in my actual past use of 'and' shows that the quand hypothesis is mistaken: when I now judge a sentence of over one hundred words formed with 'and' to be false because one of its subsentences is false I am (the sceptic says) misinterpreting my own past use – in the past I meant *quand* and so I should now judge the sentence in question *true*. Thus the sceptic suggests that I am now using 'and' *in*correctly if I take it to mean conjunction: what shows that he is wrong, that I always meant conjunction? Again, it seems that conscious states and dispositions to use will not serve to refute the sceptic, because they cannot determinately select the meaning we commonly ascribe to 'and', for reasons that are by now familiar. It should be easy to see how similarly contrived sceptical hypotheses can be generated for adverbs, demonstratives, and so on – just choose some unencountered parameter and define a nonstandard meaning with respect to it. No doubt these nonstandard meanings are bizarre and 'unnatural', but Kripke's claim is that they appear not to be logically excluded by the available facts about our use of words. I think then that we can allow Kripke to generalise his sceptical paradox across all categories of expression – *no* type of word can be supposed to have a determinate meaning, according to the semantic sceptic.

Secondly, although Kripke typically formulates his paradox as a claim about the notion of *meaning*, nothing essential would be lost if we replaced 'means' with 'refers to' throughout. Thus the problem about '+' can be reformulated as a question about what constitutes my *referring* to addition rather than quaddition when I use this word, and whether my present use is correct or incorrect depends upon which mathematical function was the *reference* of '+' in the past. For predicates generally we can formulate the paradox as the claim that there is no unique *property* which is the reference of a given predicate: to take Kripke's own example, the sceptic denies that anything makes it the case that my word 'table' *refers* to the property of being a table and not the property of being a *tabair*, where something has the property of being a tabair if either it is a table and is not in the Eiffel Tower or is a chair and is in the Eiffel Tower. The case of names is indeed most naturally formulated in terms of the notion of reference: what fact constitutes my referring to Kripke with 'Kripke' and not to Kripnam? And if we stretch the notion of reference in the manner of Frege, then we can ask what makes 'and' refer to conjunction and not to some other nonstandard truth-function. Reference, like meaning, has the requisite kind of normativeness, since normativeness for Kripke is just a matter of using a word in accordance with the semantic properties with which one earlier used it. Kripke's basic problem obviously does not distinctively concern the Fregean notion of *sense*; it is not the question what facts constitute the semantic difference between 'Hesperus' and 'Phosphorus', or something of that sort. His fundamental question concerns what it consists in for a word to stand in a determinate semantic relation to some extra-linguistic item (functions, properties, individuals, etc.). While I think this second point is uncontroversial enough, it does, I will suggest, introduce a perspective on the problem that might otherwise have escaped us.[2]

My third point is less straightforward than the first two, and its significance for Kripke is correspondingly greater – for it points up a real lacuna in Kripke's presentation of his paradox. The point is that it is necessary for Kripke to apply his paradox at the level of *concepts*: that is, he has to argue that the notion of possessing a determinate concept is likewise devoid of factual foundation – there is no 'fact of the matter' about which concepts I possess and am exercising in having a particular *thought*. Thus, for example, when I take myself to be having a thought in the content of which the concept of *addition* figures, this is an assumption with no basis in the facts – for nothing about me establishes that it is not the concept of *quaddition* that occurs in the content of my thought. Whether my thought is *true* obviously depends upon whether it is the concept of addition or quaddition that occurs in it, and Kripke's sceptic must claim that nothing does determine which of these concepts is being exercised in that thought and hence whether my thought is true or false. It is necessary for Kripke to apply the anti-factual thesis to concepts and thoughts for (at least) two reasons. One is that the paradox would be of relatively

[2] Generalising the paradox to all categories of expression does not *require* us to use the notion of reference in the broad Fregean way, nor does it even require use of a single semantic predicate applicable to all expressions. In fact, no single semantic predicate naturally covers the full range, not even 'means' or 'expresses'. But nothing prevents us using different semantic predicates for different kinds of expression, and then formulating the paradox in these different terms; in particular, 'refers' is the natural predicate for singular terms.

little interest if it had no implications for concept possession: for if the idea that ascriptions of concepts to people correspond to facts-in-the-world were in good order, then there would be no general threat to our belief that our minds can house determinate representations of extra-mental states of affairs – the general notion of *intentionality* would not be under threat.[3] It would merely be that the notion of a semantic property of a linguistic item is in trouble, but not because there is anything amiss with the idea of *content* in general: although nothing makes it the case that yesterday I *meant* addition by '+', still there is a fact of the matter about which *concepts* and *thoughts* I then had and exercised – the same or different from those I have and exercise today. The second reason follows immediately upon this first reason: if the factuality and determinacy of concepts were not under threat from the paradox, then it would seem that we have a ready reply to Kripke's semantic sceptic, namely that '+' means addition in my language simply because I associate with '+' the *concept of addition* (and not quaddition): that is, when I use '+' in sentences the thought I have and communicate is a thought whose content contains the concept of addition. Thus the factuality of concepts could be used to establish the factuality of meaning: the sought-for constitutive fact consists precisely in the *concepts* I exercise when I use the words in question – for the meaning is just the concept expressed.[4] If this deflationary response is to be convincingly blocked, the semantic sceptic will have to become a conceptual sceptic; he will have to turn his attentions to *thought*. In point of fact, Kripke does in at least one place formulate the conclusion of his argument in terms of concepts, though it cannot be said that his premises give any notice of this enlargement of scope: thus he says 'Wittgenstein's main problem is that it appears that he has shown *all* language, *all*

---

[3] Suppose (as seems to me very plausible) that there can be thought (concepts) without language: we should want to be able to direct the paradox at the content of such thoughts, as well as those of the language-endowed.

[4] This is the familiar (and by no means discredited) idea that concepts are inherently non-linguistic, and that meaning comes about when words get to *express* concepts. If concept possession is unproblematically factual, then meaning will also be (assuming that the relation of 'expression' is itself determinate). We don't want Kripke's sceptic to be antecedently committed to rejecting this picture of how meaning comes about, just because he wants his paradox to extend to concepts (holding, say, that concepts are 'internalised words' or some such).

concept formation, to be impossible, indeed unintelligible' (p. 62).[5] I suspect that Kripke inserts the sceptical claim about concepts in this way because he is aware that he *needs* to say this if his paradox is to do its sceptical work successfully. The position here is essentially analogous to Quine's indeterminacy thesis: Quine does not want to confine himself merely to the claim that the semantic properties of *words* are indeterminate; he wants to apply his thesis to the content of propositional attitudes too (indeed he had better apply it so if the thesis is to be ultimately defensible even as a *semantic* indeterminacy claim[6]).

It cannot be said, however, that Kripke explains how this need is to be met, how the extension of the paradox to concepts is to be carried out; and brief reflection shows that the exercise is by no means trivial. The chief problem is that the initial statement of the paradox in terms of constancy of meaning across time has no natural application to concepts, unless we presuppose some questionable claims about what it is to have a concept. The metalinguistic question, remember, is whether my present use of a given sign conforms with my past linguistic intentions in respect of that sign, i.e. whether a certain syntactically identified linguistic item has retained or changed its meaning over time. But at the level of thought this sort of question makes dubious sense: for we cannot sensibly ask whether my present employment of a concept in thought conforms with my past intentions in using it. The reason for the asymmetry is obvious: we have not, in the case of concepts, the idea of a single meaning-bearing item (word) about which we can press the question what establishes constancy in its meaning; there isn't the gap between a concept and its content that there is between a word and its meaning – a concept *is* (so to speak) its content. Constancy of meaning is a matter of some sign expressing the same concept over time, but constancy of concept cannot in turn be conceived in this way. We might, of course, try to restore the parallel by adopting a view of concept possession which mirrors the having of meaning by words – we

---

[5] *Cf.* also Kripke, p. 54. However, the rest of the book addresses itself exclusively to the 'metalinguistic' question of meaning something by a word.

[6] See W.V. Quine, *Word and Object* (MIT Press : Cambridge, Mass, 1960), chap. 2. The same goes for D. Davidson: see, e.g., his 'Belief and the Basis of Meaning', in *Inquiries into Truth and Interpretation* (Clarendon Press: Oxford, 1984).

might, that is, invoke the idea of a language of thought. We could then ask what establishes that a certain syntactically identified item in this internal language has the same meaning over time, and then attempt to go through the same set of arguments Kripke gives for public language meaning. But this would be to take a stand on an issue about which Kripke's sceptic would presumably prefer to stay neutral; it would be best for him if he could develop his paradox without committing himself to this controversial conception of concept possession. And besides, the issue of normativeness, the crucial issue for Kripke, has no clear content in application to the language of thought: what does it mean to ask whether my current employment of a word in my language of thought (i.e. the exercise of a particular concept) is *correct* in the light of my earlier inner employment of that word? What kind of linguistic mistake is being envisaged here? And it is arguable that this is as it should be, because it is unclear how Kripke's normativeness requirement *could* operate at the level of thought; what could be (relevantly) meant by asking whether my present employment of a concept is in accordance with its previous content?[7] There is just no analogue here for the idea of linguistic incorrectness (as opposed to the *falsity* of a thought): linguistic incorrectness (of the kind we are concerned with) is using the same word with a different meaning from that originally intended (and doing so in ignorance of the change), but we cannot in this way make sense of employing a concept with a different content from that originally intended – it would just be a *different concept*. It is this asymmetry between meanings and concepts which makes Kripke's exclusive concentration on the metalinguistic question a serious omisson; for the original intuitive statement of the paradox, in terms of constancy of meaning over time and normativeness, simply does not carry over to concepts – and yet it is imperative for the eventual success of the sceptic's argument that this extension be feasible.

Fortunately for Kripke, however, I think that we can at least develop an *analogous* sceptical argument at the level of thought, though its intuitive force is more than somewhat

---

[7] In fact, it seems to me that this point highlights a real problem for the language of thought theorist: it shows a basic difference between the vocabulary of a public language and the repertoire of concepts a person possesses. This difference is connected with the fact that concepts do not have the *conventionality* of language.

reduced by the form it is required to take; indeed, I believe that when the sceptical argument is applied to concepts its central weakness stands forth more plainly than it does in the metalinguistic version. What we must do is to drop the initial formulation in terms of constancy of meaning across time and normativeness and simply ask directly what it is that constitutes possessing and exercising one concept rather than another. We ascribe concepts and thoughts to ourselves and others, but what sort of fact is it that makes these ascriptions true? What rules out nonstandard assignments of extensions to our concepts? The sceptic will hope to give these questions bite by observing that the applications we have hitherto made of our concepts underdetermine the specific ascriptions of concepts we normally take for granted; our applications hitherto do not exhaust the (actual and possible) extension of the concept, so what is to prevent the sceptic trading upon this fact to contrive alternative assignments of concepts to us which equally fit our actual applications – ascribing to us the concept of quaddition rather than addition, say? I normally (for example) take my classifying red things together as an exercise of my concept *red*, but what shows that it is not the concept *gred* that is being exercised, where this concept is manifested by classifying red things together up to a future time *t* and green things thereafter? For any behaviour that we take to manifest a given concept *could* be interpreted so as to constitute the manifestation of a different concept, by the familiar Goodmanesque technique. And whether we ascribe to the person a true or a false thought depends upon which concepts we take him to be employing in any behaviour we take to be expressive of the thought in question. So it seems that my applications of my concepts hitherto do not suffice to *constitute* my possessing the commonly ascribed concepts as opposed to the nonstandard ones. But if this is so, then actual application cannot resolve the indeterminacy between employing a concept *C* in a *false* thought and employing some other (nonstandard) concept *C'* in a *true* thought: when I group a green object with uniformly red objects have I falsely judged that object to be red and hence applied the concept *red*, or is it that my thought was *true* and was rather a judgement that the object was *gred* and hence involved *that* concept? (This is the *analogue* for concepts of the notion of normativeness for meaning – the question what it is that accounts for the notion of a mistake.[8])

But what of the other two categories of fact Kripke considers and rejects in connexion with linguistic meaning? It is clear that qualitative states of consciousness will not serve to constitute possessing a specific concept, for essentially the reasons Wittgenstein gives and Kripke rehearses. Neither, it seems, will dispositions avail us: for dispositions are finite while concepts may have infinitary consequences; and people can be disposed to apply concepts incorrectly, so that we cannot simply read off from concept application which concept it is that is being applied. The problems here are essentially those urged by Kripke in respect of meaning, and of course this is only to be expected given the intimacy of the relation between concepts possessed and things meant. I think therefore that the semantic sceptic *can* defend himself against the easy reply that takes concept possession for granted; he cannot, it is true, set up his sceptical paradox for concepts in just the way he did for meaning, but he can still mount an argument to the effect that there is no kind of fact to constitute possessing and exercising one concept rather than another. If God could look into our minds he would not see there what concepts we possess and hence what thoughts we have – if, that is, our minds can harbour only the sorts of fact Kripke contemplates.[9]

I have so far expounded Kripke's sceptical paradox as a constitutive or metaphysical claim; it is a thesis about what it *is* to mean something and (hence) for linguistic use to be correct. But Kripke also presents an epistemological thesis, to the effect that I cannot now *justify* my present linguistic inclinations – nothing about my past use can now be cited by me as a *reason* to apply a word as I am now inclined. This alleged epistemological problem results from the circumstance that everything now available to me in memory is compatible with my having meant something different. Now this epistemological claim is clearly distinct from the metaphysical claim that there

---

[8] It is just an analogue, however, and not a species of the same genus, since (as I have said) we do not have, in respect of concepts, the notion of a syntactic item which the thinker intends to employ with a constant meaning over time; all we have for concepts is the notion of a *false* application of the concept (a factual not a linguistic error).

[9] It should be clear that the point holds for all sorts of propositional attitude, including the appetitive and volitional, since all have conceptual content.

is no *fact* about me that constitutes my meaning something, and it is by no means obvious that an answer to the metaphysical problem would simultaneously be an answer to the epistemological problem. For we do not generally suppose that once we have an account of the nature of the subject-matter of a class of sentences we have thereby solved the epistemological problems associated with those sentences: to explain what the truth of statements about the external world (for instance) consists in is not yet to solve the problem of *justifying* our claims to know truths about that sector of reality. So it is not to be *assumed* that any fact that might be produced to constitute my past meaning will be such that it can now be cited as a justification for my present use; for the constitutive fact might be of a kind that is not ordinarily available to memory, or it just might not be suitable to serve as a *reason* for present use (suppose it was a brain state). Conversely, it is not guaranteed that an answer to the epistemological problem will provide us with an answer to the metaphysical problem; for it might be that what serves as a reason for using a sign in a certain way does not add up to a *fact* that constitutes meaning something. Kripke proceeds as if the two questions were quite inseparable, on the assumption that what supplies a fact must also supply a reason and *vice versa*; but this is a substantive assumption which should not be accepted uncritically.[10] In particular, we should not let our efforts to rebut the constitutive sceptic be constrained by the necessity to answer at the same stroke the epistemological sceptic; and I think we shall see as we proceed that this warning is not empty. Let us then consider what replies we might make to the constitutive sceptic, clear in our minds that the epistemological question is separate and additional; we shall return to that latter question later.

What is very striking about Kripke's sceptic is an assumption he makes which, once it is brought to light, ought to make us suspicious of his whole way of proceeding; this assumption both is essential to the argument and is itself unargued for. I mean the assumption that if there are semantic facts they will

---

[10] Compare the question of what pain *is* and the question of how I *justify* my current belief that in the past I had a pain. It *might* be that we should answer the first question by reference to a physical state of the brain, while answering the second by citing the behaviour I manifested in the past; at least we should not exclude such a divergence of answers simply by the way we set the issue up.

have to be *reducible* to facts specified non-semantically: for the sceptic is in effect demanding an answer to the question 'what does meaning/reference consist in?' which does not just help itself to the notions of meaning and reference. Thus the candidate answers Kripke considers all attempt to say what constitutes a given semantic fact without simply *using* semantic concepts directly (or indeed indirectly) – *viz.* actual application, states of consciousness, dispositions to use. The kind of reply that is being implicitly judged illicit is one that simply uses semantic concepts, as follows: what it consists in to mean/refer to addition by '+' is for the speaker to *mean/refer to* addition by '+' – *this* is the sort of 'fact' that meaning consists in.[11] Remember that Kripke's sceptic is out to show that semantic discourse is not fact-stating; then his implicit assumption is that semantic discourse cannot be regarded as fact-stating *just as it stands*. The sceptic is assuming that unless semantic facts can be captured in non-semantic terms they are not really facts; but why should this assumption be thought compulsory? So the question for Kripke is why we cannot give the truth conditions of 'he means addition by "+"' simply by *re-using* that sentence, frankly admitting that no other specification of truth conditions is available – precisely because semantic statements cannot be *reduced* to non-semantic ones.[12] Unless this question can be answered Kripke's sceptic is wide open to the objection that he is mistaking *irreducibility* for non-factuality: he finds that he cannot provide a non-semantic fact to constitute a semantic fact and then concludes that there are *no* semantic facts, when the correct conclusion ought to be that semantic facts cannot be reduced to non-semantic facts. The sceptic thus needs to defend an undefended and undisclosed

---

[11] This assumption is implicit from the very beginning of the sceptical challenge (see Kripke, p. 11f), but it is concealed by presenting the problem in terms of the 'directions I previously gave myself' in respect of '+': we are invited to consider the actual thoughts I had and computations I performed in the past, and to observe that my past meaning cannot be read off from these. In this way, Kripke's sceptic directs our attention away from the idea that the fact in question may just be an irreducible fact. And he further conceals his reductionist assumption by pretending that 'there are no limitations, in particular, no behaviourist limitations, on the facts that may be cited to answer the sceptic' (p. 14).

[12] This would be to adopt what Dummett calls a 'naive realist' view of facts about meaning: see his 'Realism', *Synthese* 52 (1982), pp. 78, 105f. Naive realism, as defined by Dummett, is realism about a class of statements combined with an irreducibility thesis in respect of those statements.

premise, namely that semantic discourse cannot be regarded as
irreducible, this premise being tantamount to the claim that
semantic discourse is not factual just as it is (without benefit of
translation into other terms). For otherwise we can take him to
have established in a new way what many have already and
independently suspected: that semantic concepts are indeed
irreducible to non-semantic concepts.[13]

The dialectical position here can be usefully compared with
Quine's attack on the factuality of semantic discourse. Quine
explicitly assumes that all genuine facts are physical facts
(distributions of elementary particles and their physical
properties), and then argues that semantic ascriptions cannot
be reduced to statements of physical fact (including behavioural
statements); it follows that semantic ascriptions do not state
facts. The truth-value of semantic statements is *indeterminate*
with respect to the physical facts, so such statements cannot
correspond to facts at all.[14] Kripke's sceptic claims that
semantic ascriptions are indeterminate with respect to a wider
range of facts – including, notably, facts about consciousness –
and then concludes that such ascriptions are unfactual. What
both Quine and Kripke assume, the former more explicitly
than the latter, is that the factuality of semantic ascriptions
waits upon their reduction to some favoured class of fact-
stating propositions; such ascriptions cannot be taken to be
factual *independently* of finding any such reduction. It is thus
open to us to take Quine's indeterminacy arguments as
showing the hopelessness of a behaviourist or physicalist
reduction of semantic discourse; similarly, we may take
Kripke's arguments to show that *no* reduction of *any* kind is
possible – semantic statements correspond to irreducibly

---

[13] See, e.g., R. Chisholm, *Perceiving: A Philosophical Study* (Ithaca: Cornell, 1957),
chap. 11, for the suggestion that we cannot break out of the circle of intentional notions
by explaining these notions in quite other terms.
[14] Thus Quine: 'One may accept the Brentano thesis [i.e. the irreducibility of the
intentional] either as showing the indispensability of intentional idioms and the
importance of an autonomous science of intention, or as showing the baselessness of
intentional idioms and the emptiness of a science of intention. My attitude, unlike
Brentano's, is the second' (*Word and Object*, p. 221). It seems that Kripke's sceptic has
fundamentally the same attitude as Quine, but he is less forthright in admitting it.
(Actually Quine compares his doctrine of indeterminacy of translation with
'Wittgenstein's latter-day remarks on meaning', p. 77, note 2. Here he seems to be
anticipating Kripke's interpretation of Wittgenstein.)

semantic facts. Kripke's sceptic thus owes us at the least an answer to the question 'why make the reductionist assumption?'.

In fact there is an *ad hominem* point to be made here, namely that Kripke himself has been prominent in resisting reductionist philosophies in general and semantic reductionism in particular. Recall, for example, his antipathy to materialist and functionalist reductions of mental phenomena, and his approving quotation in *Naming and Necessity*[15] of Bishop Butler's dictum 'Everything is what it is and not another thing' (this is actually quoted in the context of urging a general distrust of attempts to explain philosophically central concepts 'in completely different terms' (p. 94)). In the light of these declared views one might have expected Kripke to be the first to seize upon the semantic sceptic's reductionist assumption and to press for a defence of it. And about semantic reductionism in particular Kripke has been no less explicit: discussing his own theory of names, in terms of chains of reference-preserving links, he tells us that he doubts that necessary and sufficient conditions can be found for reference which do not themselves employ the notion of reference; this is indeed why he contents himself with a 'picture' of reference, instead of a *reduction* of it, in which the concept of reference does not ineliminably feature.[16] Is not Kripke's sceptic assuming precisely what Kripke himself elsewhere strongly questions? That the sceptic is doing precisely this becomes more evident when we remember our reformulation of the sceptic's question in terms of the notion of reference and its extension to singular terms such as proper names: for the sceptic is in effect asking for a non-semantic analysis of what it is for a word to refer to a particular object (or property in the case of predicates; compare Kripke on natural kind predicates[17]),

---

[15] Blackwell: Oxford, 1980. Kripke says: 'I'm always sympathetic to Bishop Butler's "Everything is what it is and not another thing" – in the nontrivial sense that philosophical analyses of some concept like reference, in completely different terms which make no mention of reference, are very apt to fail' (p. 94). This seems a salutary point for Kripke's sceptic to keep in mind.

[16] See *Naming and Necessity*, pp. 94-7.

[17] *Op. cit.*, pp. 135f. It is interesting to compare Kripke's account of what determines the reference of general terms in this work with the treatment he gives to such terms in his book on Wittgenstein: if the sceptic were right about (say) 'table', then Kripke's own earlier account of the semantics of (say) 'tiger' would be undermined, since there would be no fact (in particular, no causal fact) that determines the extension of such a term. And Kripke clearly does not, in the earlier work, suppose that we need to explain the meaning or reference of 'tiger' by means of community assertibility conditions!

and this is precisely the kind of demand Kripke rejects as reductionist in *Naming and Necessity*. So my *ad hominem* point is this: why not take a leaf out of Kripke's (other) book and direct it against his semantic sceptic? Since I myself strongly sympathise with Kripke's anti-reductionism about reference in that other book, this seems to me an entirely reasonable response.

The unmotivated reductionism sustaining Kripke's sceptic is if anything more glaring when we consider concepts. For the *semantic* sceptic at least began with a more or less intuitive and untendentious question about past meaning and current use, and this question does not in itself commit us to the reductionist presupposition (or at least it need not); but the conceptual sceptic cannot, as I pointed out earlier, proceed in this way – he must make an outright demand for a suitable constitutive fact to make ascriptions of concepts true. And this demand invites the following deflationary retort: the constitutive fact corresponding to the statement 'he possesses/is exercising the concept *cubical*' is precisely the fact that he possesses/is exercising *the concept cubical*; or again, what makes true an ascription to someone of the thought that 5 added to 7 equals 12 is precisely the fact that he has *the thought that 5 added to 7 equals 12*. These truistic replies give expression to the conviction that there is no reduction to be had of the concept of concept or that of a thought having a content; hence the factuality of concept ascription must rest upon nothing other than the existence of irreducibly conceptual facts – facts specified using frankly 'intentional' notions. Why, after all, should we *expect* that the notion of a propositional attitude with a specific conceptual content should be explicable in terms of such notions as actual application, state of consciousness or disposition? Is it not more reasonable to expect that no explication in 'completely different terms' will ever capture what it is to have and exercise a concept?[18] Seeing the matter in this light, we are therefore entitled to ask Kripke's sceptic why he does not take himself to have provided a proof of the irreducibility of concept possession – not of its unfactuality. There is, at any rate, a challenge here that has not been met, nor even properly acknowledged.

[18] To maintain an irreducibility thesis about semantic or intentional facts is not, of course, to rule out the possibility of *any* kind of theory of meaning, or of the possession of concepts; it is rather to say that any such theory will perforce employ irreducibly intentional notions.

It is not only meaning and concepts that resist the kind of reductionism Kripke is tacitly presupposing; there are other psychological concepts which seem not to be capturable by any fact on Kripke's list of candidate constitutive facts. And this being so we have independent confirmation that (psychological) factuality does not require the sorts of grounding Kripke considers: that is, we need to adopt an irreducibility thesis with respect to these other concepts too (or if we do not this is something that has to be *shown*). Consider traits of character: bravery, kindness, irascibility, meanness of spirit, etc. Is it to be supposed that *such* properties of a person can be explained in terms of facts from Kripke's three categories? Well, that does appear rather unlikely: certainly actual behaviour will underdetermine the ascription of character traits, as can be seen by contriving rival sceptical hypotheses about the traits someone has. We ascribe the trait of (say) bravery to someone on the basis of his behaviour in a circumscribed range of situations on a finite number of occasions; but a sceptic might object that this behaviour is (logically) compatible with the ascription of *quavery* to the person, where someone is quave just if he acts bravely in all the kinds of situation hitherto examined but in a cowardly way in other situations (i.e. 'quave' means 'brave up to *t* and cowardly thereafter'). That is to say, the sceptic trades on the acknowledged underdetermination of traits by actual behaviour to define a non-standard ascription of a trait and then challenges us to *show* why the commonsense ascription is the correct one; and whatever we may want to say about the epistemological aspect of this challenge, it is clear that the sceptic is quite right to deny that actual behaviour could *constitute* (or logically determine) bravery. The point here is that character traits, like meaning, have consequences that go beyond their actual manifestations, so that we cannot hope to *define* them simply by reference to their actual manifestations.[19] This kind of scepticism has obvious repercussions for the notion of the *stability* of character traits over time; for it seems

[19] This point is implicit in Wittgenstein's comparison in 187 of meaning and being disposed to jump in the water if someone had fallen in: Wittgenstein does not here show any concern that such 'dispositions' or traits might not be genuinely factual just because they cannot be explained in terms of their *actual* manifestations; nor does he worry that I never gave myself any 'directions' or 'explicit instructions' about what to do if Smith falls in the water – I need never have considered this possibility and yet the counterfactual will still be true of me.

that we could mount an argument analogous to Kripke's argument about semantic or conceptual constancy with respect to character-trait constancy: what makes me so sure that my present action issues from the same trait as that which I had yesterday, in view of the fact that I have never in the past performed an action of that kind? Perhaps yesterday I was *quave* and would have fled from the kind of adversary now confronting me – I stand fast now only because I no longer have that trait (suppose my present adversary is red-haired and I have never come across a red-haired adversary in the past). It is clear too that states of consciousness will not serve to constitute the fact of being brave: surely it is not necessary to enjoy any particular kind of experience when one has the trait of bravery (or is acting bravely), and equally surely it is not sufficient – being brave is just not a state in which some experiential item 'comes before the mind'. Concepts of traits of character are not concepts *of* conditions of consciousness; as Wittgenstein might say, states of consciousness do not have the *consequences* of character traits.[20] The dispositional suggestion might appear more hopeful, as it did for the case of meaning; but I doubt that this suggestion will work either, at least if dispositions are construed as Kripke construes them (which is all that is needed for a fair comparison). Let us consider the kinds of counterfactuals that might be supposed to capture the trait we are after: they would presumably be of the form 'if he were in circumstance *C*, he would do such-and-such'; e.g. 'if he were in circumstances requiring aggressive action, he would act aggressively'. It is I think obvious on reflection that the truth of such counterfactuals is neither necessary nor sufficient for being brave: not necessary because the person may have false beliefs about the kind of situation he is in (he makes a mistake), and not sufficient because it is perfectly conceivable that the required aggressive action results from something other than bravery (e.g. some sort of drug).[21] Besides, our concept of

---

[20] *Cf.* 'Meaning it is not a process which accompanies a word. For no *process* could have the consequences of meaning' (p. 218).

[21] This claim would need more discussion to be properly substantiated, but I take it that the *sorts* of considerations necessary to establishing it are fairly familiar: in particular, the 'holism of the mental', and the possibility of making the counterfactuals true by means of facts other than those for which the counterfactuals are supposed to provide sufficient conditions. The case of traits would thus parallel that of propositional attitudes, for which dispositional analyses are notoriously problematic.

bravery is not tied to specific kinds of action in the way envisaged; we allow all *sorts* of actions to count as manifestations of bravery. And then there is the point that the trait of bravery can be modified or overridden by other traits (e.g. prudence) or desires (e.g. an altruistic desire to help the man who is wounded) in such a way that brave action is not forthcoming, though the trait of bravery nevertheless persists. Our concept of bravery is, as it were, much richer than anything that can be delivered by analogues of the kinds of simple dispositions Kripke considers in the case of meaning; and it seems to me highly doubtful that adding counterfactual epicycles will substantially improve the prospects of a dispositional *analysis* of ascriptions of traits. Let us suppose then, if only for the sake of argument, that traits are not identifiable with dispositions, and ask what we should conclude from this: should we conclude that this reductive failure, taken together with the other two failures, shows that there is no *fact of the matter* about what character traits a person has? Should we conclude that 'he is brave' is not made true by any real condition of the person, that our discourse about character traits is in peril of non-factuality? I venture to suggest that few of us would take that radical conclusion to be entailed; rather we would conclude, perhaps with some surprise, that traits of character are just not reducible to facts of these kinds – and that so far as we can see they are not reducible to facts of any *other* kind either.[22] This would be to conclude, in effect, that 'he is brave' is made true simply by the fact of his being *brave*; there *is* no other way to specify the appropriate constitutive fact – nor is this anything to be especially alarmed about. After all, why do we have a specific vocabulary for character traits if this vocabulary is in principle dispensable in favour of some analytical substitute? It is, at any rate, sufficiently clear that to draw a sceptical conclusion about character traits analogous to Kripke's about meaning would be questionable to say the least: it would be simply to ignore the possibility of an irreducibility thesis. In fact the same sort of question arises with respect to concepts of

[22] I here disagree with Dummett, who once said that 'only a philosophically quite naive person would adopt a realist view of statements about character' ('Realism', p. 150, in *Truth and Other Enigmas* (Duckworth: London, 1978)): that is to say, an irreducibility thesis about 'brave' would be philosophically naive (it would indeed be a form of 'naive realism': see note 12).

propositional attitudes – belief, desire, hope, intention, etc. – namely, whether *these* concepts are reducible in the kinds of ways Kripke considers. And it is very far from clear that they are: it is doubtful, for example, that *belief* can be explained in terms of actual behaviour, or conscious states, or dispositions – for reasons which should by now be pretty obvious. But such irreducibility is not obviously or uncontroversially a good reason for pressing a claim of non-factuality: perhaps belief too is a *primitive* kind of fact, not capturable in other terms.[23] In the case of propositional attitudes, reductionists have recognised the need to advertise and defend their reductionist presuppositions before an irreducibility result can be converted to a non-factuality thesis; what I am saying against Kripke's sceptic is that he does not bring this kind of presupposition into the open where it can be seen for what it is.

Kripke formulates his sceptical conclusion as the thesis that there is nothing 'in my mind' that constitutes my meaning one thing rather than another (or having one concept rather than another), or again that there is nothing in my 'mental history' that makes it the case that in the past I meant addition rather than quaddition: if God had access to all the facts concerning my mind, he would not thereby have access to my meaning, since no fact about my mind constitutes my meaning one thing rather than another. Now it might be said, in response to the irreducibility suggestion, that *this* at any rate is still true: maybe meaning (reference) is an irreducible fact but it is not a properly *mental* fact – it is not a fact of a kind to be seen by God when he looks into my mind. And it may be thought that this is still sufficiently paradoxical to warrant a *modified* sceptical thesis, *viz.* meaning is admittedly a fact but not a fact about what is in my mind. However, I think it is clear that even this modified sceptical conclusion is not warranted; it gains what plausibility it has by tacitly assuming a questionable conception of what it is to 'belong to the mind'. This is at bottom the conception that equates 'mental' with 'content of consciousness': finding that meaning (referring) is not a kind of *experience* – something that comes before the mind – the modified sceptic concludes that it

[23] Or again, suppose that the concept of knowledge persisted in eluding philosophical analysis: should we then conclude that ascriptions of knowledge to people do not state facts – that knowledge 'vanishes into thin air'? How could the results (or lack of them) of philosophical analysis have such power?

is not something mental; but this move can be blocked simply by insisting, I think reasonably, that the realm of the mental is not confined to that of the experiential. The image of God peering into my mind that is invoked by the sceptic is the image of God observing the stream of my conscious experience, and it is true enough that what I mean and understand is not to be found *there*; but it does not follow that it is not, so to speak, in some other part of my mind – the part that houses *non-*experiential mental phenomena.[24] I think, therefore, that we may persist in speaking of meaning and referring and understanding as 'in my mind' and as forming part of my 'mental history'; so the irreducibility suggestion is not after all open to the modified paradox that meaning is not a *mental* fact.

Kripke does eventually come round to considering some kind of irreducibility thesis about meaning, but I do not find his treatment of it satisfactory. He begins by considering the suggestion that meaning something is a *sui generis* type of experience 'with its own special *quale*, known directly to each of us by introspection' (p. 41), somewhat like seeing yellow or having a headache. This suggestion is quickly and persuasively dispatched: introspection does not in point of fact encounter any such experience, and if it did it would not 'have the consequences of meaning'. But, of course, this is hardly the most favourable version of an irreducibility thesis – think again of an irreducibility thesis concerning character traits; and it is not the form that Kripke's own irreducibility thesis about reference (in *Naming and Necessity*) takes. Rather, the thesis will be that meaning (referring) belongs with the other sorts of mental concept for which an experiential account is inappropriate – belief, intention, bravery, etc. – and it is irreducible in (roughly) the way these are. Kripke does in fact at one point state what is the natural nonreductive view of meaning: 'it is simply a primitive state, not to be assimilated to sensations or headaches or any 'qualitative' states, nor to be assimilated to dispositions, but a state of a unique kind of its own' (p. 51): but I do not think that he gives the view its due. He begins by conceding that 'such a move may in a sense be irrefutable',

---

[24] This is, of course, just a metaphor; its literal purport is as follows: it is not only experiential phenomena ('states of consciousness') that are correctly characterised as 'mental' – there are non-experiential mental phenomena too (e.g. the propositional attitudes).

but then urges that it is 'desperate' and that it leaves the notion of meaning 'completely mysterious' (p. 51). Let me first remark that these accusations of desperation and mysteriousness are not fair as they stand: for it cannot in general be maintained that a claim of primitiveness on behalf of a concept is *eo ipso* desperate or mysterious – as we all know *some* concepts *have* to be taken as primitive.[25] What Kripke needs to show (and doesn't) is that a claim of primitiveness is desperate and mysterious in the present case. His position here resembles that of Quine on the analytic-synthetic distinction: one well-known response to Quine points out that not all concepts are definable by moving outside the family of concepts that are up for explication (consider the family of truth-functions), and that this is not in itself a particularly bad or mysterious thing.[26] Is not Kripke adopting essentially the same attitude here as Quine did to analyticity and synonymy in 'Two Dogmas of Empiricism', alleging mystery when no definition can be found 'in completely different terms'? And, as I observed earlier, does not Kripke himself elsewhere make a claim of primitiveness in respect of the concept of reference, urging that this is not something to get alarmed over if we have a right conception of the limitations of reductive philosophical analysis? In fact, since we can formulate Kripke's semantic scepticism in terms of the relation of reference, it seems that he is here in effect accusing his other self of desperate ploys and mystery-mongering; but I myself would say that this self-criticism is unjust.

Kripke follows up his accusation by trying to spell out just what the alleged mystery consists in. His first point is that meaning something 'is not supposed to be an introspectible state, yet we are supposedly aware of it with some fair degree of certainty whenever it occurs' (p. 51) – and that this in itself is mysterious. It is not easy to see just what Kripke's point is here, but I think it is something like the following: once we abandon the idea that meaning is an irreducible *experiential* state we have no account of the nature of our first-person knowledge of

[25] I mean merely that in any system of definitionally related concepts some of these concepts are not themselves defined. This does not imply any great mystery, so long as the undefined concepts are not in some way intrinsically suspect (so we may, for example, take some truth-functional connectives as primitive and define the rest on this primitive basis: there is nothing 'desperate' or 'mysterious' about *this*).

[26] See H.P. Grice and P.F. Strawson, 'In Defence of a Dogma', *Philosophical Review* LXV (1956), esp. pp. 147f.

meaning – we have no conception of how the non-experiential primitive state of meaning something is an object of distinctively first-person knowledge.[27] This point is surely misguided; for one thing it proves far too much. For we do not generally suppose that first-person knowledge of psychological states – the kind of knowledge one has just if the state actually obtains – is always of a 'qualitative' state of consciousness: consider the knowledge we have of our beliefs, thoughts, intentions, hopes, etc. – knowledge which displays a first-person/third-person asymmetry but which is not of anything *experiential* in character.[28] That is to say, there is a legitimate notion of 'introspection' which does not involve what Kripke describes as 'attending to the qualitative character of our own experiences' (p. 41): it is the kind of 'introspection' we employ when coming to know what we intend, believe and mean (we do not of course need to say that this faculty is absolutely infallible). How to give a philosophical *theory* of this kind of knowledge is of course a difficult and substantive question, but the lack of a theory of a phenomenon is not in itself a good reason to doubt the *existence* of the phenomenon. I therefore see no mystery-mongering in the claim that there are primitive non-experiential mental states which display a distinctive first-person epistemology. Why, indeed, should this be found any *more* mysterious on reflection than our capacity to know about our *sensations* whenever they occur? This too raises genuine and difficult philosophical questions, but Kripke does not say that the existence of the states known about is therefore in doubt, or that a claim of primitiveness (irreducibility) for sensations

[27] All we would achieve by (*per impossibile*) reducing meaning to an experiential state would be to assimilate one kind of introspective knowledge (first-person avowal) to another; we would not thereby have answered the question how we come to know our own mental states at all (make such avowals). And does the sceptical solution make the problem of accounting for our first-person knowledge of meaning any *more* tractable?

[28] Here I am disagreeing with Wittgenstein's well-known remark: 'It can't be said of me at all (except perhaps as a joke) that I *know* I am in pain' (246). This remark is, in fact, crucially ambiguous between: it would be literally *false* to say this, and: it would be odd or misleading or humorous to say this. I would agree with Wittgenstein under the second interpretation, but resist (for familiar reasons) the inference to the first interpretation. Of course, if we interpret Wittgenstein merely as warning us not to assimilate this kind of knowledge with other kinds (e.g. of the material world), then again I think he is quite right – but then he is putting the point needlessly hyperbolically.

leads to insoluble epistemological mysteries.[29] Our first-person knowledge of sensations seems to me to be no more pellucid and unproblematic than our first-person knowledge of our intentions – and of our meanings and concepts.

Kripke's second objection to the idea of a primitive non-experiential state of meaning is harder to evaluate because it raises some difficult questions about infinity and how we grasp it. This is the objection that there is a 'logical difficulty' in the very idea of a state of meaning addition by '+' because 'such a state would have to be a finite object, contained in our finite minds' (p. 52), and 'it remains mysterious exactly how the existence of *any* finite past state of my mind could entail that, if I wish to accord with it, and remember the state, and do not miscalculate, I must give a determinate answer to an arbitrarily large addition problem' (p. 53). Kripke's point here, insofar as I have a firm grasp on it, is a point about a sort of conceptual collision between the fact that our minds are 'finite' and the infinity of the objects we seem capable of referring to or meaning; thus he speaks of 'the problem of how our finite minds can give rules that are supposed to apply to an infinity of cases' (p. 54).[30] Now I have no wish to deny that our possession of infinitary concepts raises philosophical difficulties – notably how an infinite object such as the number series can be represented by a finite object (the mind or brain) – but I think that this is not a problem on which Kripke can legitimately rest his case; for this is a *special* problem about *mathematical* language and concepts, not a *general* problem about meaning as such – most words, after all, do not have (like '+') infinite extensions! Kripke's original paradox was intended to apply to *any* word or concept, and it concerned the normative hold of

[29] In assuming that first-person knowledge of meaning, construed as primitive state, must derive from 'attending to the "qualitative" character of our own experience', Kripke is able to charge that such a state, like experiences in general, could never determine a unique meaning (pp. 41–2); but this consideration lapses if we refuse so to characterise the primitive state of meaning something.

[30] Such (seeming) problems have encouraged views such as intuitionism and finitism – views which deny that we can have concepts capable of comprehending an actual infinity of objects. But these views are distant from those recommended by Kripke's sceptic. What he chiefly relies upon is the claim that any finite state could be interpreted in a nonstandard way. But if the state is specified simply as (e.g.) meaning addition by '+', then this is not so, since this specification just *does* determine a unique meaning (with infinitely many normative consequences); *it* is not susceptible of nonstandard interpretation.

present meaning over future use; the paradox would be of a quite different character if it came to rest upon the question how a finite mind represents an infinite object. This latter problem is a specific problem about *infinity*; it is not a general problem about the notion of *meaning*. It is true, of course, that the meaning of any word will have 'indefinitely many' consequences for use in future and counterfactual situations, and that the primitive state of meaning something by the word (or referring to something) will have in some way to 'generate' these consequences; but I cannot see that this raises any irresoluble 'logical difficulty' – at least none that could justify abandoning the notion of meaning altogether. For consider, by way of analogy, our beliefs and desires: do not they have 'indefinitely many' (normative and causal) consequences for action in different circumstances? A given desire may interact with any of a great many different beliefs to produce different actions in different circumstances, but this 'productive power' does not seem especially problematic or mysterious. Indeed, ordinary non-psychological states, dispositions and capacities (powers) appear to give rise to essentially the same kind of productivity: the same state or disposition placed in different circumstances at different times will produce 'indefinitely many' effects (token events); but is there really a 'logical difficulty' in the idea that (say) solubility is a property which can be manifested on 'indefinitely many' occasions, both future and counterfactual?[31] What happens in each of these cases is that the property in question – meaning, desire, solubility – *interacts* with the circumstances in which it is present in such a way as to determine a range of effects of certain kinds; we do not have to suppose that in some 'queer way' these effects are already present in the state in some shadowy form.[32] When a dog acquires the habit of extending a

---

[31] In the case of physical dispositions, the productivity is purely causal – there is no normative aspect to it; but this does not affect the point I am making. When a state has intentional content its causal productivity is coupled with a normative aspect which determines whether an event (say an utterance) is correct or incorrect. If it be asked how this normativity works, then the answer (according to the irreducibility thesis) is that it is simply in the nature of meaning to have normative consequences (as it is in the nature of moral values to determine what is right conduct).

[32] A concrete example might help here. Suppose I refer to Smith with 'Smith'; then there will be indefinitely many occasions on which this semantic fact determines what would be a correct use of 'Smith', e.g. occasions on which Smith is presented to me and

paw on demand it presumably comes to instantiate some 'finite state' which is the (causal) basis of its behaviour in 'indefinitely many' future and counterfactual situations: it acquires a 'disposition' to perform actions of a certain type in appropriate circumstances, and there seems no special problem about how the finite state underlying the disposition can have this kind of productivity. Somewhat similarly, according to Wittgenstein's conception of meaning, it is our natural propensities that underlie our meaning, and these propensities have the capacity to generate linguistic behaviour in 'indefinitely many' situations.[33] It seems to me, then, that Kripke has no cogent objection to the primitive state suggestion, i.e. to the idea that meaning or referring is an irreducible property of a person; and if I am right in this, then we have at least one solid line of resistance to the constitutive semantic sceptic.

The irreducibility thesis is one kind of 'straight solution' to Kripke's sceptical problem; it draws the sceptic's attention to a kind of fact he overlooked when he claimed that there are no facts to constitute meaning, namely facts about *meaning*. But are there any other possibilities for a straight solution? I believe that the prospects for a reductive or quasi-reductive straight solution are by no means as bleak as Kripke suggests. I shall consider three suggestions, noting their strengths and weaknesses; each of them has some claim to bolster our faith in the factuality of semantic ascriptions.

I begin with the suggestion that we make appeal to the 'causal theory of reference', a suggestion that seems eminently natural in view of Kripke's own (elsewhere expressed) views on what it is to refer to something with a name or a natural kind term.[34] If the relation of reference holds between a name and an object, then there is this normative consequence: the name is

---

I recognise him as Smith, and hence call him 'Smith'. Similarly for the recognitional application of predicates. Here we have semantic properties that interact with occasions of recognition and dictate correctness of use.

[33] See again 187 in which (in effect) semantic productivity is compared with counterfactuals about what someone would have done in virtue of possessing a trait of character. What ground the counterfactuals associated with meaning, according to Wittgenstein, are our spontaneous and natural ways of reacting, as these are fixed by our 'form of life'. These seem to me adequate materials for providing the requisite productivity.

[34] See *Naming and Necessity, passim.*

correctly used only in application to that object. Now we would have a basis for this normativeness if we had an account of what the relation of reference consists in: if reference is constituted by some relation R, then the use of a name in application to a particular object is correct just if the name stands in R to that object. We have agreed with Kripke that R cannot be derived from the actual application of the name, nor from states of consciousness, nor from simple linguistic dispositions; but what about Kripke's own suggestion, put forward in *Naming and Necessity*, that R is some kind of *causal* relation? Now I do not want here to go into the question whether the causal theory is right, nor into whether what Kripke suggests deserves to be called a 'causal' theory (as opposed to a 'chain of communication' theory); let us, for the sake of argument, suppose that such a theory is correct – reference is some kind of causal relation.[35] Then why not say that R is the (or a) causal relation, and hence that a use of a name is correct just if it involves applying the name to the object which lies at the origin of the causal chain leading up to that use? In the case of a natural kind predicate we can likewise say that such a predicate is correctly applied to an object just if that object is of the same kind as the original sample which initiated the causal chain leading up to that use. Does this type of theory exclude the kinds of nonstandard extension contrived by the semantic sceptic? It seems to me that it does, since it will not be true that the nonstandard extension figures as the *causal origin* of the use of the name or predicate. Thus the nonstandard extension *Kripnam* for 'Kripke', considered earlier, will not qualify for the simple reason that Putnam is causally isolated from my present use of 'Kripke' (or we can suppose as much): the sceptical hypothesis was that 'Kripke' correctly applies to Putnam after some future time t, but the causal theory can exclude this possibility by observing that it is *Kripke* who lies at the origin of the causal chain leading up to my present use of 'Kripke' – I need have had no causal contact with Putnam at all, still less the kind of causal contact that determines reference. Similarly, my current use of 'tiger' has a sample of *tigers* at its causal origin and not any aardvarks, so that the

---

[35] In fact, I disagree with causal theories: see my 'The Mechanism of Reference', *Synthese* 49 (1981). The point I am making in the text could however be recast in terms of the theory favoured in that paper (the 'contextual theory').

sceptic is defeated if he claims that 'tiger' might correctly apply to aardvarks after some future time t. Quite generally, a causal link theory of reference seems to have the resources to answer Kripke's constitutive sceptic; for it specifies a kind of fact which might be supposed to underlie the semantic relation of reference, and it does so in such a way as to meet the normativeness adequacy condition.

Why does Kripke not consider this kind of suggestion? It cannot be because he rejects the causal theory (or picture) of reference. Two possible explanations present themselves: first, he tends to formulate his sceptical problem in terms of the notion of meaning and not that of reference, thus closing off a natural line of reply; second, he concentrates on mathematical examples, for which a causal account of reference is notoriously problematic.[36] Neither explanation, however, justifies Kripke's neglect of the causal reply to his sceptic: first, because the sceptical problem *can* be readily reformulated (at least for some categories of expressions) as a problem about the semantic property of reference; second, because the problem is supposed to afflict *all* kinds of expressions (and concepts), not just the mathematical. Maybe there is a residual and special problem about what constitutes reference in mathematical language; but this does not affect other sorts of language and is anyway only to be expected in view of the peculiar issues that arise in the philosophy of mathematics. So it seems to me that the causal theory is at least a serious *candidate* for a straight solution: it supplies some conception of the *sort* of fact that reference might be supposed to consist in. Whether we prefer this solution to the irreducibility thesis obviously depends upon our general attitude to irreducibility theses and upon our estimate of the plausibility of the causal theory; these are not matters I propose to adjudicate here: my purpose is simply to lay out the available options for responding to Kripke's sceptic.[37]

---

[36] See P. Benacerraf, 'Mathematical Truth', *Journal of Philosophy* LXX, (1973). I suspect that a good deal of the initial plausibility of the sceptic's case comes from reliance upon special features of mathematical terms and concepts, since mathematics is already philosophically puzzling in a number of respects not shared by ordinary empirical discourse: it wouldn't look so compelling, I think, if the sceptic *began* with (say) proper names and natural kind predicates.

[37] In Kripke's version of the causal theory, that theory is explicitly nonreductive (see *Naming and Necessity*, p. 97). We may therefore construe Kripke's causal 'picture' as

The second suggestion I want to mention is interesting chiefly as a demonstration that Kripke must extend his paradox to concepts if he is to block certain kinds of reply to the sceptical paradox: the suggestion is that we explain semantic facts in Gricean terms, i.e. in terms of the propositional attitudes which accompany the use of sentences.[38] This proposal is natural because the Gricean programme is precisely a programme of semantic *reduction*: it claims to reduce semantic facts to psychological facts of certain kinds, in such a way that semantic vocabulary can always in principle be replaced by psychological vocabulary, which latter vocabulary provides an adequate conceptual *analysis* of that semantic vocabulary. In short, a Gricean is precisely someone who is out to tell us what meaning *consists in* in 'completely different terms'. Again, let us not concern ourselves with the prospects and motivation for such a reductive programme; let us assume for present purposes that it is both well-conceived and feasible. Then it seems that the Gricean has a reply to the question what it is to mean addition by '+', or to mean today by '+' what one meant by it yesterday: it is to utter sentences containing '+' with the intention to get one's audience to believe something involving (the concept of) *addition* by means of their recognition of that intention (this is intended only as a rough statement of the basic idea). For example, for me to mean by '5 + 7 = 12' that 5 *added* (not *quadded*) to 7 equals 12 is for me to utter this sentence with the intention of producing in my audience the belief that 5 *added* (not *quadded*) to 7 equals 12 by means. . . . And similarly for what it is to mean the *same* thing by '+' over time. Now this Gricean analysis of meaning *does* answer Kripke's 'metalinguistic sceptic'; for it does tell us what sort of fact meaning something consists in. But of course it does so only by presupposing that *concept possession*, on the part of the speaker and his audience, is itself unproblematic; for it simply *uses* the notions of intention and belief with determinate conceptual content. So Kripke has to extend his scepticism to

---

telling us something substantial about what reference is, but doing so without breaking out of the intentional circle. This seems to me the best strategy for convincingly resisting the semantic sceptic's claim: for it ministers to his worries about factuality without conceding his reductionist presupposition.

[38] See H.P. Grice, 'Meaning', *Philosophical Review* LXVI (1957), and subsequent work in this tradition.

concept possession if he is to rebut the Gricean reply. Indeed, the Gricean reply strongly suggests that the *primary* locus of the sceptical paradox must be at the level of concepts or thought, since the Gricean reduction (assuming it successful) would convert the semantic problem into a special case of the conceptual problem. Not only does Kripke himself not see the matter this way but, as I indicated earlier, the reductionist assumption is even more glaring and objectionable-seeming when the paradox is aimed directly at concepts. So I think we should say that while the Gricean reply does not as it stands offer a straight solution to the underlying or extended sceptical argument, it does help to bring out the true character of that argument – I believe to its detriment.[39]

The third suggestion invokes the notion of *capacity* in order to give a straight solution; let us initially consider this suggestion in application to concept possession. We have become familiar enough with the idea that having a concept is having a certain sort of capacity; the idea perhaps has its origins in Wittgenstein's discussions of these matters.[40] The conspicuous presence of the notion of capacity (technique) in Wittgenstein's writings makes it somewhat surprising that Kripke does not bring up the suggestion that facts about capacities might supply what the sceptic says cannot be supplied; perhaps he assumes that this is just the dispositional suggestion in other words and so does not feel the need to treat it separately. If this is his assumption, then (as I shall explain) I think it is mistaken; the capacity suggestion is distinct from the dispositional suggestion and is better placed than it is to provide a suitable constitutive fact. The identification of concepts with capacities can of course take a variety of forms, depending upon the type of concept in question and the type of capacity

[39] Possibly Kripke does not consider this Gricean reply because it is alien to Wittgenstein's own views; certainly Wittgenstein's text shows no trace of the kind of idea later developed by Grice and others. Also, such theories give a priority to thought over language, which is not in line with Wittgenstein's own views about the relation between thought and language (see, e.g., 25, 327–32, 342).

[40] For a discussion of this type of view of concepts, see P.T. Geach, *Mental Acts* (Routledge and Kegan Paul: London, 1957), esp. chap. 5. Geach himself agrees with some versions of this type of view, but disagrees with others. Views of this type are primarily distinguished from one another by what they take concepts to be capacities *to do*; but for our purposes these detailed questions can be ignored – we are concerned with this as a general approach to concepts.

deemed appropriate; let us for simplicity consider the simplest and most familiar case, *viz.* observational concepts and the recognitional capacities associated with them. A natural idea then is that to possess the concept *red* or *square* is to have the capacity to discriminate, recognise or identify red or square things and to classify them accordingly: such a capacity might be manifested by calling the objects by the same name ('red', 'square') or by a non-linguistic action such as grouping the objects into the appropriate classes. Thus in teaching a child an observational concept one expects to produce in the child a capacity to classify objects according to the concept – one sees for example whether the child puts a new red object in a pile along with those already classified as red or calls a new object by the appropriate predicate. Thus having an observational concept is conceived as a capacity to make a distinctive discriminative response upon being (perceptually) presented with objects falling under the concept in question; so if the capacity theorist is asked what kind of fact concept possession consists in, he will reply by citing capacities of the kind described. Now I do not wish to assert that this kind of account of concepts is free from all difficulties, even for the simple case of observational concepts; but I do think that it deserves a hearing by Kripke's sceptic, for it has the look of something that supplies just what we need: we can say that a thought has a content involving the concept *red* and not *gred* in virtue of the fact that the thought involves the exercise of a capacity to recognise *red* things and not *gred* things (the person may not even *have* this latter capacity or indeed he may be incapable of coming to have it, e.g. if he cannot keep track of time – 'gred' being defined by reference to a temporal parameter). The capacity to discriminate red things is a *different* capacity from the capacity to discriminate objects belonging to some nonstandardly defined class (the extension of the sceptic's alternative concept), and so we can find a basis for the distinction between possessing the concept *red* and possessing some nonstandard concept compatible with all the applications made hitherto. In Kripke's favourite example, the suggestion would be that it is the concept of *addition* that I exercise when I do computations involving '+', and not the concept of *quaddition*, because the capacity that gets brought to bear is the capacity *to add* and not *to quadd*, where the former capacity is conceived as a capacity

to recognise what is the *sum* of pairs of numbers. It is then easy
to see how, once we have applied the notion of capacity to
concepts, we can give an account of meaning employing the
same materials: to mean addition by '+' is to *associate* with
'+' the capacity to add, i.e. to exercise *that* capacity in response
to questions involving '+'; to mean red by 'red' is to exercise the
capacity to discriminate red things when asked to judge
whether 'red' applies to a presented object.[41] No doubt this is
crude and incomplete as an account of concepts and meaning,
but it does seem to provide us with the beginnings of an answer
to the question what *kind* of fact meaning and concept
possession consist in.

We might be reminded at this point of Dummett-type
questions about meaning in relation to recognitional capacities:
for Dummett has suggested conceiving linguistic understanding
as a recognitional capacity – the capacity to verify or falsify the
sentence concerned – and this is tantamount to the suggestion
that concept possession be explained in terms of capacities to
verify and falsify sentences.[42] And it is not really surprising that
Dummett should make play with something that might serve to
answer Kripke's sceptic, since Dummett's own favourite
question is what knowledge of meaning *consists in*; Dummett
in effect presses for the same kind of reductive account of
meaning as does Kripke's sceptic, though Dummett does so *via*
the notion of *knowledge* of meaning.[43] But if we do direct the
Dummettian conception of meaning and concepts at Kripke's
sceptic, we immediately encounter a question which ought to

[41] This association may be explained in different ways, but there is doubtless some
sense in which it is conventional: on the view under consideration, the meaning of a
word in a language can be represented as a mapping from words to mental capacities
(concepts), which may be set up by whatever establishes linguistic conventions. No
question is begged by invoking this notion of association, since Kripke's problem is
clearly *not* what determines a unique mapping from words to (determinately
possessed) concepts (if it were, it would not be difficult to solve).

[42] See Dummett, 'What is a Theory of Meaning? (II)', in *Truth and Meaning*, eds. G.
Evans and J. McDowell (Clarendon Press: Oxford, 1976).

[43] Thus Dummett wants an account of meaning which does not take any semantic
concept as primitive: more specifically, the content of linguistic knowledge (knowledge
of the meaning of sentences) should be explicable without attributing to the speaker
primitive grasp of semantic concepts – and indeed without taking his grasp of the
concepts expressed by the sentence as primitive (see 'What is a Theory of Meaning?', in
Mind and Language, ed. S. Guttenplan (Clarendon Press: Oxford, 1975)). In effect,
Dummett is here rejecting 'naive realism' about meaning and concepts.

give us pause: namely, does the capacity suggestion have verificationist or anti-realist consequences? The danger is that we may be forced to choose between Dummettian verificationism and Kripkean semantic scepticism: for if we answer Kripke by adopting Dummett's conception of understanding, then we seem to commit ourselves to verificationism; whereas if we abandon the capacity suggestion, then we do not have at least *this* answer to the Kripkean sceptic.[44] Consider '+' again: is it true that my understanding of '+' consists in or involves a capacity to add arbitrary pairs of numbers? Well, it certainly seems wrong to ascribe to me the capacity to give the sum of *any* pair of numbers, for essentially the reasons Kripke brings against the dispositional theorist: some numbers are simply too big for me to take in (in standard notation) and some computations are too lengthy for me to perform in my lifetime; for these reasons I lack the ability to add *arbitrary* pairs of numbers. One response to this concession is Kripke's: there is no fact for meaning addition by '+' to consist in – the capacity suggestion doesn't work, at least for infinitary cases. Another response is Dummett's: keep the capacity suggestion and go verificationist or finitist or anti-realist, i.e. maintain that there is in reality no more to my grasp of the meaning of '+' than the finite capacities for verification which I actually have – the meaning of '+' thus turns out to be other than what we naively and realistically supposed. This is an unwelcome dilemma for a realist who wants to believe in the factuality of meaning, and I think we should do our best to avoid it. Fortunately, our options are not closed: we can either drop the capacity suggestion and have recourse to our other replies to Kripke's sceptic; or we can construe the capacity suggestion more liberally than hitherto – we can abandon the observational model and propose a more catholic and flexible conception of the sorts of capacities in which concept possession consists. The natural way to develop the latter alternative would be to go for a more 'holistic' account of what it is to possess a concept, including perhaps the logical principles into which reasoning

---

[44] Rather as we seem forced to choose between Dummettian verificationism and Quinean indeterminacy when we try to construe understanding in terms of a capacity to recognise the truth: see my 'Truth and Use', in *Reference, Truth and Reality*, ed. M. Platts (Routledge and Kegan Paul: London, 1980), pp. 32–3.

with the concepts concerned embeds.[45] I shall not here pursue
the question how satisfactory this modified capacity suggestion
would be as an account of concept possession and meaning; my
purpose has been merely to point out that there are possibilities
here that Kripke's sceptic has not explored. Even if there were
difficulties of principle in the way of extending the capacity
suggestion to the non-observational parts of language, still the
applicability of that suggestion to observational concepts
would be a substantial victory against Kripke's sceptic: for his
claim was that we have *no* account of what sort of fact meaning
consists in, and for observational predicates at any rate it seems
that we do. The account may be rough and incomplete, but it
does show that there are *some* words for which we have an
adequate enough reply to the sceptic – even accepting his
reductionist presuppositions.

I have yet to explain why the capacity suggestion is distinct
from the dispositional suggestion. The reason is that it appears
wrong to analyse capacities in terms of the sorts of counterfactuals Kripke considers when he is articulating the dispositional
suggestion. To suppose that such an analysis is correct is to
suppose that someone has the capacity to φ if and only if were
conditions C to obtain he would φ, where conditions C do not
include the (circular) condition that the person is exercising the
capacity to φ. Thus in the case of recognitional capacities the
idea would be that someone has the capacity to recognise red
things if and only if were a red object perceptually presented to
him he would classify it as red. There are grounds for thinking
this type of analysis neither necessary nor sufficient for having
the capacity in question. The basic problem here is that what a
person is disposed to do depends upon a lot more than the
capacities he has: gross dispositions of the kind considered by
Kripke reflect the summation of factors operating on a person
to produce his behaviour; they do not capture the separate
contributions of the various factors which together lead to

---

[45] This is, in effect, Quine's position: see his 'Two Dogmas of Empiricism', in *From a
Logical Point of View* (Harvard University Press: Cambridge, Mass., 1953). Dummett
criticises holism in a number of places, e.g. 'Frege's Distinction between Sense and
Reference', in *Truth and Other Enigmas*, pp. 134f. Any version of holism that had a
chance of working would have to be moderate, not extreme: it would not constitutively
link possession of a concept *C* with *every* other concept possessed by the person in
question, but only with some distinguished proper subset. I shall not here inquire into
the details of how this would go.

behaviour. The concept of a disposition, at least of the simple kind we are considering, is (so to speak) a *vector* concept – it aggregates distinct factors or forces to give a gross result; and a person's capacities are just *one* factor operative in determining his behaviour on a particular occasion. More concretely, the same overall disposition could result from different capacities if other extraneous factors intervene, and different dispositions could result from the same capacity for the same sort of reason. One important way in which capacities and dispositions can come thus apart is through the possibility of *mistake*: two people could both have the capacity to classify red things on the basis of their appearance, but one of them fails to do so when presented with a red object because he believes his senses to be functioning abnormally – he is then *able* to do what he is not *disposed* to do (as determined by the appropriate counterfactual). Or again, I have the capacity to dial telephone numbers, but in some circumstances I make mistakes; it is not a necessary condition of possessing an ability that one *always* exercise it correctly – other factors can interfere in such a way as to falsify the counterfactuals that purport to capture what it is to have the capacity. For similar reasons a counterfactually specified disposition is not *sufficient* for having an ability: we can conceive of set-ups in which a person is disposed to φ in conditions C but he has not the ability to φ – he gets the disposition from some source other than the possession of the ability. Thus God or a brain scientist could bring about in you a disposition to φ in condition C otherwise than by endowing you with the *ability* to φ: he just causes φ-ing behaviour in you whenever you try to φ without setting up in you any *competence* at φ-ing. The general point here is that the notion of a capacity is more subtle and restrictive than anything that can be delivered by the sorts of counterfactuals Kripke considers in relation to the dispositional suggestion.[46] Indeed, capacities elude dispositional analysis in ways strikingly similar to the ways meaning does according to Kripke – a consideration which ought to reinforce the idea that meaning and capacity are notions that belong together. (None of this is to say that capacities are not dispositional in a weaker sense, i.e. not

---

[46] The same can be said of character traits and propositional attitudes: the materials provided by a counterfactually specified dispositional analysis are simply too coarse to yield up these concepts.

'occurrent'; it is only to deny that capacities are dispositional in the specific sense discussed by Kripke.)

I suppose that someone will want to protest that the capacity suggestion fails to answer Kripke's sceptic because the same kinds of questions arise about what it is to possess one capacity rather than another: that is, actual behaviour underdetermines capacity possessed, and states of consciousness and dispositions likewise do not determine one's capacities. Therefore, it may be said, capacity ascriptions are just as unfactual as ascriptions of meaning. I think it is clear that this protest is misplaced: it can be prompted only by an unargued reductionism about the notion of *capacity* – a reluctance to accept that capacities might be factual just as they stand. And there is plainly no interest in a kind of scepticism which insists, with respect to *any* constitutive suggestion that is produced, that we provide a reductive answer to the question what *that* sort of fact consists in: the assumption of an unduly restrictive conception of the realm of the factual becomes altogether too blatant. So it seems to me that no questions are begged by taking capacity concepts as primitive for present purposes.[47]

Does the capacity suggestion account for normativeness? The notion of normativeness Kripke wants captured is a transtemporal notion: it is the idea of present use being in accord with past meaning; a linguistic mistake accordingly consists in no longer using a word with the meaning one originally intended (without of course intending to introduce a change of meaning by explicit stipulation). We have an account of this normativeness when we have two things: (*a*) an account of what it is to mean something at a given time and (*b*) an account of what it is to mean the *same* thing at two different times – since (Kripkean) normativeness is a matter of meaning now what one meant earlier. Put in these terms, it is easy to supply what we require: to mean addition by '+' at *t* is to associate with '+' the capacity to add at *t*, and to mean the same by '+' at *t'* is to associate with '+' the *same capacity* at *t'* as at *t*. A

[47] Capacities are, of course, distinguished (individuated) by what they are capacities *to do*; so there is no particular difficulty in saying what a *difference* of capacity consists in. This leaves open two further questions, however: what *grounds* the capacity, i.e. what its physical basis is; and how we *test* whether someone has a given capacity. It does not seem to me that we have to answer either of *these* questions to be entitled to invoke capacities in the way I have to answer the sceptic. But I see no difficulty of principle in answering these questions, if I were pressed to do so.

linguistic mistake would thus consist in (unwittingly) coming to associate with a given word a different capacity (i.e. concept) from that associated with that word earlier: this might happen if by some drug (as Kripke would say) I tomorrow come to associate the capacity to recognise green things with the word 'red' – so that if someone asks me then whether 'red' applies to an object I establish whether it is green and if it is I say 'yes'. In the same way I might undergo a mental change which causes me to deploy my capacity to *quadd* in association with the word '+'; I would then be using '+' wrongly, i.e. wrongly relative to my previous use of it. Linguistic normativeness, in the sense invoked by Kripke, is a matter of a standing intention to use words with the same meaning over time unless by explicit intentional change of meaning; this standing intention is fulfilled if one's association of words with capacities remains constant over time (the same could be said, *mutatis mutandis*, with respect to the other constitutive suggestions we have considered).[48]

We are not, I think, forced to make a choice from among the possible responses to Kripke's sceptic I have set forth; each may be supposed to capture one aspect of the truth about concepts and meaning (reference), and each allows us to beat off the sceptic's attack. Probably the irreducibility response is the most significant in exposing the true character of the scepticism; and I suspect (though I have not claimed to show it) that we cannot ultimately dispense with an irreducibility claim if we are to preserve the full factuality of the notion of meaning.[49] The other suggestions help bring out the *kind* of thing meaning is, but I think they are best seen as providing us with a 'picture' of meaning and not as amounting to a full-

[48] It might be asked how the capacity suggestion accounts for normativeness *at* a time, without reference to what was meant earlier. Suppose that at *t* I associate with '+' the capacity to add; then, on the capacity view, I mean addition by '+' at *t*. I use '+' *correctly* at *t* just if I apply '+' to pairs of numbers such that I will exercise my capacity to *add* them if I am asked (and certain other conditions are fulfilled); I would use '+' incorrectly at *t* if I broke the conventional association by using it to report the result of my (say) exercising the capacity to *subtract* the second number from the first.

[49] If semantic or intentional notions are indeed irreducible, then we can *only* preserve the factuality of meaning and concepts by at some point using these notions primitively. What we might hope for, beyond this, is some account of how these concepts mesh with others – in particular, how their instantiation is constrained by other sorts of fact (e.g. physical). In other words, we might combine some sort of supervenience thesis with insistence upon irreducibility.

blown *reduction* of it: and this is I think enough to justify our confidence that talk of meaning is not talk of the mythical – we do not have to worry that meaning 'vanishes into thin air', as Kripke puts it (p. 22). We do not then have to succumb to that 'eerie feeling' (p. 21) Kripke reports upon contemplating his sceptical paradox.

So far I have confined my discussion to the constitutive question: I now wish to make some brief remarks about the epistemological question. This question concerns the character and quality of the *justifications* we commonly rely upon in ascribing meaning and concepts to ourselves and others: is there room here for an interesting form of epistemological scepticism? I shall argue that there is no real novelty in the brand of epistemological scepticism Kripke brings against our customary ascriptions of meaning. Let us first consider first-person knowledge of past meaning, this being Kripke's original way into his sceptical problem: can I now justify my belief that yesterday I meant addition by '+'? This is not, as Kripke is careful to point out, a question about the reliability of memory – we can assume that scepticism about memory is not at issue; the question is rather whether, assuming memory to give us access to past facts, there is anything *available* to it about my past use of signs which might be used to justify my present semantic convictions. And then Kripke's epistemological sceptic contends that be my memory never so perfect it will not tell me whether my present use is faithful to my past meaning – for the facts available to memory are compatible with alternative hypotheses as to what I meant, i.e. facts about my past use, states of consciousness and dispositions to use.

Two replies may I think be made to this sceptical challenge. The first is that the sceptic is far too restrictive in the sorts of facts he takes to be (in principle) available to memory: why not say, taking a cue from the irreducibility thesis, that I can now remember precisely what I *meant* yesterday? For there is surely nothing wrong with the general claim that one can remember what one meant by a word: I might remember, for instance, that I used to mean *uninterested* by 'disinterested'. And if this is generally allowable, then I *can* now justify the correctness of my present inclination with '+' – simply by re-calling that in the past I meant *addition* by '+' and not quaddition. This seems no more problematic in principle than remembering what I believed or intended or felt; it is remembering a fact about my 'mental history'. All that is required of me is that I store in memory what I earlier *knew*, namely that it was addition that I meant. So if a sceptic presses me to justify my present use in terms of some fact about my past use I can reply by observing that I have a clear memory of having meant addition; and this seems sufficient to reduce the sceptic to silence. If he asks me for some other kind of justification – some remembered fact from which I might *infer* my past meaning – then we can oblige him (though we need not) by citing the causal origin of my present use, or the Gricean intentions with which I uttered sentences in the past, or the capacities I associated with the word in question. Thus I remember that Kripke was the cause of my initial use of 'Kripke'[50] (I have no memory of ever having been in causal contact with Putnam); I remember that I used to intend to produce in my audience beliefs about addition when I uttered sentences containing '+'; and I remember that I used to exercise my capacity to recognise red things when asked whether 'red' applies to a perceived object. Of course my memory might, logically, be deceptive, but that is not to the point – if it were then we would be dealing with a *general* scepticism about our knowledge of the past in memory. In short, the suggested constitutive facts seem capable of serving equally as responses to the epistemological sceptic, since they are facts about which the speaker had knowledge at the earlier time.[51]

The second reply we might make is to question whether the sceptic is entitled to seize upon the alleged fact that the evidence about the past to which we now have access

---

[50]This is most straightforward in the case in which the speaker was present at the initial baptism and so (in principle) can remember who was at the origin of the causal chain. For cases in which this is not so, e.g. long-dead historical figures, the speaker will have (typically) no memory-based knowledge by reference to which he can justify his current use of the name. In such cases it seems right to say that his use may be *determined* as correct or incorrect by the facts concerning the actual causal history of the name, but he may not himself be able to *give* a justification of the desired kind for his use of the name. This would be a case in which the constitutive and epistemological questions come apart. (Such cases do not seem to arise when we restrict ourselves, as Kripke in fact does, to the idiolect.)

[51] But even if the suggested constitutive facts did not do double duty, this would not vitiate their claim to answer the sceptic: what matters is whether the suggested facts render current use right or wrong, not whether the speaker is in a position justifiably to *assert* which of these obtains.

underdetermines what we then meant. The replies I just made did not concede this to the sceptic, since the remembered facts were held to be *constitutive* of past meaning; but we can also question the idea that evidential underdetermination is in itself a good reason for scepticism – or a good reason to claim that we are here confronted with an interestingly *novel* kind of scepticism. It is true enough that my past applications of a sign do not logically exclude sceptical alternatives as to what I earlier meant; but is this not a familiar epistemological problem in those cases in which our knowledge is admittedly inferential? In fact, is this not essentially the standard epistemological problem concerning inductive knowledge, i.e. knowledge of that which transcends what we have directly observed? It is not that I have a general solution to this kind of epistemological problem, nor that I believe such problems spurious; my point is just that this kind of scepticism has been with us a long time – so no essentially *new* problem is raised by the underdetermination of meaning by actual use (similarly for capacities and their actual exercise). This point becomes more evident when we switch to the third-person case. Suppose we allow, as seems reasonable, that the evidence I have for another's meaning consists in his actual applications of his words; then the sceptic will be able to contrive alternative ascriptions of meaning which are logically compatible with this evidence, simply by considering the possibility of a future divergence of use from that predicted by the standard ascription of meaning. This is so simply because the use that meaning determines transcends the use upon the basis of which specific meanings are ascribed.[52] But this is surely not at all surprising when we consider the ascription of capacities and

---

[52] Because of the normative aspect of semantic properties, we need, as ascribers of meaning, to move from what the speaker *actually* does with his words to what he *ought* to do with them, since this is what determines his meaning; and for this we need to employ criteria for judging linguistic mistakes. No doubt this is a holistic and heuristic matter, not to be algorithmically settled by simple and local tests. The case of meaning is not unique in this respect: consider determining someone's moral values on the basis of what he actually does, or what an agent judges rational given only his behaviour (think here of the complexities introduced by the normative phenomenon of weakness of will). It is not surprising, when one distances oneself from one's unreflective practice in ascribing such properties to others, that it can seem that there is here massive and ineradicable underdetermination of theory by evidence. Still, it is something we readily learn how to do in the course of making sense of others.

dispositions to people and things. Just consider the ascription of solubility to salt: we commonly suppose that salt would dissolve in water at any place or time (subject to the usual assumptions about background conditions), but we have not tested salt for solubility everywhere in the universe or at all future times; and so a sceptic might urge that our evidence does not logically exclude the ascription to salt of *quolubility*, where a substance is quoluble if it is soluble at all places other than place *p* or times other than time *t*, at which place or time it explodes. By hypothesis we have never tested salt for solubility in those circumstances, so what makes us so sure that salt would dissolve and not explode in the untested conditions? What indeed. Clearly there is an epistemological question here which trades upon the underdetermination of what we believe by our evidence for it (i.e. there is no logical entailment), but it is a question with which we are thoroughly familiar. It seems to me that the question about meaning is not different in kind: when we ascribe a particular meaning to someone's words we expect him to behave in the future in a certain way, and this expectation is not grounded in any *logical entailment* from the evidence that prompts it. If we think of meaning in terms of capacities, then the problem is what justifies an ascription of one capacity rather than another given that both ascriptions are logically consistent with the evidence we have. The problem is not I think unreal, but it is not a new problem; at best it is an old problem applied to a new subject-matter.[53] (Actually, of course, problems of the underdetermination of meaning by behaviour had already been raised by Quine in connexion with the compatibility of stimulus meaning with rival interpretations of terms; what Kripke's sceptic adds is the inductive or future-oriented dimension.[54]) However, with respect to the original first-person sceptical problem, it seems to me that we are rather better off; for we can appeal to remembered facts about past

[53] Kripke says: 'Wittgenstein has invented a new form of scepticism. Personally I am inclined to regard it as the most radical and original sceptical problem that philosophy has seen to date, one that only a highly unusual cast of mind could have produced' (p. 60). As will be clear from the text, I think this is at best an exaggeration.

[54] We might say: Quine plus Goodman equals Kripke. That is to say, once we notice the inductive underdetermination of meaning by use, we have the prospect of 'grue'-like semantic predicates – which is of course exactly what 'means quaddition' is. Ascriptions of meaning are *predictive* of use, and so raise the standard inductive problem (along with the extra normative dimension).

meaning (etc.) and hence justify our conviction that today we are using words correctly.[55] Of course such memory claims are always fallible, but it is an uninteresting form of scepticism which would try to make capital out of fallibility alone.

I turn now to Kripke's sceptical solution. If our reflections so far have been correct, there is no need of such a solution; the alleged paradox has been resolved by means of a straight solution. Kripke's reason for proposing an assertibility conditions account of the significance of semantic sentences, an account in which the community figures essentially, therefore lapses: we have been given no cogent reason to revise our naive belief that ascriptions of meaning and rule-following are made true by individualistic facts. But we can still ask, independently of the threat of a sceptical paradox, whether there is anything to be said for characterising the assertibility conditions of semantic sentences in terms of community responses – and indeed whether the notion of a community has *any* essential role to play in explaining what it is for someone to mean something or to follow a rule. Let us begin by getting some possible objections to the sceptical solution out of the way.

I would not think it proper to object to Kripke's sceptical solution on the quite general ground that it can *never* be correct to replace a fact-stating model of a specific region of discourse with some kind of 'non-cognitivist' model. For I think it is entirely possible that some one kind of sentence exerts an illicit grip on our conception of other kinds, so that we are prone, as philosophers, to assimilate all kinds of sentences to that one kind. Thus sentences concerning the observable material world are apt to strike us as providing a model for all other kinds of sentence, by dint perhaps of their centrality and ontogenetic primacy; and it may well be that, e.g., mathematical discourse has been wrongly assimilated to this model. I take it that Wittgenstein himself held something of the same view in his insistence that different language-games should be approached

---

[55] As with Quine's indeterminacy thesis, the (alleged) problem is apt to lose its force when considered from the first-person perspective: we seem to have 'privileged access' to our own present meanings (*I* know I mean rabbits by 'rabbit' and addition by '+' even if *you* must be forever unsure what I mean). Compare the question of the intrinsic character of my colour experience.

without prejudice as to their functioning, and that they may turn out to differ radically in how they work.[56] Some philosophers have indeed suggested that the case of mathematics should be treated by giving up a fact-stating or referential conception of the meaning of mathematical sentences and replacing it with an account of their assertibility conditions (proof-conditions) and their utility in empirical applications.[57] This kind of 'non-cognitivist' proposal can be motivated by considering what sorts of facts would have to be supposed stated if referential truth conditions were assigned to mathematical sentences, *viz.* facts about a super-sensible non-spatial world of abstract entities. We can perhaps solve the metaphysical and epistemological problems raised by the fact-stating conception in this area by adopting a 'sceptical solution', i.e. explain mathematical meaning in terms of proof and empirical applications. Ethical discourse is another area in which it has seemed desirable to some to reject a fact-stating model in favour of (in effect) an assertibility conditions theory (emotivism). These views may or may not be correct, but I do not think they can be dismissed just on general semantic grounds.[58] Similarly, we can certainly consider the *possibility* that semantic discourse itself is not fact-stating but has some other interpretation (actually this is Quine's view, put in other terms[59]).

A second objection that I think can be answered is that

---

[56] See, e.g., 24, 65; in 1 Wittgenstein in effect suggests that mathematical language works quite differently from other kinds of discourse. And his treatment of sensations largely consists in questioning the assimilation of words for sensations to words for material objects (see esp. 290–1).

[57] This is the view of H. Field, *Science Without Numbers* (Blackwell: Oxford, 1980). There is some similarity between Field's view and Wittgenstein's as expressed in 1: both emphasise empirical applications and wish to do away with a Platonist ontology.

[58] Of course there are plenty of sentences that are meaningful without being fact-stating, e.g. imperatives; and there are others that are grammatically indicative but functionally non-fact-stating, notably explicit performatives. J.L. Austin, indeed, was largely occupied with shrinking the domain of the fact-stating ('constative') and hence recognising different sorts of meaningful sentence: see his *How to Do Things with Words* (Oxford University Press, 1962).

[59] Quine does not suppose that semantic sentences are simply meaningless, or that 'true' cannot be applied to them (he is a redundancy theorist about 'true'), but he denies that they succeed in stating facts; their role is rather that of a practically useful 'dramatic idiom' which at present we cannot dispense with (see *Word and Object*, p. 219). This is, effectively, a kind of sceptical solution to a sceptical paradox: the speech act of ascribing meaning is to be seen not as fact-stating but as a kind of non-literal dramatisation of the result of our projecting ourselves into the state of mind of the other.

Kripke's non-cognitivist theory accounts for only *some* uses of semantic sentences, namely those in which we ascribe meaning to a person's words in the context of certifying him as a member of our linguistic community; it does not account for the employment of semantic notions in other contexts, notably when doing linguistic theory. That is, it seems that when we are doing *pure* semantics, e.g. in model-theoretic metalogic, we cannot be using semantic words in the way Kripke's sceptical solution suggests – for we are not in such a context ascribing meaning to anyone at all, let alone certifying community membership. How then can Kripke explain the significance of these 'pure' uses? We can see what Kripke ought to say to this objection (he does not raise the objection himself) if we compare semantic discourse with the case of mathematics again. Someone who wishes to explain the significance of mathematical sentences in terms of their empirical applications has to face the fact that some mathematics is *pure*: that is, there are meaningful uses of mathematical sentences outside the context of empirical applications. Now it must I think be admitted that the existence of formal semantics and of pure mathematics does raise a *prima facie* difficulty for views which emphasise the concrete applications of semantic and mathematical vocabulary, but it is possible to predict the sort of reply that might be made to this objection: the natural suggestion is that the pure uses are in some way *parasitic* on the basic uses in concrete applications. Thus it will be said that semantic concepts take their rise from the sorts of community application Kripke sketches but that they can then take on a measure of autonomy: their proper home is in the context of community ascriptions, but they can be abstracted away from this and considered more theoretically (e.g. in constructing formal theories of truth). Somewhat similarly, it will be said that mathematical concepts are conceived in the womb of empirical applications, but that once these concepts are born into the world they can take on a life of their own and hence be investigated in abstraction from particular applications. The availability of this kind of dependency thesis with respect to pure semantics and pure mathematics thus makes it difficult to press the objection that the non-cognitivist account covers only some of the ground; so I think that Kripke need not be especially worried by this objection.[60]

The third inconclusive objection I want to mention is that the sceptical solution involves a vicious regress.[61] The sceptical paradox threatens to undermine our ascription of rules to ourselves and others; the sceptical solution aims to preserve such ascriptions in the face of their unfactuality by providing an alternative account of what is involved in the ascription of rules. The alternative account uses the idea of assertibility conditions for a semantic sentence (or criteria for ascribing a semantic predicate); but this idea is precisely the idea of *rules* for assertion (or ascription) – so has not the sceptical solution presupposed what it undertook to explain? It is certainly true that the sceptical solution itself employs the notion of a rule of assertion in its account of the meaning of 'he is following rule *R* in using sign *S*'; but this is objectionable only if the claim was to give a *reductive analysis* of the notion of a rule, or to dispense with this notion altogether. However, this is not how the sceptical solution is intended: it is intended only as a descriptive account of the language-game of ascribing mastery of rules to people, not as an account of what following a rule *consists in*. There is thus no objection to applying the account to itself: that is, we can legitimately ask what are the rules for asserting that someone is correctly following the rules for asserting that another is following a rule – and we can expect to be given assertibility conditions for when assertibility conditions (i.e. assertion rules) are being correctly followed. There is indeed a regress here, but it is not vicious, since we are not setting out to explain what a rule *is* in non-circular terms; all we are doing is descriptively specifying the assertibility conditions and point of ascribing rules to people – and there is no good reason why this specification should not in turn be applied to rules for asserting that rules are being followed. What this objection does clearly bring out, though, is the *status* of the sceptical solution: it cannot be taken as any kind of eliminative

---

[60] Much the same could be said about the notion of rule employed in formal game theory: here games are studied in abstraction from anyone actually playing them, but it might yet be maintained that the notion of rule thus studied essentially arises from the actual playing of games.

[61] This point was made to me by Hartry Field; I do not know how seriously he took it.

analysis of the notion of correct rule-following (nor does Kripke take it this way).[62]

More telling objections concern the role of the *community* in the assertibility conditions Kripke suggests for rule-ascription. In the case of first-person ascriptions Kripke suggests that the appropriate criterion is simply that one is confidently inclined to apply the sign in a particular way; so, at this level, there is no distinction to be drawn between *seeming* to oneself to be using a sign correctly and *really* using it correctly – there are no conditions under which a person could assert of himself that he is using the sign incorrectly.[63] But this does not capture our concept of rule-following, since we do allow that someone might follow a rule incorrectly and yet take himself to be doing the right thing; we thus need to find room for this distinction somewhere in our practice of ascribing rules to people.[64] Kripke's suggestion is that the distinction emerges when we shift to the third-person case: it resides in the possibility that a given person's rule-following behaviour might not coincide with that of the community, and in particular with that of the ascriber. Thus we will say of a child that he *thinks* he is following the rule of addition, but in fact has not properly grasped that rule, when his profession of mastery is accompanied by a failure to produce the kinds of computational response we ourselves produce when confronted with addition problems. In other words, the normative aspect of rules is located in agreement and disagreement with a community of rule-followers. Now the first question I want to put is whether these community assertibility conditions are in fact correct: is

---

[62] Contrast the assertibility conditions of 'pain' and 'rule' in this respect: we do not, it seems, have to *use* the notion of pain in specifying the former, but we must use the notion of a rule of assertion in specifying the latter. The reason for this difference is that the notion of a linguistic rule is a notion we must appeal to when giving the meaning (assertibility conditions) of sentences about linguistic rules; whereas the linguistic rules for using 'pain' do not somehow involve the notion of pain essentially.

[63] See Kripke, p. 87f.

[64] Actually we can distinguish three sorts of mistake about rule-following: (i) taking oneself to be following a rule *R* and really following no rule at all (acting randomly); (ii) taking oneself to be following *R* and really following *R'*; (iii) taking oneself to be applying *R* correctly and really applying it incorrectly (the behaviour is rule-governed but goes wrong for some reason). Each kind of mistake will need to be given appropriate assertibility conditions by the sceptical solution; if it works for one kind of mistake, however, then it will work for all, so that we need not concern ourselves with the differences between the three sorts of mistake in what follows.

agreement with the behaviour of others the right test for whether a given person is really following the rule he thinks he is following (or following any rule at all)? This question divides into two: (*a*) do we *need* to appeal to the community in order to find assertibility conditions for 'he is really following rule *R*'? and (*b*) does the introduction of the community actually give us the right results? How we answer these questions will determine whether rule-following is to be conceived as an individualistic or as a social notion, at least in respect of assertibility conditions; I shall argue that it is individualistic.

The claim, then, is that I will judge that you (e.g.) mean addition by '+' if and only if I observe that your responses with '+' agree with mine sufficiently often (or with those of the community to which I belong). My first objection to this is that the reference to my own responses is strictly *redundant* in this assertibility condition: for the correct condition is simply that I observe that you give the *sum* of pairs of numbers sufficiently often.[65] This condition is, of course, entirely individualistic in that it refers only to the person to whom the rule is ascribed and to his behaviour – no mention here of me or my community. Moreover, unless Kripke's community condition somehow embeds this individualistic condition it cannot give the right results: it is only if your agreement of response with me is *correlated* with your giving the sum of pairs of numbers that it is right for me to use such agreement as a basis for ascribing the rule of addition to you. The point here is a general one about the ascription of psychological states: suppose we say that I should ascribe pain to you if and only if you behave in the way I do when I take myself to be in pain, i.e. we build agreement of response into the assertibility conditions of 'he is in pain'. It is

[65] This assertibility condition should not be read in such a way as to *presuppose* that the speaker has the concept of addition: that is, we should not assume that the computational behaviour is intentional under a description in which the concept of addition figures; the condition is rather that the speaker gives what is *in fact* the sum of pairs of numbers sufficiently often. A test for whether someone has and is exercising a given concept should not be formulated in such a way as to presuppose that the concept is possessed. It should also be noted that the suggested criterion is too crude as it stands; one important qualification, or supplementation, is that the speaker should not give evidence of being the sort of creature who adopts deviant rules that might lead to quus-like behaviour in the future (e.g. he should be a human being with a certain natural sense of similarity). These criteria are not, of course, intended to be proof against classical underdetermination scepticism, but rather to capture our actual practice in ascribing meaning and rules to people; so they are intended to be fallible.

easy to see in this case that we do not really *need* to appeal to such inter-personal agreement; it would suffice to say that the criteria for pain ascription relate to the person's behaviour individualistically considered (groaning, etc.). Moreover, the agreement of response criterion gets it right only if it correlates with the usual behavioural criteria.[66] This point can be brought out by asking what we would say if the two sorts of criteria came apart. Thus suppose I know or believe myself to be prone to (possibly systematic) mistakes in computations with '+'; then I shall *not* regard your agreement with me as either necessary or sufficient for you to be correctly said to grasp the rule of addition – indeed, we can envisage circumstances in which agreement with me would be a good reason for me to ascribe a *different* rule to you. Or again, if I suffer from a sensory defect that occasionally makes me apply the wrong observational term, then I shall not take agreement with me as a test of whether you have the same concept as me. What I *shall* take as the right test is your applying the word sufficiently often in situations in which it *does* apply, given that it has the ascribed meaning.[67] It is the same with pain ascription: agreement with my behaviour when I am in pain is not a good test of whether you are in pain if (for example) I am paralysed or have been given a drug that makes me behave cheerfully when in pain; what matters is how *you* behave – agreement with me is at best

[66] Compare the ascription of veridical perception to another. It might seem, superficially, that the criteria for such ascriptions involve inter-personal agreement: I judge whether your experience is veridical by testing whether it agrees with mine, and I am primitively entitled to take my own experience as veridical. However, closer examination undermines this idea; the criteria relate rather to the disposition and state of the other's sense organs and his success in dealing with the world around him. So the criteria of perceptual *correctness* do not essentially involve reference to the perceptual state of the ascriber (or the community).

[67] There is thus an element of charity built into our usual criteria of meaning ascription. However, I would not want to say that such charity is an absolutely necessary feature of meaning ascription; it can be overridden by evidence of sensory defect or other sources of (intelligible) error. For example, if a person is known to suffer from a visual defect that causes him to see square things as rhomboid, then I think we should interpret the word he applies to (really) square things as meaning *rhomboid* not *square*. But I will not enter into a full defence of this general position here; for present purposes we can stick with the simple charitable criterion proposed in the text. (In fact, Kripke's criterion is charitable to exactly the same degree, since agreement is with what the ascriber himself takes to be a correct use of the word in question.)

incidental. It therefore seems to me that the best description of our assertoric practice with sentences like 'he thinks he has got the hang of the rule of addition but in fact he hasn't' is individualistic: we assert this sentence if (i) he professes to have mastery of the rule of addition but (ii) he shows himself generally unable to give the sum of pairs of numbers when asked to answer questions of the form '$n + m = ?$' – that is, he fails to do this most of the time and there is no special reason to suppose there to be some impediment to his implementing his mastery of addition. So the language-game of correcting others' self-ascription of rules can be adequately described without building the community into assertibility conditions in the way Kripke suggests. In ascribing rules to people we proceed by establishing whether they behave as one would who has grasped the rule, and a person may fail this test while thinking that he has grasped the rule. This point seems to me obvious enough if we just ask ourselves how we do in fact ascribe concepts and meanings to others; I suspect that Kripke overlooks it because of his enthusiasm to construct a position which fits his (mistaken) interpretation of Wittgenstein: he is trying hard to find a place for the community to come in, in order to make sense of Wittgenstein's alleged adherence to some kind of community conception of rules, and so he incautiously introduces it in a context in which its necessity is more apparent than real. At any rate, I think it is clear that it is not *essential* to make reference to the community in giving the criteria for (e.g.) meaning addition by '+'; and it is the claim that it *is* essential that is supposed by Kripke to have the consequence that we cannot make *sense* of someone following a rule 'considered in isolation'.[68]

My next criticism is that the sceptical solution fails to answer Kripke's own original question. That question concerned the notion of a present use of a sign being in accord with what was earlier meant by it – transtemporal normativeness, as it might

[68] It is important for Kripke to maintain the stronger thesis, since the weaker thesis does not deliver an *essentially* social notion of rule-following: the claim has to be that we *cannot* provide adequate assertibility conditions for correct rule-following unless we bring in the community; it would not be enough to maintain merely that we *can* have reason to attribute correct rule-following to someone which involves reference to the community. For one thing, this would make too many properties community-involving, e.g. pain and veridical perception, not to speak of ordinary physical properties of people.

be called – and the sceptical solution is supposed to protect this notion from the ravages of the semantic sceptic. Cast in terms of assertibility, what we then want from the sceptical solution is an account of when it is right to assert that meaning has remained constant over time: under which conditions may I assert that yesterday I meant addition by '+' and not quaddition? Now what is notable about Kripke's eventual account of normativeness is that it locates correctness in agreement with the community *at a given time*: and this raises two problems. First, it is not clear how the community view of normativeness is to provide an account of transtemporal normativeness: how does it determine whether my present use accords with my past meaning? What we have to say, it seems, is that in the past I was declared to mean addition on the strength of my agreement with others, and that now I am declared to mean addition on similar grounds; but this raises the old question of whether the earlier declaration was correct – perhaps I meant *quaddition* then, but I had not been tested on numbers big enough to bring this out. That is, we seem to have made no progress with the original sceptical problem; it has simply been *assumed* that my past behaviour justifies an ascription of addition and not quaddition. Second, it seems to me that essentially the same problem of transtemporal normativeness comes up with respect to the whole community: for can we not ask what justifies our assumption, as a community, that yesterday *we* meant the same by our words as we do today? What about a sceptic who questions whether the community of English speakers meant addition by '+' yesterday?[69] It is clear on brief reflection that this semantic sceptic could dismiss the sorts of answers Kripke considers when dealing with individual constancy of meaning – actual applications, states of consciousness, dispositions. And yet we *do* I think recognise a distinction between a whole community using words as it originally intended and its (unintentionally) failing to do so – that is, we have the idea of a community-wide transtemporal linguistic

---

[69] Following Kripke, we could give this sceptical claim colour by supposing that we are all under the influence of a drug that causes us to misinterpret our past use (*cf.* Kripke, pp. 9–10): perhaps we *all* meant quaddition by '+' yesterday. Or again, perhaps we are collectively deceived about our present rule-following powers – we take our behaviour to be rule-governed but it is in reality random (a *collective* impression of a rule is not the same thing as a rule). For signs of uneasiness about this kind of point, see Kripke's note 87, p. 146.

mistake. The trouble, evidently, is that Kripke's community account of normativeness does not extend to the question of transtemporal community correctness of use: whatever *seems* right to the community must *be* right. It may be that we now all agree in our responses with '+', but that in the past we meant something different, so that our present use fails to accord with our past linguistic intentions: but this is a possibility that Kripke cannot make room for, since he has not supplied assertibility conditions for 'it seems to all of us that we are using '+' as we originally intended, but it is possible that we are not'.[70] So he has not solved the original sceptical problem; he has merely suggested assertibility conditions for 'he thinks he is following *R* but is not' at a *given* time.

I distinguished earlier between the constitutive and the epistemological semantic sceptic. Kripke's sceptical solution is designed to solve the constitutive problem by questioning the assumption that semantic statements have meaning by virtue of stating facts: these statements do not require what the sceptic has shown to be impossible. But there is still the question whether the sceptical solution makes any progress with the *epistemological* sceptic: does it help in showing that I am after all *justified* in my naive belief that I am using words correctly, or that others are? What is not clear to me is whether Kripke himself believes that he has offered any solution to *that* problem, as distinct from the constitutive problem. For, though the epistemological formulation is preferred when the argument is originally presented, it has disappeared from view by the time the sceptical solution is proposed, the emphasis being all on the constitutive problem. It is worth pointing out, however, that no real progress has been made with the original epistemological problem. The epistemological problem, as Kripke presents it, is fundamentally a problem of evidential underdetermination: actual application is compatible with

[70] It is, of course, no help to appeal to *other* communities and their agreement or disagreement with the given community, since the same problem recurs at this level: might not two or more communities be mistaken in their self-ascriptions of rule-following (after all, a community is just a collection of individuals, *each* of whom can be mistaken)? That this question does intelligibly arise for whole communities shows that the notion of rule is not like the notion of (say) marching in step, since we clearly cannot make sense of the idea of a whole army marching out of step though the members agree with each other in the way they march. Following a rule is more like veridically perceiving, in the present respect.

rival hypotheses about what is (or was) meant. The sceptical solution does not help with *this* problem because it does nothing to augment the evidential basis: it simply describes our *de facto* practice of ascribing rules in a way that advertises the very underdetermination upon which the sceptic trades. That you have agreed in your responses with '+' with me up to now does not logically guarantee that you will continue to do so: perhaps when you get to a pair of numbers neither of us has yet encountered you will give a response of the quaddition kind and sincerely aver that this is the *right* response – the response indeed which you expected *me* to give. Similarly, my past use of '+' is logically compatible with my having meant quaddition; that I do not in practice ascribe quaddition to myself in the past is something the sceptic still wants justified. The appeal to community agreement thus does not enhance the quality of our reasons for ascribing rules as we do; in fact, it displays precisely the same degree of underdetermination that we saw to obtain in respect of the applications a person makes of his signs when he is 'considered in isolation'. As I say, it is not perhaps clear that Kripke *is* offering to solve these epistemological problems, but it is worth making it explicit that he does not; so the community does not help us here either.[71]

Let me now summarise my position on Kripke's community conception of the notion of rule; there are two main points at which I have resisted the introduction of the community. First, in rejecting the sceptical paradox I have suggested straight solutions which make no essential reference to the notion of community agreement: meaning is thus, in the relevant sense, an individualistic fact about a person. Second, I have resisted (essentially) incorporating the community into the *assertibility* conditions of rule-ascriptions: since *truth* conditions of an

---

[71] The sceptical solution dispenses with the need for facts to make ascriptions of rule-following true, and so is no longer threatened by the upshot of the sceptical paradox: but it does nothing to show that our ordinary *criteria* for ascribing rules to ourselves and others are robust enough to withstand the sceptical attack in its epistemological form. For there is still nothing about my past use of '+' that enables me to provide conclusive reason to assert that I meant addition. But if the sceptical solution is allowed the liberty to relax the standards of epistemic warrant, then why could we not have done the same when we were first confronted with the sceptical paradox? The epistemological question serves to get semantic scepticism off the ground, but it is effectively dropped by the time the solution is proposed, and so we don't notice that the original question has not been answered.

individualistic sort have been supplied, this has not been strictly necessary in order to make sense of the possibility of socially isolated rule-following; but it is as well to convince ourselves in addition that the community will not enjoy a resurgence at the level of assertibility conditions. It would, of course, be rather surprising if the truth conditions were individualistic and the assertibility conditions were *essentially* social – for how can inherently individualistic facts be knowable *only* on the basis of community-involving evidence? – but we have seen that this is not a puzzle we need to worry about. So I think that Kripke has provided no compelling reason to depart from the natural idea that which concepts a person possesses depends simply upon *facts about him*: we can thus form a conception of someone possessing concepts and following rules without introducing *other* persons into our thought, at least so far as Kripke's arguments are concerned.[72]

It will be evident by now that I am generally opposed to a community conception of rules. In a final effort to persuade my readers that this is the right view to take, I want to conclude by considering some other community theses and indicating why I find them implausible. Kripke has presented what I take to be the most developed and systematic defence of this general idea, but there are other versions of the community conception that some have found attractive, and I should address myself, however briefly, to them. I believe that once they are clearly stated their attractions will rapidly fade, since the tendency here is to adopt positions which confuse the trivially true with the manifestly false. I shall formulate these variants of the community conception in terms of truth conditions, i.e. in terms of what states of affairs are logically (conceptually, metaphysically) possible; I do so because the versions I have come across do not take the form of a sceptical solution in the style of Kripke – they are simply views about what it *consists in* to follow a rule. However, if the truth conditions of 'he is

---

[72] A vivid way to appreciate the force of what I am calling the natural view is to imagine what it would take to create (in a God-like way) rule-followers or concept-possessors. According to the community view, nothing you can do in the construction of an individual can justify the assertion that he has concepts or means anything *until* you create other individuals: Adam had, so to speak, to wait for Eve before he could follow rules (in particular, have thoughts). But how could the creation of other individuals wreak such a momentous change in the first created individual? Either he already has concepts or the creation of others is not going to remedy his deficiency.

following R' are agreed to be individualistic (assuming such sentences to have truth conditions) then it is a short step to an individualistic account of assertibility conditions: for (as I indicated a paragraph back) it is hard to see how if rule-following can *obtain* in logical independence of a community it could *assertibly* obtain only in virtue of inter-personal criteria (e.g. agreement). Put abstractly, it is hard to see how a monadic fact could be known to obtain only and essentially on the basis of relational criteria: if the truth of a sentence S depends upon an object a being F, then how could it be that we can only *judge* that a is F by establishing that a is R to some b? At any rate, I shall be recommending that we take an individualistic view of the notion of rule-following with respect both to the fact and to the criteria for the fact. It is well to remember when considering this question that *concepts* are also at issue, not just linguistic meaning: we are then asking whether it is logically possible for someone to have concepts independently of any community.

Let us first put on one side views of meaning and concepts which *sound* like community conceptions but which are not so in the sense in which we are interested. Chief among these is the idea, attributable to Wittgenstein, that rules are essentially *public*, in the sense that which rules a person follows must be ascertainable by others on the basis of 'public criteria', *viz.* behaviour and its context.[73] This is the idea that grasp of a rule must be manifest in what is inter-personally accessible – i.e. to others as well as to oneself – so that there can be no such thing as intrinsically *unknowable* (by another) rule-following. In this sense we might also want to say that pain (not the *concept* of pain) is essentially public: pain must be manifestable in public criteria available to another – it is logically impossible to have pain which is unknowable by another.[74] But of course these

---

[73] See 243f. Remember that what Wittgenstein argues to be necessary for a meaningful language of sensations are 'natural expressions of sensation' (256), i.e. various kinds of behaviour that show a person to be in pain: this necessary condition is clearly not 'social' in the required sense, though it is 'public', i.e. ascertainable by others. A given person's sensations could have natural behavioural expressions without there actually being any community of people to exploit these expressions to determine whether the speaker is using his sensation words consistently; the absence of a surrounding community would not make his language 'private' in the relevant sense (i.e. such that nobody else *could* understand it).

[74] I do not say I agree with this claim; in fact it does not seem to me impossible to describe cases in which the character of a person's sensations (e.g. colour sensations) is unknowable to others (inverted spectrum cases, etc.).

claims (right or wrong) are not *community* theses: they do not imply that one could not follow a rule or be in pain 'in social isolation', nor do they remotely suggest the model of being in fashion or marching in step as the kind of thing rule-following or pain is. If this is not obvious, then consider a parallel claim about properties of physical objects: suppose it claimed that such properties must be public, i.e. knowable by observers in some way; this would *not* be to say (absurdly) that (e.g.) a table cannot be *square* in 'social isolation' – that it needs the company of other square things or some such. I think therefore that the so-called private language argument does not in itself have a community conception as its conclusion: the conclusion is just that semantic rules require public criteria in the sense I have explained; this does *not* imply that the person following the rule must be a member of a linguistic community, nor that there must be others who follow the same rule or correct the given person's rule-following behaviour, nor even that any other rule-followers exist.[75] The demand for public criteria no more implies these things than does a like demand for being in pain or for having a physical property like squareness. To put it in Dummettian terms, the requirement that meaning be 'exhaustively manifest' in use does not imply that a person could not mean something by a word unless he stood in some relation to a community – it does not even imply that any linguistic community exists.[76] Neither does the requirement of rule *shareability* have community implications. Suppose it claimed (not implausibly) that there cannot be a rule which is

---

[75] Neither, I think, does Wittgenstein himself ever make these mistaken inferences, or accept what is thus inferred. Indeed, in 243 Wittgenstein contemplates the real possibility of 'human beings who spoke only in monologue'; here he seems to allow that someone might have a language and never use it to communicate with others, and so never correct other peoples' use of language. Nor does he suggest that such uncommunicative speakers could only exist in *groups*. This section seems to me to go against a good deal of the usual interpretation of Wittgenstein's general position: language is not, for Wittgenstein, 'essentially social', as this phrase is usually intended.

[76] The requirement of exhaustive manifestation is intended to ensure the 'communicability' of meaning (see Dummett, 'The Philosophical Basis of Intuitionistic Logic', in *Truth and Other Enigmas*, esp. p. 216); but this does not make Dummett into a 'community theorist' about meaning, since his requirement concerns the third-person *knowability* of meaning. Nor would he become a community theorist, in the relevant sense, by insisting that the essential *purpose* of language is to act as a vehicle of communication between people, since this does *not* imply that meaning is impossible outside of a community context.

necessarily grasped by just one person: if rule R is grasped by person x, then it must at least be logically possible for some other person y to grasp R. This is *a* sense in which it might be said that rule-following cannot be essentially *private*.[77] Does this supply us with a nontrivial community thesis? To see that it does not, consider again sensations and physical properties: we might hold, plausibly enough, that these also are essentially shareable in the sense defined (it must be at least logically possible for more than one individual to satisfy the corresponding predicates); but it would be an obvious error to infer from this that these concepts are inherently *social*, since the shareability requirement is compatible with the actual non-existence of other individuals. If this were a good ground for advancing a community thesis then *all* general properties would be social, just in virtue of their (potential) multiple applicability – this would, indeed, be a simple consequence of their being *universals*. What we need for a genuine community conception is the idea that following a rule is a notion, like that of being in fashion or marching in step, that inherently involves reference to individuals other than the individual to whom the ascription is made: and the requirements of third-person knowability and of shareability do not entail anything of that kind.[78] Let us then consider some theses which indisputably do deserve to be classified as community conceptions.

The strongest community thesis is presumably this: it is not possible for an individual to follow a rule R unless he is a participating member of a rule-following community in which R is also followed by others. This thesis would reflect the idea that to follow a rule R *is* just to conform one's actions to those of others certified to follow R – rule-following consists in a kind of collective agreement. So strong is this thesis that it excludes

[77] Frege's thesis that the sense of 'I' is private to each person who uses it, so that you cannot grasp what I grasp when I think 'I am hot', seems to be an instance of an allegedly unshareable rule or concept: see his 'The Thought: A Logical Inquiry', in *Philosophical Logic*, ed. P.F. Strawson (Oxford University Press, 1967). This thesis certainly creates *prima facie* problems for the communicability of thoughts about oneself.

[78] Neither does the idea that rule-following has to be in principle *correctable* by others, if indeed this goes beyond knowability and shareability; for, again, this requirement does not imply either the existence of a community or the necessity to explain rule-following by reference to the practices of a community (compare the in principle correctability of one's sense-impressions by others).

the possibility of someone introducing a rule which only he follows, say a word which only he (in fact) understands: thus the thesis declares impossible a creative mathematician who discovers a new mathematical function which he names and perhaps goes on to investigate (think of the discovery of exponentiation), or a zoologist who comes across a hitherto unknown species and gives it a name. Such newly introduced expressions are not of course *incapable* of being grasped by persons other than their original introducer; but they would be cases of words which only one member of a linguistic community in fact understands. I take it as obvious that this strong thesis is self-evidently absurd, and I doubt that it has ever been (explicitly) held: it makes nonsense of the idea that a member of a rule-following community can be *innovative* in the rules he follows. A natural weakening of the thesis, which avoids the objection from innovative rule-following, would be that an individual can follow a rule *R* only if he is a member of a community the other members of which follow *some* rules – they need not include *R*. This weaker thesis allows for *unique* grasp of a particular rule, but it excludes *solitary* rule-following, i.e. rule-following by an individual who is not a member of a rule-following community; it therefore excludes Robinson Crusoe from the class of rule-followers, since he is not (on his island) a participating member of a linguistic community. I take it that this weaker thesis is also clearly wrong: for it would, I think, be totally implausible to maintain that Crusoe somehow *loses* his rule-following capacities when he wakes up on his island in social isolation, that his words no longer have meaning (what if you went alone to a desert island for a holiday?). Again, I doubt that anyone can have held such a view.[79] What may have been maintained is a weaker thesis yet, namely that Crusoe qualifies as a rule-follower only because *at some earlier time* he was a member of a rule-following community – specifically, he was brought up in such a community.[80] The idea behind this thesis might be that

---

[79] Kripke, p. 110, seems to think that this view has been held, e.g. by R. Rhees in 'Can There Be a Private Language?', *Proceedings of the Aristotelian Society*, Supp. Vol. XXVIII (1954). But Rhees's concern appears to have been with the different question of whether a solitary individual could *invent* a language.

[80] Rhees, *op. cit.*, seems committed to this thesis, as does P. Winch: 'it makes no sense to suppose anyone capable of establishing a purely personal standard of behaviour *if*

society is essential for induction into the activity of rule-following (notably in learning a language) but that once acquired the capacity takes on a certain autonomy – other people are no longer needed. This thesis cannot be dismissed as self-evidently absurd, and it does appear to have been explicitly maintained; it does, however, seem to me very implausible, construed as a claim about what is logically or conceptually possible. The thesis lets in Crusoe, but it excludes the possibility of an infant reaching rule-following maturity outside of any community, as in the case of Romulus and Remus; it excludes the possibility that a human being might introduce rules for himself to follow and *never* have been a member of a rule-following community.[81] Now the question here is not whether a human infant could, as a matter of biological and psychological law, come to follow rules without the benefit of adult instruction – for this is a purely empirical question; the question is whether there is any *conceptual* obstacle to the kind of creativity that would be necessary for rules to be introduced totally *ab initio*. That is, we are not concerned with the possibility that some rules might be innate in the human infant and become operational during maturation (as Chomsky holds for the case of some grammatical rules[82]); what we are asking about is whether the very *notion* of grasping a rule requires sometime membership of a community of rule-followers. And it seems to me that it does not require this: I find it perfectly possible to imagine that Romulus, upon reaching the age of reason, hits upon the idea of distributing sign-posts around his island as an *aide-memoire*. He wants to avoid the marshes, so he writes an arrow in the sand and undertakes to walk in the direction of its head when he comes across it in

---

he had never had any experience of human society with its socially established rules', *The Idea of a Social Science* (Routledge and Kegan Paul: London, 1958), p. 33. I find the reasons given by these authors for this view hard to follow, and I do not think the view has the authority of Wittgenstein (see Chapters 1 and 2).

[81] This case is discussed by A.J. Ayer in 'Can There Be a Private Language?', *Proceedings of the Aristotelian Society*, Supp. Vol. XXVIII (1954). I am in substantial agreement with Ayer on this point, though I think he is wrong to suppose that rejecting the community thesis affects Wittgenstein's private language argument, since (as I have argued earlier) that argument does not presuppose the existence of a community to correct what the individual speaker does with his (sensation) words.

[82] For a recent statement, see N. Chomsky, *Rules and Representations* (Columbia University Press: New York, 1980), esp. Chapter 5.

future; he follows his rule correctly in the future if he conforms his actions to his original intentions in respect of the arrow; and he may discover on occasion that he has followed his rule *in*correctly when, misremembering his original intention, he finds himself wallowing in the marsh (he mistakenly thought that his original intention was to follow the *tail* of the arrow). Nor do I see any conceptual obstacle to his introducing properly linguistic signs for his own use, e.g. to keep records of the weather: all he needs is a good reason to introduce the signs and the intelligence to operate with them. That he has never had contact with other rule-followers does not seem to me to put a logical wall between him and the activity of following rules. Certainly it seems implausible to insist that rules must necessarily be *taught* if they are to be grasped: for who taught the teachers? Of course I am merely reporting my intuitions of logical possibility here, not providing any real *demonstration* that lifelong solitary rule-following is possible; but it seems to me fair to cleave to these intuitions unless some argument can be produced which overturns them – and I know of no argument that looks like succeeding in this.[83]

It might now be said that the community conception should not have required *membership* in a community at all, not even sometime membership; what it should require is rather the mere *existence* of a rule-following community to which the candidate individual rule-follower stands in various relations – notably agreement of response.[84] The idea here is that rule-following on the part of an individual should be conceived as a kind of behavioural similarity or isomorphism, and that does not in itself require actually *interacting* with those with whom

---

[83] I am not here wishing to denigrate intuitions of logical possibility; indeed, in the end, they are all one has to go on in deciding modal questions. But since many philosophers have not had these intuitions, or have supposed them illusory, I should acknowledge the fact that I have not provided anything like a *proof* that *ab initio* solitary rule-following is conceptually possible (I am not sure I know what such a proof would look like).

[84] This is close to Kripke's official view (see p. 110), where the existing community is that of he who contemplates the isolated individual's rule-following. Kripke does appear to think that in any possible world in which an individual follows a rule there must in *that* world exist other rule-followers whose actions agree with those of the given individual; he is not saying that when we in the actual world judge that a solitary individual in another possible world is following rules we consider him in relation to *our* actual community. In fact, Kripke appears to be considering only the ascription of rules to physically isolated individuals within the actual world.

one's behaviour is isomorphic. It seems to me, though, that this conception is counter-intuitive in essentially the same way that the previous theses were seen to be: for could not the rest of the human race be wiped out while you sleep and yet the next day you awake with your rule-following capacities intact? And if it is said that it is only required that other rule-followers should have existed *sometime*, then what of the seeming possibility that God could have created a single rule-follower alone in the universe for all time? These possibilities do not really call for much more than the original Romulus and Remus case; they simply delete other people and invite us to agree that this could not materially alter the condition of these already isolated rule-followers. Think of it this way: suppose you were to discover that solipsism is true – you are the only person there is (has been and ever will be); would this be to discover that you have never followed a rule, that you have neither language nor concepts? If so, then this is not in fact a discovery you *could* make, since a discovery is a thought with conceptual content – and the suggestion is that if solipsism is true you *have* no concepts and thoughts. Surely this is grossly implausible: for one thing, it invites a surely spurious refutation of solipsism by contraposition. I would say that considering the (epistemic) possibility of solipsism is a way of seeing that the existence of others is *not* logically necessary for the possession of concepts, language and rules. (I hope no-one will want to suggest that rule-following at least requires the *appearance* of other people!) So I think it is too much to require the *actual* (sometime) existence of others for individual rule-following.[85]

Someone might concede this degree of individualism but still insist that the community enters the concept of rule at least *notionally*: that is, we count someone a rule-follower only because his practice agrees with that of a *possible* or *hypothetical* or *conceivable* community of rule-followers.[86] More fully,

---

[85] I am not saying of the solitary rule-follower that his impression of following rules is infallible, so that he is in principle uncorrectable by others; on the contrary, others could correct him *if they existed*. In the case of a solitary rule-follower, there are public *criteria* for correct rule-following, which may conflict with the individual's own convictions; it is just that there is nobody around (in that possible world, so to speak) who can take advantage of this opportunity for correcting the individual's own sincere avowals.

[86] This seems to be the view of C. Peacocke, 'Rule-Following: The Nature of Wittgenstein's Arguments', in *Wittgenstein: To Follow a Rule*, eds. S.H. Holtzman and

when we judge someone to follow a rule *R* the content of our judgement includes the idea that the given individual stands in a relation of behavioural isomorphism with some notional community – this community need not *actually* exist. There are at least two problems with this maximally weak community conception: first, it has not been properly motivated – *why* build inter-personal relations into the content of a rule-ascription? – second, the thesis is in imminent danger of triviality and vacuity. The first problem is best appreciated by comparing the ascription of rules with the ascription of (say) pain: why not say equally that the thought of a given individual in pain involves the idea of behavioural similarity to some notional pain-feeler? The second problem emerges from the first: *of course* there is a sense in which the ascription of a rule to someone contains the thought of a possible other rule-follower; but it does so in an entirely trivial sense, namely the sense in which the ascription of pain to someone contains a like thought – as indeed the ascription of squareness to physical objects does. This sense amounts to no more than the idea that these properties – rule, pain, squareness – are *universals* that may be multiply exemplified, by possible objects if not by actual ones. But we surely do not want to say that just because I will admit that *other* objects *could* be square (not just the object I am presently ascribing 'square' to) I am thereby committing myself to a *community* conception of squareness! So I think that the notional community provides us with no substantial sense in which rule-following is a social concept. Neither does it provide any content for the notion of a *mistake* in the application of a rule, since for *any* piece of putative rule-following behaviour on the part of a given person we can envisage *some* possible community which behaves with the sign in question just as the given person does; so we cannot use the idea of a notional community to determine *which* rule an individual is following, or indeed whether he is following any. The introduction of the notional community is an attempt to

C.M. Leich (Routledge and Kegan Paul: London, 1981), pp. 93–4. Peacocke takes himself to be expounding Wittgenstein here, rather than advancing his own view; however, he seems to think the view not obviously inadequate. On this and other matters, both exegetical and substantive, see Malcolm Budd's excellent paper, 'Wittgenstein on Meaning, Interpretation and Rules', *Synthese* 58 (1984).

preserve the idea of the essentially social character of the concept of a rule while avoiding the implausibilities to which this idea leads; but it does this only by sacrificing its claim to be a substantive community conception.

It seems to me in conclusion, then, that the proposed community conceptions fall into two groups: those that are reasonably plausible but are not properly described as community conceptions, and those that are genuine community conceptions but are intrinsically implausible. My own view is that rule-following may be conceived, as I think it is pre-theoretically, in entirely individualistic terms. I should emphasise that I do not believe that Wittgenstein himself would have dissented from this conclusion: insofar as he has a view on the individual/social opposition, he is an individualist – though I think that in fact this issue is rather remote from his real concerns. There are, as I argued in Chapter 3, questionable aspects of Wittgenstein's treatment of rule-following, but adherence to the community conception is not one of them: Wittgenstein would be the last person to lapse so far from common sense.

Index